Abstracts of the
TESTAMENTARY PROCEEDINGS
of the
PREROGATIVE COURT OF MARYLAND

Volume VIII: 1697–1700

Libers: 17, 18A

by
V. L. Skinner, Jr.

CLEARFIELD

Printed for
Clearfield Company by
Genealogical Publishing Co.
Baltimore, Maryland
2007

ISBN-13: 978-0-8063-5318-0
ISBN-10: 0-8063-5318-X

Made in the United States of America

INTRODUCTION

Purpose of the Prerogative Court.

The Prerogative Court was the central point for
probate for Provincial Maryland. It was
mirrored after the Prerogative Court of
Canterbury. There was a judge as well as
clerk(s) of the court. Initially, all probate
was brought directly to the Prerogative Court,
located in the Provincial Capital. As the
Province became more populous, all documents
were still to be filed with the Prerogative
Court; however, administration of probate was
delegated to the various county courts. Even
so, there are documents only in the Prerogative
Court and not in the appropriate county, and
vice versa.

Documents filed in the Prerogative Court.

The following documents were filed in the
Prerogative Court: administration bond, will,
inventory, administration accounts, and final
balances. The testamentary proceedings contain
the administration bond and the docket for the
court. If the administrator is lax in filing
documents, then a summons is also recorded.

Equity Court

The Prerogative Court was also the court for
equity cases--resolution of disputes over the
settlement and distribution of an estate. The
case was brought before the judge and could take
several years to resolve. Often depositions
were taken and recorded in the minutes.

Notes on the Abstraction.

1. The left hand column contains the liber/folio
number. The folio numbers are presented just as
they appear in the actual document, e.g., 32a,
78½.

2. The right hand column contains the
abstraction text.

3. Various libers specify a particular session
for the Prerogative Court, e.g., 1678; or,
September Court 1742. This information is
presented as "Court Session:" followed by the

appropriate session. Should no session have
been specified, then the phrase "no date" is
used.

4. An ellipsis (...) is used to indicate a
continuation of the previous information, but no
relevant genealogical information is present.

5. The following symbols are used in the
abstraction:
    ?   difficult to read.
    #   pounds of tobacco.
    !   [sic].

Abbreviations.

The following abbreviations have been used
throughout this abstraction:

AA - Anne Arundel Co.   administration
ACC - Accomac Co.   MA - Massachusetts
BA - Baltimore Co.   MD - Maryland
CE - Cecil Co.   MO - Montgomery Co.
CH - Charles Co.   NE - New England
CR - Caroline Co.   NEI - "non est
CV - Calvert Co.   inventar" (not
dbn - de bonis non   found)
DE - Delaware   NY - New York
DO - Dorchester Co.   NYC - New York City
ENG - England   p - planter
FR - Frederick Co.   PA - Pennsylvania
g - gentleman   PG - Prince George's
HA - Harford Co.   Co.
IRE - Ireland   PoA - power of
KE - Kent Co. MD   attorney
KEDE - Kent Co. DE   QA - Queen Anne's Co.
LaC - letters ad   SM - St. Mary's Co.
    colligendum (for   SMC - St. Mary's City
    temporary   SO - Somerset Co.
    collection &   TA - Talbot Co.
    preservation of   VA - Virginia
    assets)   WA - Washington Co.
LoA - letters of   WO - Worcester Co.

This volume is a continuation of the series,
covering 1697 to 1700. A continuation of the
delegation of authority to the counties occurs.
In general, only the entry of the various
documents is recorded. Appraisers are no longer
assigned by the Prerogative Court.

17:1   <u>29 May</u>. MM John Hall (g, BA) & Daniell Palmer (g, BA) exhibited will of Mary Utie, constituting her daughter Susanna Utie (infant, age 1½ years) executrix & petitioners overseers, proved by 4 witnesses. Mr. Marke Richardson (g, BA) for self & his wife Susanna petitioned that administration of estate of George Utie ought not be committed to petitioners, but to said Richardson & his wife.

17:2   Said Susanna Richardson is the grandmother to the child; said John Hall is uncle. Said Palmer wrote the will. Said Richardson is also principle creditor to said George Utie. Charles Carroll is procurator for John Hall. Robert Carvile is procurator for Marke Richardson. Ruling: joint administration was granted to Marke Richardson & his wife Susanna & John Hall & his wife Martha. Daniell Palmer is to remain overseer.

17:3   Mr. Edward Boothby to administer oath.

    <u>2 June</u>. Exhibited will of Henrieta Mary Lloyd (TA), constituting her mother Madam Ann Neale, her 2 brothers MM James & Anthony Neale, & her 2 sons Richard Bennett & Philemon Lloyd executors, proved by 3 witnesses. Madam Neale & Mr. Anthony Neale are not here. Mr. Bennett has gone to ENG. MM James Neale & Philemon Lloyd were granted administration. Madam Ann Neale & Mr. Anthony Neale summoned to show cause why they do not join the administration. On 4 August, Madam Ann Neale & Mr. Anthony Neale renounced administration.

    Charles Brooke (SM) vs. Richard Marsham. Plaintiff demands his due from his father's estate. Said Marsham married the administratrix. Said Marsham summoned.

17:4   Allen Robinett (AA) vs. estate of Edward Snellen (carpenter, AA). Caveat exhibited. Said Robinett is greatest creditor.

Exhibited inventory of Maurice Hooper (cooper, KI), by appraisers Math. Erreckson & Hugh Elburn.

4 June. Cateryne Herman widow of Col. Casparus Herman petitioned for LoA on his estate. Appraisers: Mr. Jacob Vangaesill, Mathias Vanderheyden. LoA to be sent via Mr. Manthrop.

17:5 Said Catherine was granted administration on estate of Casparus Augustin Herman (CE). Mr. Edward Blay to administer oath.

John Edmondson, Maj. Thomas Ennalls, Thomas Hicks, & William Sharp securities to Sarah Pindar vs. said Sarah administratrix of Edward Pindar (DO). Attachment of contempt issued, to render accounts.

5 June. John Baptista Carbery (g, SM) who married relict of Cuthbert Scott (SM) exhibited inventory, dated 8 August 1691, by appraisers William Roswell & Stephen Gough. Said inventory was found amongst his wife's papers.

10 June. John Sumerland (AA) administrator of Thomas Wood (AA) exhibited accounts. Also exhibited nuncupative will, sworn to by Dr. Wolfran Hunt.

17:6 Grace Lewis (CV) widow of Andrew Lewis was granted administration on his estate.

12 June. William & Thomas Mackell (both of DO) executors of John Mackell (DO) exhibited accounts.

14 June. Mr. Richard Middleton (coroner, PG) to server attachment of contempt to Thomas Greenfeild administrator of Richard Charlett.

Mr. Samuell Hopkins (SO) to examine accounts of Elisabeth Racliffe executrix of Charles Rackliffe.

Court Session: 1697

Said Hopkins also to examine accounts of Elisabeth Dunkean administratrix of James Dunkean.

Edward Lloyd (g, TA) exhibited that his mother Henrieta Maria Lloyd (now dec'd) was granted administration on estate of his father Philemond Lloyd (TA). Said Edward Lloyd was granted administration dbn on estate of his father Philemond Loyd, as eldest brother. Mr. Robert Gouldesborough to administer oath.

17:7   23 June. Ann Watkins widow of John Watkins (AA) was granted administration on his estate. Securities: William Burges, Richard Jones.

1 July. Joshua Cecill (PG) exhibited bond of Thomas Clarke administrator of Dennis Smith (PG). Security: Charles Tracy.

Said Cecill also exhibited inventory of William Cooper, by appraisers John Cuccens & Benjamin Berry.

Mr. Thomas Greenfeild (g, PG) was granted LAC on estate of Capt. William Pen. Accounts were exhibited.

9 July. Mr. Samuell Hopkins (SO) exhibited:
- will of Capt. John King (SO), constituting his friends Maj. Robert King & Mr. John West executors, proved by 4 witnesses. Said King & West were granted administration. Security: Miles Gray. Also inventory, by appraisers John Bozman & Miles Gray.

17:8   . . .
- will of Richard Davis (SO), constituting his son Richard executor, proved by 4 witnesses. Said son Richard was granted administration. Securities: Ephraim Wilson, George Lane. Also inventory, by appraisers Ephraim Wilson & George Lean.
- will of Michaell Disharoone (SO), constituting his widow Joane

Court Session: 1697

Disharoone executrix, proved by 3
witnesses. Said Joane was granted
administration. Securities: Philip
Carter, Thomas Humfris. Also
inventory, by appraisers William
Elget & Thomas Ralfe.
* accounts of Elisabeth & Charles
Racklife (SO) executors of Charles
Racklife.
* accounts of Elisabeth Walle (SO)
executrix of William Tomkins.

24 July. Exhibited inventory of William
Cockey (AA), by appraisers Edward Fuller
& William Penington.

29 July. Thomas Jones vs. Arnold Elzey
(SO). Continuance was granted.

17:9   The Governor ordered the following
summons, regarding the estate of Col.
George Wells (BA), having found that the
executor is not capable of administering
said estate: Benjamin Wells (executor),
Blanch Wells (widow), George Wells
(son), James Phillips (overseer). Date:
17 July 1797.

2 August. Mr. Elias King (KE)
exhibited:
* bond of Mary Long administratrix of
David Long (KE). Security: John
Parsons. Also inventory, by
appraisers William Comegys & Thomas
Wyeat.
* bond of Elisabeth Carsey
administratrix of James Carsey (KE).
Security: John Shaw. Also
inventory, by appraisers William
Comegys & Thomas Wyeat.

4 August. Christopher Vernon (AA) was
granted administration on estate of
William Hinton (AA), as greatest
creditor. Securities: Richard Jones,
Henry Wriothesley. Appraisers: John
Chapell, John Trundle.

17:10   3 August. The following returned
summons: George Lingan (sheriff, CV),
Nicholas Lowe (sheriff, TA), Richard
Beard (sheriff, AA), Capt. John Bayne

Court Session: 1697

(sheriff, CH).

4 August. Exhibited inventory of John Estell (TA), by appraisers John Needles & Richard Endley.

Exhibited inventory of Thomas Cooke (TA), by appraisers Nicholas Milburne & Robert Ungle.

John Elsey (CV) exhibited that he has not brought in the papers of Mr. Briscoe because he has been very ill. Mentions: Mr. Parrott.

17:11   Hugh Ellis (CV) exhibited that he is ready to pay legacies to the orphans of Mordica Hunton. Mentions: estate of (N) Cosden. Philip Clarke procurator for Elisabeth & Ann Hunton, 2 of the orphans of said Mordica exhibited libel.

Richard Keene exhibited that he has been so lame that he cannot ride that far. Continuance was granted on estates of: (N) Hopewell, (N) Thatcher, (N) King, (N) Hill. Date: 1 August 1697.

Exhibited will of Francis Hill (SM), constituting his daughter Elisabeth Hopewell executrix, proved by 2 witnesses. Richard Keene who married said Elisabeth was granted administration. Security: Timo. Morry.

Samuell Manthrop for Madam Katerine Herman (CE) administratrix of Casparus Augustin Herman was granted continuance.

17:12   Mr. William Sharp (TA) administrator LAC of William Dorrington (DO) exhibited inventory, by appraisers Jacob Loockerman, Charles Powell, & John Steevens. Also exhibited will, constituting his son William Dorrington (under age) & his daughter Ann Dorrington (under age) executors. Mr. John Rawlings to examine said orphans for the administrator during their minority.

Mr. Baker Brooke (SM) petitioned for LoA via his brother directed to Col. Lowe. Securities: MM Charles Brooke, Raphaell Haywood.

17:13 Date: 8 July 1696. Also exhibited will of Garrett Comberford, proved by 2 witnesses. Said Baker was granted administration. Col. Henry Lowe to administer oath.

Mr. Robert Mason (SM) was granted administration on estate of Michaell Dent, as greatest creditor. Securities: Philip Clarke, George Muschamp. John Dent (father of dec'd) renounced administration. Date: 23 June 1697.

William Morgann who married Elisabeth Large (now dec'd) relict & administratrix of Robert Large (SM) was granted administration dbn on his estate. Securities: Owen Guyther, John Savidge. Also exhibited accounts. Thomas Large renounced administration on estate of his father Robert Large. Date: 3 June 1697.

17:14 Exhibited bond of Grace Lewis administratrix of Adrew Lewis (CV). Securities: Jacob Pattison, Richard Leake.

Exhibited inventory of Col. Edward Pye (CH), by appraisers John Haryson & Will. Thompson.

Exhibited inventory of John Heard (SM), by appraisers Stephen Gough & John Tant.

Exhibited inventory of Anthony Andrews (SM), by appraisers Charles Smith & Thomas Rose.

Thomas Rose (SM) who married relict & administratrix of Emanuell Pitcher (SM) exhibited additional accounts.

William Carr (TA) executor of Joseph Wiggott (TA) exhibited additional accounts. John Tiley is the other executor.

Court Session: 1697

17:15 Anthony Neale renounced administration on estate of Madam Henrieta Maria Lloyd (will made on 26 June last), due to remoteness of his residence from the estate. Date: 10 June 1697. Witnesses: Ric. Hobart, Roger Brooke, Jr. Mr. Roger Brooke, Jr. attested to said renunciation before John Courts. Date: 26 June 1697. The renunciation was sent via his brother Neale; refers to Madam Lloyd as sister Lloyd. Also cites refusal by his mother. Date: 23 June 1697.

17:16 Col. John Bigger (CV) to Esq. Cheseldyn. Date: 25 June 1697. Said Bigger exhibited that Dr. Simon Wootton is dec'd in Jomaicia. Said Wootton made a will, constituting Capt. Thomas Wharton (ENG) executor. Said Wharton sent PoA to said Bigger. Said Wootton's wife has gone home to ENG; said Wootton's daughter died 2 years ago. Said Bigger is greatest creditor.

17:17 Said Bigger was granted administration. Mr. William Parker to administer oath. Appraisers: Franc. Hutchings, Rogert Skinner. Securities: Hugh Ellis, William Head. Also inventory, by appraisers Francis Hutchings & Robert Skinner. Also exhibited will of said Wootton (chirurgeon, CV). Bequests: wife Susanna Wootton, William Fisher (under 21) son of brother John Fisher, Ann Bardwell (widow), Thomas Wharton, daughter Ann Wotton (under age 18) land.

17:18 Executor: friend Thomas Wharton for daughter Anne. Date: 13 January 1695. Witnesses: John. Hyde, William Clapcott, (N) Buckle. [LoA paragraph in Latin.] PoA from Capt. Thomas Wharton to Col. John Bigger. Date: 31 December 1696 before Jeremiah Jenkins (notary).

17:19 Witnesses: William Cooper, Jeremiah Hawthorne.

17:20 Mr. Samuell Hopkins (SO) exhibited:
• will of Peter Bodkin (SO), constituting John Hendry executor, proved by 3 witnesses. Also bond by John Hendry & William Robinson executors. Security: John Webb.

Also inventory, by appraisers Edward
Green & John Webb.

- bond of Ann Wallter administratrix
of Thomas Wallter (SO). Security:
Thomas Wallter. Also inventory, by
appraisers John Panter & John Jones.
- bond of Mary Down administratrix of
Robert Down (SO). Securities:
Richard Jeffres, John Ricketts.
Also inventory, by appraisers Thomas
Winder & Philip Cawser.
- bond of James Round administrator of
Howell Francis (SO). Security:
Samuell Watkins. Also inventory, by
appraisers John Francklin & Thomas
Morris.
- will of Henry Miles (SO),
constituting his son Samuell Miles
(under age) executor, proved by 3
witnesses.

17:21   ...

- bond of John Hendry administrator of
John Parker (SO). Securities:
William Robinson, John Webb. Also
inventory, by appraisers Edward
Green & John Webb.
- bond of William Brittingham
administrator of Nathaniell Innis.
Securities: Stephen Horsey, John
West, Nathaniell Horsey.
- bond of Thomas Jones administrator
of Stephen Luffe (SO). LoA formerly
granted to said Jones & Capt. John
King (now dec'd). Securities:
Mathew Scarbrough, Peter Dent.
- accounts of John Onorton
administrator of William Onorton.
- accounts of Jane Price
administratrix of Edward Price.
- accounts of Alice Hall executrix of
Charles Hall.
- accounts of Elisabeth Porter
executrix of William Porter.
- accounts of Johnson Hill who married
relict of John Tarr.
- accounts of Frances Holland
executrix of Richard Holland.

17:22   5 August. Mr. Hugh Sherwood (TA)
executor of Judith Brooke was granted
continuance.

Court Session: 1697

Absolon Kent (CV) administrator of
Richard Gibbs exhibited accounts. Also
inventory, by appraisers Frances Maldin
& Simon Wootton.

Charles Brooke exhibited that an account
was made up on behalf of petitioner
against Mr. Henry Brent. Also that
Richard Marsham (PG) married
administratrix of said Brent & is liable
to pay said account, but said Marsham
refuses. Administrators of said Brent
to pay said Brooke. Mr. Richard
Marsham exhibited additional accounts of
Henry Brent.

17:23   Mr. Thomas Greenfeild administrator of
Richard Charlett exhibited accounts.
Continuance was granted. Also exhibited
PoA from Mr. Richard Kings (merchant,
London) to said Greenfeild.
• William Smith, Jr. (g), age 32,
deposed before Sir John Houblon
knight & Lord Mayor, at the request
of Richard Kings (citizen, merchant
tailor, London) executor of Richard
Charlett (Swanson's Creek, CV) that
he saw said Kings deliver PoA to
said Greenfeild. Date: 26 December
1695 at London. Signed: (N).
Goodfellow.

17:24   ...
• PoA from said Kings to said
Greenfeild.

17:25   ...
Date: 26 December 1695. Witnesses:
William Smith, Jr., John Williams,
Philip Rogerson.

Sarah Pindar (DO) administratrix of
Edward Pindar exhibited additional
accounts. Since no one appeared against
her, the attachment was dismissed.

Exhibited bond of Mr. Benjamin Wells
administrator of George Wells.
Securities: Edward Boothby, James
Philips.

Robert Gouldesborough procurator for
John Fisher vs. Col. John Bigger
administrator of Simon Wootton. Libel

Court Session: 1697

exhibited.

17:26 7 August. Exhibited will of Col.
William Digges (CH), constituting his
widow Elisabeth Digges & his son Edward
Digges executors, proved by 3 witnesses.
Said Elisabeth & Edward were granted
administration. Appraisers: Maj. James
Smallwood, Mr. Anthony Neale. Mr.
Robert Yates (g, CH) to administer oath.

10 August. Mr. Seth Biggs (g, AA)
exhibited bond of William Liddell & his
wife Jane relict & administrators of
Nicholas Terrett (AA). Securities: John
Deaver, Henry Sury. Also inventory, by
appraisers said Deaver & said Sury.

Richard Chishire (AA) administrator of
Charles Roberts exhibited accounts.

Mr. William Palmer (g, CV) exhibited
will of William Hickman, proved by 3
witnesses. Also inventory, by
appraisers John Scott & James Heigh.

17:27 11 August. Mr. James Cranford (CV)
administrator of John Abington appeared,
to exhibit accounts. His Excellency the
Governor ordered that the accounts
should not pass until the appraisers
have been examined by His Excellency.
William Turner & Elisha Hall appraisers
were summoned. James Cranford & George
Lingan were summoned to appear before
His Excellency & said Cranford is not
permitted to plead his case in this
court.

Gabriell Parrott (AA) administrator of
Daniell Longman exhibited additional
accounts.

MM Robert Carvile & William Bladen
procurators for MM James Pattison &
Garrett Vansweringen vs. James Cullens
executor of Marke Cordea. Continuance
was granted, to complete the accounts &
to exhibit exceptions.

Madam Blackiston administratrix of
Nehemiah Blackiston exhibited additional

accounts.

George Plater, Esq. administrator of
Robert Doyne (CH) exhibited additional
accounts.

17:28 13 August. Thomas & Abraham Warren vs.
Notley Warren (CH). Attachment issued
to said Notley.

Samuell Watkins vs.   William Morrison.
Dismissed.

John Edmondson vs.   Joseph Rogers.
Dismissed.

Richard Keene vs.   Joseph Edloe.
Dismissed.

His Excellency the Governor & the
Councill ordered that no papers from Mr.
John Llewelling concerning the records
of this Office ought to be received
until further notice.

Mr. Philip Clarke procurator for John
Hodges son & heir of William Hodges (KE)
vs. Richard Mason (KE) & John Hurt
(KE). Libel exhibited. Said Mason &
Hurt summoned to show cause why the will
of said Hodges should not be set aside &
said John given LoA. George James & his
wife Jone, Robert Atckison, Robert
Browne, James Wroth, & Mary Peak
summoned to prove said will.

17:29 Mr. William Dent (CH) exhibited his
letter regarding inventory & accounts on
estate of Col. Chandler by Capt. George
Brent. Author is friend to children.
The widow paid the debts prior to her
marriage to said Brent. Said widow
married & went to VA.
17:30 Said widow is now dec'd & children are
of age (or nearly so). Mentions:
daughter Jane, son William (eldest son,
over age 17).
17:31 Capt. George Brent (VA) who married
Mary Chandler had falsely obtained
administration on estate of Col.
William Chandler. Mr. William Dent
exhibited exceptions on 2 July 1697.

Ruling: accounts are null & void. Said
Brent summoned.

17:32 Michaell Butterworth (SM) was granted
administration on estate of William
Taylor (SM). Securities: Robert Carss,
James Symons. Appraisers: Henry
Poultery, Capt. Thomas Attaway.

23 August. Mr. Edward Boothby (BA)
exhibited:
* will of Nicholas Corbin (BA),
  constituting his widow Alice Corbin
  executrix, proved by 2 witnesses.
  Said Alice was granted
  administration. Also inventory of
  said Nicholas Corben, by appraisers
  Jonas Bowen & John Mounfeild.
* will of Richard Adams, Sr.,
  constituting his widow Mary Adams &
  son Charles Adams executors, proved
  by 3 witnesses. Said Mary & Charles
  were granted administration. Also
  inventory, by appraisers Thomas
  Smith & Samuell Sicklemore.
* bond of Charles Adams administrator
  of Richard Adams, Jr. Securities:
  William Lenox, John Boone. Also
  inventory, by appraisers Thomas
  Smith & Samuell Sicklemore.

17:33 ...
* Mary Jones relict of Thomas Jones
  (BA) was granted administration on
  his estate.
* bond of William Pickett
  administrator of Joseph Gallion
  (AA). Securities: Thomas Heath,
  Moses Groom.
* bond of Mr. Marke Richardson
  administrator of Mary Utie relict of
  George Utie. Securities: Samuell
  Browne, Roger Mathew, James
  Phillips, Anthony Drew.
* bond of Mr. John Hall & his wife
  Martha administrators of said Mary
  Utie. Securities: Anthony Drew,
  Thomas Browne.
* oath of Marke Richardson & his wife
  Susanah administrators of Mary Utie.
  Also renunciation of Mr. Hall.
  Date: 6 July last.
* oath of said Hall, having

reconsidered, sworn 10 July last.
- will of Thomas Darbin (BA), constituting his friends Richard Cromwell & Mr. Fitzsymons overseers, proved by 3 witnesses. Mr. Roger Newman was granted administration, as greatest creditor.
- accounts of Joseph Peake who married Jane executrix of her mother Jane Long.
- accounts of Robuck Lynch administrator of Samuell Greenwood.

17:34   3 September. Mr. Richard Boughton (CH) exhibited:
- bond of Mary Meeks administratrix of Francis Meeks (CH). Security: Richard Harrison. Also inventory, by Richard Harrison & Edward Ming.
- bond of Mary Hunt administratrix of Richard Hunt. Security: Thomas Hunt.
- inventory of Thomas Mudd, by appraisers William Thompson & Samuell Luckett.
- inventory of Philip Cooksey, by appraisers William Smith & Thomas Price.
- inventory of Dr. William Hall, by appraisers Ralph Shaw & John Godshall.

Mr. Edward James (KI) exhibited renunciation of Catherine Batchelour (Wye River, TA) widow of William Batchelour (d. 23 April 1696), recommending Edward James (KI). Date: 19 August 1697. Witnesses: William Denton, Charles Murphy. Said James was granted administration, as greatest creditor. Security: Nicholas Sporne. Appraisers: Andrew Price, John King. Mr. Richard Tilghman to administer oath.

17:35   15 September. Samuell Duvall (AA) who married Elisabeth relict & executrix of Daniell Clarke (AA) petitioned for Capt. Nicholas Gassaway to prove will & swear appraisers. Appraisers: Gabriell Parrott, Robert Hopper.

Court Session: 1697

17 September. Mr. John Rawlings (DO)
exhibited:
- will of William Read (DO), proved by
  3 witnesses. Jane Read relict was
  granted administration. Securities:
  John Taylor, Henry Wheeler. Also
  inventory, by appraisers Edward
  Williams & Anthony Rawlings.
- bond of Susanah Willmott
  administratrix of Henry Willmott
  (DO). Securities: Henry Wheeler,
  Obadiah King. Also inventory, by
  appraisers Morrice Mathews & Edward
  Wright. Also accounts.

17:36 ...
- accounts of Mary Aldridge
  administratrix of Henry Aldridge
  (DO).
- accounts of Mathias Alford &
  Christian executrix of Elias Godward
  (DO).

23 September. Mr. Samuell Hopkins (SO)
exhibited:
- will of Henry Leaton (SO), proved by
  4 witnesses. Mary Leaton was
  granted administration. Securities:
  John Rencha, John Winsor. Also
  inventory, by appraisers John Panter
  & John Jones.
- will of John Lawes (SO), proved by 3
  witnesses. Katherine Lawes widow
  was granted administration.
  Securities: Jones John William
  Waller. Also inventory, by
  appraisers John Panter & John Jones.
- bond of Henry Rich administrator of
  John Williams (SO). Security:
  Alexander Maddox. Also inventory,
  by appraisers Edmund Howard & Fran.
  Throwgood.

17:37 ...
- bond of John Miskall administrator
  of his father Teague Miskall (SO).
  Securities: Mr. Samuell Hopkins,
  Richard Wharton. Also inventory, by
  appraisers Samuell Collins & John
  Clarke.

8 October. Col. Nicholas Greenberry
(AA) was granted administration on
estate of William Fuller, as greatest

Court Session: 1697

creditor. Securities: Robert
Gouldesborough, Philip Clarke.

11 October. Kenelm Cheseldyn exhibited:
- bond of Mary Thompson widow &
executrix of Robert Thompson (SM).
Securities: John Bayley, James
French. Also inventory, by
appraisers James French & John
Bayley, sworn before Jos. Guibert
(g).
- inventory of Robert Large (SM), by
appraisers Richard Atwood & Capt.
Henry Smith, sworn before Richard
Benton (g). Also, William Morgan
administrator exhibited accounts.

17:38 . . .
- Elisabeth Phips (widow, SM) was
granted administration on estate of
Thomas Moseley. Also inventory, by
appraisers John Cheverell & Richard
Forrest.
- inventory of John Vanreswick (SM),
by appraisers Stephen Gough & Thomas
Kirkley. Mentions: James Browne.
- inventory of William Moss (CV), by
appraisers Daniell Sheridin &
William Harbert. Administrator:
Michaell Taney.

Mr. John Thompson (CE) exhibited:
- will of Robert Crooke (CE),
constituting Henry Eldersley & his
wife Parnell & their daughter
Elisabeth Moss executors, proved by
4 witnesses. Securities: Thomas
Skillton, Robert Hewes.
- inventory of Jacob Young, by
appraisers Cornelius Comegis &
William Boorne.

17:39 . . .
- will of Edward Jones (g, CE),
constituting his widow Dorothy Jones
executrix, proved by 4 witnesses.
Securities: John Veezey, Owen Hewes.
- bond of Sarah Mounts widow &
administratrix of Laurens Mounts
(CE). Securities: Sampson George,
Charles Gorsuch. Also inventory of
said Laurence Mounts, by appraisers
Thomas Witton & John Sequence.
- bond of Mary Mackachy widow &

Page 15

administratrix of John Mackachy
(CE). Securities: James George,
Henry Peterson.

- will of Thomas Nicholson (CE),
constituting his widow Elisabeth
executrix, proved by 3 witnesses.
Said Elisabeth was granted
administration. Securities: Hugh
Finch, John Ryland. Also inventory,
by Thomas Peirce & Thomas Perrey.
- bond of Emanuell Smith who married
relict of Edward Teege (CE).
Securities: Benoni Clarke, Henry
Peterson.

17:40 ...

- inventory of John Brace (CE), by
appraisers John Standly & John
Waggitt.

Mr. Richard Boughton (CH) exhibited:
- will of John Cornish (CH),
constituting his widow Martha
Cornish executrix, proved by 1
witness. Securities: Peter
Mackmilion, George Brett. Also
inventory, by appraisers Peter
Mackmilion, George Britt.
- inventory of Robert Hill (CH), by
appraisers Thomas Hunt & Richard
Eastop.
- list of debts of Col. Pye.
Administrator: Maj. Nicholas
Sewall. Mentions: Henry Wharton,
Edward Digges.

17:41 Mr. Elias King (KE) exhibited:
- will of Walter Jones (KE),
constituting his widow Alice Jones
executrix, proved by 3 witnesses.
Said Alice was granted
administration.
- inventory of William Jones (KE), by
appraisers Charles Tilden & Thomas
Pyner.
- will of Robert Certain (KE),
constituting his widow Mary Certaine
executrix, proved by 2 witnesses.
Said Mary was granted
administration.
- bond of Elisabeth Whitall widow &
administratrix of John Whitall (KE).
Security: John Hollensworth. Also

Court Session: 1697

inventory, by appraisers William
Hackett & Walter Lodge.
- accounts of John Wells administrator
of William Richards (KE).
- accounts of Col. John Hinson
executor of Maj. Joseph Weeks.
- inventory of Lambert Willmer by
administrator Simon Willmer.
- inventory of John Tilletson, by
appraisers Nath. Wright & John
Chaires.
- inventory of John Power, by
appraisers James Smith & John
Hainer.

17:42 Mr. Samuell Withers (TA) exhibited:
- will of Richard Sweatnam (TA),
constituting his brother Edward
Sweatnam (g, KE) & Mr. Hans Hanson
(g, KE) executors, proved by 3
witnesses. Said Hanson renounced
administration. Said Edward was
granted administration. Securities:
Simon Wilmer, Richard Tilgham.
Mentions: orphans of dec'd, Jane
(widow of dec'd).

17:43 ...
George Robotham, Esq. & Michaell
Miller to summon said Jane & any
others. Date: 23 October 1697.
- will of Thomas Bowdle (TA),
constituting his widow Phebe Bowdle
executrix, proved by 2 witnesses.
Said Phebe was granted
administration. Securities: Joseph
Leech, Joseph James.
- John Edmondson was granted
administration on estate of
Cornelius Mulraine, unadministered
by Jesse Holton. Securities: James
Benson, William Edmondson. Also
exhibited accounts.
- accounts of Mary Bagg administratrix
of Thomas Bagg (TA).

17:44 ...
- bond of William Moore administrator
of Henry Newland (TA). Securities:
William Rich, Stephen Richant.
- bond of William Harrison
administrator of James Harrison
(TA). Securities: William Troth,
Stephen Durdon.

- bond of John Hacker administrator of Edward Smith (TA). Securities: William Hatfeild, Thomas Evans.
- bond of Ann Tyley administratrix of John Tyley (TA). Securities: William Bellford, Michaell Baker.
- bond of William Bellford administrator of Edmond Stringer. Securities: Michaell Baker, Ann Tyley.
- accounts of John Long administrator of William Dale.
- inventory of John Qwann, by appraisers John Davis & Philip Massee. Also accounts by Christopher Santee administrator of John Quann. Estate is overpaid.
- accounts of John Glover administrator of Henry Boston (TA).
- inventory of William Allin (d. 1690, TA), by appraisers Nicholas Milburne & Anthony Rumball. Also accounts by John Newman who married Jane relict & administrators.

17:45   Mr. Thomas Smithson (TA) exhibited bond of Mr. Edward Loyd administrator of Philemond Loyd (TA). Securities: Col. George Robotham, Mr. William Coursey. Appraisers: Capt. James Murphey, Capt. John Davis. Date: 24 August 1697.

Mr. Philemond Loyd (TA) one of executors of Hen. Maria Loyd exhibited that £3374.17.0 remains to be distributed equally to the widow & each of the 7 children of Col. Loyd: Edward Lloyd, Phillmond Lloyd, Hen. Mar. Blake, Alie Loyd, Anne Loyd, James Loyd, Margaret Loyd.

17:46   Mr. John Hall (BA) one of administrators of Mary Utie (BA) exhibited inventory, by appraisers George Smith & Laurence Taylor. Mentions: debt from Samuell Chew.

Said Hall who married Martha one of executors of Edward Beddle exhibited accounts.

Court Session: 1697

Mr. John Hall who married relict &
executrix of George Gouldsmith exhibited
additional accounts.

Mr. William Dent procurator for Gerrard
Fouke vs. Capt. George Brent procurator
for William Chandler (CH). Libel
exhibited. Mentions: said Chandler
exhibited caveat against estate of
Richard Chandler. Answer exhibited.

12 October. Isaack Williams (CV)
executor of Ruth Hide exhibited
additional accounts.

Exhibited inventory of Henry Thomas
(CV), by appraisers Richard Watkins &
Jacob Tyre. John Jenkins administrator
exhibited accounts. Estate is overpaid.
Dismissed.

17:47 Mr. Richard Keene (CV) exhibited: bond
of Elisabeth Howe administratrix of John
Howe (CV). Securities: John Lauterkin,
James Dixon. Also inventory, by
appraisers John Skiper & William
Hutchins.

Robert Carvile procurator for Mr.
Thomas Jones (SO) vs. Mr. Charles
Carroll procurator for Arnold Elzey.
Libel & answer exhibited.

13 October. Mr. Philip Clarke
procurator for John Hodges (KE) son &
heir of William Hodges (KE) vs. Mr.
William Dent procurator for Richard
Mason & John Hurt. Libel & answer
exhibited.

Mr. John Thompson (CE) to examine
accounts of William Jones & his wife
Sarah administratrix of Walter Meekes.

Christopher Bane (PG) executor of his
father was granted continuance.

Mr. Richard Keene (CV) to prove will of
William Keet (CH).

17:48 Thomas Blake (CV) & his wife Jane
executrix of Edward Isaack (CV)

exhibited accounts.

William Hemsley administrator of Francis
Armstrong (TA) exhibited that there is
no estate to inventory.

Peter Mackmilion (CH) executor of
Elisabeth Bullett exhibited accounts.

Sheriff (CV) to serve attachment of
contempt to Michaell Higgins
administrator of John Guyatt (CV).

14 October. MM Richard Keene & Henry
Fernly exhibited oath of Mr. Henry Lowe
& his wife to their answer to libel of
Col. Darnell.

Thomas & Abraham Warren vs. Robert
Carvile procurator for Notley Warren
(CH). Answer exhibited.

17:49   13 October. Mary Douglas (CH)
administratrix of Richard Beaumont (CH)
exhibited accounts.

Henry Lowe, Esq. (SM) exhibited oath of
Baker Brooke administrator of Garrat
Cumberford. Also oath of appraisers:
Charles Brookes, Ralph Haywood.

14 October. Ann Smith (AA) executrix of
James Smith exhibited accounts.

John Gale (AA) who married Margarett
relict & administratrix of John Atkins
exhibited accounts. Continuance was
granted.

John Batie (AA) who married relict &
executrix of Roger Bishop (AA) exhibited
accounts.

Capt. Richard Brightwell (PG) was
granted administration on estate of John
Baker (PG), as greatest creditor.
Securities: James Waple, Henry Dryden.

15 October. Mr. John Scott (CV)
exhibited bond of Mary Hickman
administratrix of William Hickman.
Securities: Marke Clare, Richard Fida.

Court Session: 1697

16 October. John Watkins (PG) administrator of Thomas Lewis was granted continuance.

17:50   Mr. Thomas Greenfeild administrator of Richard Charlett exhibited additional accounts.

John Fisher vs. Charles Carroll procurator for Col. John Bigger. Answer exhibited. Ruling: plaintiff, & administration dbn was granted to said Fisher, as next of kin.

Hugh Ellis to pay legacies in libel suit.

Thomas Skellington (TA) on behalf of Sarah Goddard exhibited petition.

Richard Kendle (DO) who married Jane relict of James Quatermus exhibited accounts.

William Watts who married Margret relict & executrix of W. Bexley (TA) exhibited accounts.

Mr. Hugh Sherwood (TA) executor of Judith Brooke exhibited accounts. Continuance was granted.

Mr. Edward Blay (CE) exhibited bond of widow & administratrix of Casparus Augustine Herman. Securities: Mathew VanderHeyden, Michaell Miller.

Thomas Warren & Abraham Warren (SM) vs. Notly Warren (CH). Search for accounts of Humph. Warren administrator of Thomas Howell.

17:51   MM William Dent & Philip Clarke for (N) Fowke vs. Capt. Brent & Mr. Carroll for (N) Chandler. Ruling: will is good as to the personal estate, but the land to distribute according to inheritance. LoA to said Fowke. Mr. Boughton to administer oath.

18 October. Gabriell Parrott vs. William Bladen procurator for John Elsey

Page 21

Court Session: 1697

(CV). Answer exhibited.

Petition of Sarah Goddard (TA) spinster
& daughter of Elias Goddard (DO). Said
Elias d. 7 March 1696, leaving a small
estate to be divided between petitioner
& her younger sister Christian Goddard.
By the persuasion of John Alford &
Mathias Alford, stranger to the
petitioner, said Christian kept from the
petitioner and/or her grandfather Thomas
Skillington her father's will. Said
Alfords have fraudulently carried away
all.
19 October. Executor to exhibit
accounts.

17:52   Mr. John Llewellin exhibited papers of
        Col. Blackiston.

        Thomas Tany (CH) administrator of his
        father Michaell Tawney exhibited
        accounts.

        Samuell Watkins procurator for Gabriell
        Parrott vs. William Bladen procurator
        for John Elzey. Ruling: said Elzey to
        pay 2/3rds to said Parrott.

        Mr. Elias King (KE) to prove will of
        Marke Benton (KE).

        Mr. Edward Loyd administrator of his
        father was granted continuance.

        Exhibited inventory of Mr. Henry
        Constable (AA), by appraisers Capt.
        John Worthington & Capt. Humphrey
        Boone.

        Maj. William Barton (PG) executor of
        Bazell Warren exhibited accounts.

        widow Mooney (CV) exhibited accounts.

        James Pattison (SM) administrator of
        Edward Ward & administrator of James
        Watkins exhibited accounts on both
        estates.

17:53   Exhibited inventory of Col. Henry
        Coursey (TA), by appraisers Maj. Thomas

Court Session: 1697

Smithson, John Johnson, & William
Coursey.

20 October. Mr. Philip Clarke
procurator for (N) vs. Hodges Mr. Dent
procurator for (N) Mason & (N) Hurt.
Ruling: former LoA revoked.
Administration dbn was granted to said
Hodges. Securities: Mr. Michaell
Miller, Robert Brewnett.

21 October. Thomas Taylor for Sarah
Pinder (DO) administratrix of Edward
Pinder exhibited additional accounts.

Mr. Philemon Lloyd petitioned for a new
appraisal of estate of Henerita Maria
Lloyd. Appraisers: Capt. James
Murphey, Maj. Thomas Smithson, Mr.
William Coursey.

Edward James (KE) exhibited inventory of
William Batchelour, by appraisers Andrew
Price & John King.

Madam Mary King was granted
administration on estate of Maj. Robert
King (SO). Appraisers: MM William
Planner, Sr., Ephraim Willson. Mr.
Stephen Horsey to administer oath.

Mr. John Rawlings (DO) exhibited
inventory of William Dorrington.
Administrator: Charles Powell.

Sisley Richardson exhibited inventory of
Simon Richardson.

17:54 25 October. Mr. Egcleston (alias Mr.
Eccleston, DO) executor of William Hill
exhibited additional accounts.

George Lingan vs. James Cranford. Said
Cranford administrator of John Abington
exhibited additional accounts. Ruling:
said Cranford to pay said Lingan the
balance.

(N) Fisher vs. (N) Bigger. Ruling:
plaintiff has administration on that
part of the estate of Symon Wootton in
this province, as next of kin. Daughter

of said dec'd is dec'd.

Thomas & Abraham Warren vs. Notley
Warren. Ruling: deferred until
verification of accounts of Humphrey
Warren (dec'd) administrator of (N)
Howell.

Elisabeth & Ann Hunton vs. Hugh Ellis.
Ruling: said Ellis to pay the orphans
their portion, & they to give security.

Col. Thomas Richardson (BA) who married
Martha executrix of Anthony Demondidier
exhibited accounts.

17:55 1 November. Inspections of returns
exhibited, from 1689 to 1692:
- Charles Hynson (clerk, KE).
  Endorsed by Mr. Llewellin on 3
  December 1692.
- John West (clerk, SO). Endorsed by
  Mr. Llewellin on 3 December 1693.
- Mr. Denton (clerk, SM).
- Mr. Henry Fernly (clerk, CV).
- Thomas Hedge (clerk, BA).
- Cleborne Lomax (clerk, CH).
- Henry Bonner (clerk, AA).
- John Thompson (clerk, CE).
- Hugh Eccleston (clerk, DO).
- Mr. Henry Denton (clerk, TA).
Date: 16 March 1697/8.

5 November. Daniell Toas (Quaker, KE)
was granted administration dbn on estate
of Daniell Carnell (TA), unadministered
by his wife Deborah & Edward Pollard
executors.

9 November. Exhibited inventory of John
Watkins (AA), by appraisers Henry
Hanslap & John Chapell.

Exhibited inventory of Nicholas Lambe
(AA), by appraisers Thomas Beason &
William Freeman.

17:56 11 November. Exhibited inventory of
Richard Wells (AA), by appraisers Morgan
Jones & Edward Mason.

Capt. William Holland exhibited bond:
- Mary Wells administratrix of Richard Wells. Securities: Marke Clare, Morgan Jones.
- John Swinster who married relict of Richard Deavour (AA). Securities: Joseph Chew, Benjamin Chew.

22 November. Margarett Marke widow of John Marke (BA) was granted administration on his estate. Appraisers: Samuell Sickamore, Abraham Taylor. Mr. Thomas Staley to administer oath.

23 November. Charles Carroll procurator for Thomas Thurston (BA) son & heir of Thomas Thurston (dec'd) vs. Samuell Brown executor of said dec'd. Libel exhibited.

Thomas Jones administrator of Stephen Luffe vs. Charles Carroll procurator for Arnold Elzey (SO). Answer exhibited.

25 November. Dr. James Benson (TA) exhibited will of Samuell Withers (TA), constituting him executor, on behalf of his 3 children: Perry Benson, Ann Benson, Elisabeth Benson. Said James was granted administration. Capt. James Murphey to prove said will.

17:57 11 December. Exhibited inventory of Daniell Clarke (AA), by appraisers Gabriell Parrott & Robert Hopper.

24 December. Mr. Francis Freeman (CV) exhibited bond of John Fisher administrator of Symon Wootten. Securities: Richard Keene, Daniell Shereden. Appraisers: Thomas Blake, Henry Fernely.

Joshua Cecill (PG) exhibited:
- bond of Mary Wales administratrix of Richard Wales. Securities: James Gambing, Isaack Williams.
- inventory of David Floyd (PG), by appraisers George Athey & William Clarke. Accounts exhibited by Henry

Gutridge who married Mary the
relict.

28 December. Exhibited inventory of
Richard Deavour (AA), by appraisers
Robert Wood & Daniell Browne.

11 December. Ann Johnson widow of
Edward Johnson (CE) vs. estate of said
Edward. Caveat exhibited. Owen Hughes
(alias Owen Hues) is the pretended
executor. Witnesses are all legatees,
except for a mad man.

17:58 6 January. Darbey Henly exhibited
additional accounts on estate of Obadia
Evens (CV). Date: 12 October 1697. He
was sworn on 11 March following.

Regarding estate of Mary Aldredge (DO).
Summons issued for: Walter Cample,
Anthony Thompson, William Dowse, John
Batten. Signed: John Rawlings.

William Dent to John Bouge. Date: 4
December 1697 at Nanzemy. Mentions:
Samuell Withers (TA, dec'd). Petition
for LoA, as greatest creditor.

17:59 Kenelm Cheseldyn to Mr. Bouge. Date: 1
January 1697/8. Directions. Mentions:
Ann Hunton vs. Hugh Ellis, Mr. Carvile.

11 February. Matthew Scarbrough to Mr.
Bouge. Petition on behalf of widow
Maynard. Mentions: numerous suits.

24 February. Dr. James Benson
administrator of Samuell Wither (TA) was
granted continuance. Mentions: major
portion of estate is in KE.

Mr. Nich. Milborne (TA) administrator
of Alderman Meadcalfe. Mentions: estate
in ENG. Said Milborne is now vey ill.
Continuance was granted.

John Edmondson administrator of William
Johnson was granted continuance. Cites:
letter dated 7 February 1697/8.

Court Session: 1697

17:60 Mr. Hopkins (SO) exhibited:
- will & inventory of Mr. James Dashiell.
- inventory of John Conner. Administrator: Levin Denwood, Jr.
- accounts of Elisabeth Robinson, Cornelius Innes, Johnson Hill, & Anne Walter.
- inventory of Daniell Selby.
- inventory of Thomas Smith.
- additional inventory of Stephen Costin.
- accounts of Dunnock Dennis administrator.

24 January. Samuell Smith (AA) was granted administration on estate of his brother James Smith for use of John Smith only son of dec'd. Securities: William Gosling, Thomas Blake. Appraisers: Jonathon Neale, James Homewood.

13 January. David Small administrator of William Cooper exhibited accounts.

24 February. Mr. Samuell Hopkins, Sr. (SO) exhibited:
- accounts of Ann Walker administratrix of Thomas Walker (SO).
- accounts of Cornelius Innis administrator of William Innis (SO).
- accounts of Elisabeth Robinson administratrix of William Robinson (SO).
- accounts of Johnson Hill who married relict of John Tarr (SO).

17:61 ...
- inventory of Stephen Costen.
- inventory of father of James Dashiell administrator.
- inventory of Daniell Selby (SO).
- accounts of Dannock Dennis administrator of Hope Taylor (SO).
- inventory of John Conner (SO). Administrator: Levin Denwood.
- inventory of Thomas Smith (SO). Administrators: Jennitt & William Smith.
- will of James Dashell (SO), proved.
- will of Thomas Smith (SO), proved by

Page 27

3 witnesses.
- bond of James Dashiell administrator of his father.
- bond of Leven Denwood administrator of John Conner.
- bond of Mary, Daniell, & Parker Selby administrators of Daniell Selby (SO).
- bond of Jennet & William Smith administrators of Thomas Smith.

2 March. Exhibited inventory of William Anderson, by appraisers Thomas Taylor & John Burges.

Exhibited inventory of William Johnson (AA), by appraisers William Courtis & Richard Sanders. Also bond ob Francis Johnson (AA) administratrix.

17:62   Mr. Thomas Robins (TA) to prove will of John Edmondson (TA), constituting Sarah, James, William, & Thomas Edmondson executors.

Mr. Richard Bennet exhibited that he is joint administrator of estate of Henrietta Maria Lloyd.

5 March. Exhibited will of Col. Nicholas Greenberry (AA), constituting his widow Ann & his son Charles Greenbery executors, proved by 3 witnesses. Said Ann & Charles were granted administration. Securities: Robert Gouldesborrough, Henry Ridgley, Jr.

Mr. John Thompson (CE) exhibited:
- inventory of John Makacky. Administratrix: Mary Makacky (widow, CE). Date: 1 November 1697.
- inventory of Edward Teege (CE). Administrator: Emanuell Smith (CE).
- inventory of Robert Crooke (CE). One of executors: Henry Elderseley.

Ann Johnson vs. estate of Edward Johnson. Caveat exhibited. Date: 11 December.

9 March. Mr. Gouldesborough procurator for Henry King & ux. vs. Joseph Peake & his wife Jane. Libel exhibited.

17:63 Col. William Pearce was granted administration on estate of Richard Thornton (CE), as greatest creditor. Date: 30 December. Security: Hugh Fouck. Appraisers: Thomas Windall, Peter Cole. Capt. Edward Blay to administer oath.

John Thompson exhibited the commission to swear Thomas Kellton, James Gray, & Jacob Vaugezell as appraisers of estate of Col. Casper Herman.
- said Thomas Killton & Jacob Vaugezlow were sworn on 26 February 1697/8. Said Gray was not present.
- exhibited bond of Katherine Herman administratrix. Sureties: Math. Vanderhayden, Michaell Miller.
Date: 28 February 1697/8.

Said Thompson also exhibited accounts of York Yorkenson & his wife Mary relict & administratrix of Jonas Mattox (CE).

Honorable Commissary Esq. Cheseldyn exhibited:
- inventory of Thomas Richardson.
- inventory of Thomas Ennis.
- inventory of John Duggins.
- inventory of William Chessum.
- inventory of Arthur Keive.
- inventory of Elias Beck.

17:64 ...
- bond of Thomas Meech.
- bond of Stanhope Rule.
- bond of Charles Goff.
- bond of Ignatius Warren.
- bond of Richard Berkhead.
- bond of Christopher Gwin.
- bond of Philip Jones.
- bond of John Bayly.
- inventory of William Taylor, by appraisers Henry Powltery & James Symmons.
- inventory of Timothy Tracy.
- inventory of William Rosewell.
- will & inventory of Col. Digges.
- inventory of Thomas Miles.

- will & inventory of John Long.
- will of John Askins.
- will of Stephen Walton.
- will of Mr. William Powell.

10 March.
- will & inventory of Richard Benton.
- inventory of Owen Newton.
- inventory of Richard Wallis (PG).
- inventory of Robert Thompson (SM).
- petition of John Medley that his father-in-law Charles Daught be granted administration on estate of his father, unadministered by his mother, for use of himself & his brothers & sisters. Date: 11 February 1697. Witness: Elias Polman.
- accounts of Edward Cole & James French on estate of John Curry.

17:65 ...
- commission to Mr. William Husbands. Date: 7 February 1697.
- William Husbands exhibited bond of Ignatius Warren administrator, bond of Richard Burket & Charles Goffe, note on estate of John Masters. Mentions: said Husbands has lately lost his Negro & his (Husbands') wife & 2 others are ill. Date: 26 February 1697/8.
- accounts of William Braborne executor of John Hambleton.
- accounts of Madam Elisabeth Bourne executrix of Mr. Samuell Bourne.
- petition of Rachall Keive (blind & bedridden) that her brother be granted administration on her husband's estate. Witnesses: Daniell Barey, William Asbestone. Date: 5 February 1697. Isaack Payne was granted administration on said estate.

17:66 ...
- accounts of Thomas Cambell executor of John Cambell.
- bond of Margrett Copnell administratrix of Edward Copnell (CV). Securities: Henry Mitchell, Charles Chrismas.
- inventory of Alexander Lewis (CV), by appraisers John Hollins & Thomas How.

Court Session: 1697

- will of Robert Foster (SM), proved
  by Mr. Richard Clouds. Ann Reeves
  executrix was granted
  administration. Security: Thomas
  Reeves. Appraisers: John Smith,
  Notly Maddox. Said Clouds to
  administer oath.
- bond of Margret Taylor
  administratrix of Walter Taylor
  (SM). Securities: John Miller, John
  Williams.
- bond of Charles Daught administrator
  of William Medly (SM). Securities:
  John Nevit, John Brown.
- will of Francis Freeman (CV), proved
  by 3 witnesses. Also bond by Ann
  Freeman administratrix.

17:67 ...

- bond of Elisabeth Keitly widow &
  administratrix of Thomas Keitly.
  Securities: John Nevitt, John
  Browne. Also inventory, by
  appraisers Stephen Gough, John Tant,
  & James Greenwell, sworn by Mr.
  William Husbands.
- Anne Medly widow of William Medly
  exhibited his inventory, by
  appraisers James Greenwell & Stephen
  Gough, sworn by Mr. William
  Husbands.

Exhibited will of Robert Bayly (SM),
constituting his widow Margret
executrix, proved. Said Margrett was
granted administration. Security: John
Bright.

Exhibited bond of William Herbert & his
wife Elinor executors of James Pattison
(SM). Securities: Thomas Grunwin,
William Lowrey.

Exhibited will of John Miles (SM),
constituting his son John Miles
executor. Said son John was granted
administration. Security: Charles Beck.
James Keech to administer oath.

Exhibited will of John Davis (CV),
constituting his widow Mary executrix,
proved by Richard Sothorne & William
Bull. Said Mary was granted

Court Session: 1697

17:68
administration. Securities: John Davis,
Samuell Williamson. Mr. James Keech to
administer oath.
Letter from James Keech, sent by John
Miles. Mentions: Mary Davis executrix
of her husband, several widows with
children in CH who desire LoA but cannot
travel to head of CH. Date: 29 March
1698. Exhibited oath of MM Robert
Clarke & John Fenix, appraisers of John
Davis.

11 March. Exhibited inventory of
William Taylor (SM), by appraisers Henry
Powetter & James Simons. Also bond of
Michaell Butterworth administrator.
Security: Charles Watts.

Exhibited inventory of John Marke (BA),
per Mr. Staley.

17:69
10 March. MM Clement Hill & Ralph Rymer
to inspect the papers of Mr. Edward Pye
(d. 14 September 1697). Mentions:
estate of Benjamin Rozier who wife
married said Pye.

Nicholas Fitzsimons & his wife Martha
exhibited will of Thomas Morgan (BA).
Said Nicholas & Martha were granted
administration. Mr. Thomas Staley to
administer oath.

Ruth Ellis widow of Hugh Ellis (d. 3rd
of last month) exhibited his will,
constituting her executrix. Said Ruth
was granted administration. Probate was
held up by sureties for estate of (N)
Cosden. Mentions: estate of (N) Hunton.
Mr. Richard Keene (CV) to administer
oath.

17:70
Mr. James Cranford deposed on 28
October 1697 that he would deliver to
Mr. George Lingan the papers, etc., on
the estate of Mr. John Abington.
Present at the delivery: Mr. Carroll,
Mr. Carvile, Mr. Lingan, Mr. Cranford,
John Bouye.

Mathew Lewis (p, CV) executor of John
Edwards (CV) exhibited his renunciation.

Date: 4 May 1695. Witnesses: George
Plater, Mark Gendron.

11 March. Mr. John Rawlings (DO)
exhibited:
- accounts of Edward Taylor
  administrator of Mordant Thetcher
  (DO).
- accounts of Jane Reed administratrix
  of William Read (DO).
- will of John Southee, proved.
- will of Henry Whigler (DO), proved.

17:71 ...
- inventory of John Southee.
- inventory of Henry Whigler. Also
  bond of Alice Whigler
  administratrix.
- bond of Charles Powell administrator
  of William Dorrington.

Katherine Robertson widow of Richard
Robertson (BA) was granted
administration on his estate. Mr.
George Ashman to administer oath.

Mr. Tilghman executor of John Swaine was
granted continuance.

12 March. Ellinor Clift (TA) was
granted administration on estate of John
Clift (TA). Mr. Thomas Robins to
administer oath.

John Gattrell (AA) petitioned for equal
distribution of estate of William
Johnson to: Francis Johnson (brother), &
said Gattrell in right of his wife
(sister).

14 March. Mr. Jacob Moreland (SM) was
granted administration on estate of
Thomas Barker (mariner, London), on
behalf of Mary widow. Securities: Col.
Henry Jowles, Mr. James Cranford.

Mr. Thomas Robins (TA) exhibited will
of John Edmondson which was returned, as
it was insufficiently proved per Mr.
William Sharp.

17:72 12 March. Mr. Robert Gouldesborough
for Henry King & his wife (BA) vs. Mr.

Philip Clarke for Joseph Peake & his wife executors of Mrs. Jane Long (BA). Libel exhibited.

Mr. William Hemsley vs. Edward Sweatnam (KE) administrator of Richard Sweatnam (TA). Libel exhibited.

Patrick Danielly (TA) vs. Charles Powell (DO). Libel exhibited.

Col. Henry Lowe & his wife vs. Mr. Charles Carroll for Col. Henry Darnall & his wife. Replication & answer exhibited.

Walter Camble (DO) was granted administration on estate of Mary Aldredge, as greatest creditor. Securities: Col. Ninian Beale, William Taylard.

Mr. William Taylard was granted administration on estate of John Masters (SM). Securities: Walter Camble, Col. Ninian Beale.

14 March. Mr. John Hall (BA) was appointed Deputy Commissary (BA).

Allice Smith (AA) was granted administration on estate of John Smith (Irishman, AA). Securities: Edward Lunn, Richard Horner. Appraisers: John Gadsby, Richard Sorrell. Mr. John Worthington to administer oath.

15 March. George Plater, Esq. administrator of Robert Doyne exhibited additional accounts.

17:73   Exhibited inventory of John Reynolds (CV), by appraisers Cornelius Walkinson & John Gillam.

16 March. Mr. Henry Denton exhibited all testamentary papers for TA for 1689, 1690, & 1691.

Mr. Philip Clarke (SM) one of administrators of Thomas Meech exhibited accounts.

Court Session: 1697

William Clark (AA) was granted
administration on estate of John Persons
(AA). Appraisers: William Pennington,
John Gardner. Capt. John Worthington
to administer oath.

Dennis Connorrll & his wife Mary (CH)
were granted administration on estate of
William Bryan (CH), as next of kin to
Elinor Bryan next of kin to dec'd. Said
Elinor for natural inability &
incapacity of mind to manage the estate
was not granted administration. Maj.
James Smallwood to administer oath.

Mr. Nicholas Lowe exhibited 5 summons.

Mr. Walter Smith (CV) exhibited will of
Thomas Hillary (CV), constituting his
son Thomas Hillary (infant) executor.
Said Smith was granted administration,
during minority of the orphan. Said
Smith was appointed overseer.
17:74 Said will was proved by 3 witnesses,
before Richard Keene.

17 March. Mr. Samuell Young (AA) who
married Mary relict of Thomas Francis
(AA) exhibited additional accounts.
Payments to Charles Whitehead are not to
be allowed.

Mr. Benjamin Hall (CH) who married
relict & executrix of James Bowling was
granted "quietus est".

21 March. Mr. Kempton Mabbet (DO)
exhibited will of Maj. Henry Tripp.
Said Mabbet is one of the witnesses.

24 March. Exhibited will of George
Norman (BA), constituting his widow
Elisabeth Norman executrix. Said
Elisabeth was granted administration.
Securities: Thomas Reynolds, Samuell
Smith. Appraisers: Richard Crumwell,
James Murrey. Mr. George Ashman to
administer oath. Said Reynolds is one
of the witnesses. Mentions: 2 orphans.

Ann Fisher (alias Ann Davis) widow of
Thomas Fisher (KI, TA) was granted

Page 35

administration on his estate.
Securities: Mr. Philip Lynes, Richard
Jones. Appraisers: William Elles,
Isaack Winchester. Mr. Edward Jones to
administer oath.

Court Session: 1698

17:75 28 March. Mr. Richard Bennett vs.
executors of estate of his mother
Henrietta Maria Lloyd. Caveat
exhibited.

Exhibited bond of Susanna Miles, Thomas
Courtney, & John Wiseman. Date: 8
February 1697. Said Susanna is
administratrix of Thomas Miles (SM).
Witnesses: Philip Cork, William
Aisquith.

17:76 John Royston (BA) who married relict &
executrix of Rouland Thornborough (BA)
exhibited accounts.

Mr. Richard Bennett (TA) vs. executors
of his mother's estate. Caveat
exhibited.

30 March. Mr. Edward Swettnam (KE)
executor of Richard Swettnam (TA) was
granted continuance.

John Hodges (KE) administrator of his
father William Hodges petitioned for
renewal of appraisers: Col. Charles
Hinson, William Glanvell.

Madam Frances Sayer executrix of Jacob
Seth (TA) was granted administration on
his estate. Thomas Smithson, to
administer oath.

Thomas Smithson, (TA) was appointed
Deputy Commissary (TA).

2 April. Nathaniell Wickham (PG) who
married Sebina relict & executrix of
Thomas Barnett (PG) exhibited additional
accounts. Mentions: 2 orphans.

17:77 Charles Greenberry son & one of
executors of Col. Nicholas Greenbery

Court Session: 1698

(g, AA) was granted a renewed
administration on estate of William
Fuller. Said Nicholas died soon after
original LoA were granted. Securities:
Robert Gouldbury, Henry Ridgley, Jr.

5 April. Mr. Edward Swettnam (KE)
exhibited his letter: Petter Clarke (now
dec'd) was overseer on his brother's
plantation. Date: 4 April 1698.
Signed: Edward Sweatnam. James Williams
vs. said estate. Caveat exhibited
before Mr. Elias King (KE), alleging a
nuncupative will.

Samuell Scidmore (AA) was granted
administration on estate of Ailce Boyce
(widow, AA), as next of kin & greatest
creditor.
17:78 Securities: Richard Killburne, Jonathon
Neale.

6 April. Mr. Richard Boughton (CH)
exhibited returns.

Robuck Linch administrator of Samuell
Greenwood (BA) was granted continuance.

Mr. George Lingan (high sheriff, CV)
exhibited returns.

Exhibited inventory of Francis Hyden
(SM), by appraisers John Baptista
Carbery & John Bailley.

Phillip Clarke procurator for Col.
George Robotham (TA) vs. Richard
Bennett administrator of John Howell.
Exceptions to accounts exhibited.

Henry King & his wife Tabitha vs. said
Phillip Clark procurator for Joseph
Peake (BA) & his wife. Answer
exhibited.

7 April. Capt. James Murphy (TA)
exhibited:
• oath of Madam Frances Sayer & Mr.
Charles Blake executors of Col.
Petter Sayer.
17:79 ...
Securities: James Murphey, Edward

Lloyd.

- oath of Ralph Dawson, Jr. & John Dawson, appraisers of Daniell Carnall. Administrator: Daniell Toas. Sureties: William Dixon, Robert Regester.
- will of Samuell Withers (TA), proved by 2 witnesses. James Benson executor was granted administration. Securities: Daniell Sherwood, John Dawson.

8 April. Mr. Robert Gouldesborough procurator for Henry King & his wife (BA) vs. Joseph Peake & his wife Jane. Replication exhibited.

Henry Fernley & his wife Margaret administratrix of John Broom (alias John Broome, CV) petitioned for continuance. Mentions: Mr. Samuell Groome. Date: 6 April 1698.

17:80 Elisabeth Haddock (AA) widow of Richard Haddock was granted administration on his estate.

9 April. Exhibited inventory of William Hinson (AA), by appraisers John & John Trundell.

John Harbottle (AA) who married Ann relict of Henry Francis (AA) was granted administration on his estate. Sureties: Henry Meredith, Richard Jones, Sr. Appraisers: Edward Fuller, William Penington. Capt. John Worthington to administer oath.

John Sherwood (TA) who married Lucy Man administratrix of Edward Man (TA) exhibited inventory, by appraisers Robert Grundy & Thomas Delehay. Also exhibited accounts.

17:81 **11 April.** Thomas Booker (TA) one of executors of Thomas Booker (TA) exhibited inventory, by appraisers Daniell Walker & Edward Latham. Mr. Thomas Smithson (TA) to examine accounts.

Court Session: 1698

Christopher Santee (TA) administrator of
John Quan (TA) exhibited accounts.

William Gilly (CV) who married Elisabeth
administratrix of Francis Higham (CV)
exhibited accounts.

Per Mr. John Scott, James Heigh (CV)
administrator of Petter Godard (CV)
exhibited accounts.

William Sharpe (TA) executor of John
Boram (TA) exhibited inventory, by
appraisers Samuell Abotthe & Francis
Chaplin. Also exhibited accounts.

17:82   12 April. John Thomas who married widow
of Edward Norris (BA) exhibited that
there is nothing to pay. Distribution
to: 2 orphans of (N) Kemp.

Maj. William Dent (CH) for William
Smith son of Adam Smith (London)
exhibited that Mr. William Smith (CH)
devised his estate to his wife during
her lifetime, then to said William.
Said wife is now dec'd. Said William
Smith (son) desires said Dent & Capt.
Phillip Hoskins (CH) to care for the
estate as per letters from Adam Smith
(father of said William Smith (infant)).
Said Dent & Hoskins were granted
administration on estate of said William
Smith (the elder). Mr. Richard
Boughton to administer oath.

17:83   Letter from Adam Smith to MM William
Dent & Phillip Hoskins. Date: 10
November 1695. Mentions: said Adam is
brother to said William Smith (dec'd).

17:84   Letter from Adam Smith to Mr. William
Dent. Date: 14 October 1696 at London.

James Edmondson one of executors of his
father John Edmondson (TA) exhibited
inventory. Continuance was granted.

17:85   John Walken (PG) was granted
administration on estate of John Forrest
(PG), as greatest creditor. Wife of
said Forrest refused administration.
Said Walken's wife is an orphan of
William Rout (CV).

Page 39

Joan Willymott executrix of Richard
Willymott (BA) exhibited that there are
no accounts.

13 April. Henry King & his wife Tabitha
vs. Mr. Phillip Clarke procurator for
Joseph Peake & his wife Jane. Rejoinder
exhibited.

Mr. Henry Bonner attorney for William
Smith vs. Margarett or Mary Wells
executrices or administratrices of
Richard Wells who was one of executors
of Leonard Coates (AA). Caveat
exhibited. Mentions: debt of Robert
Gott the other executor.

Richard Owen (DO) one of overseers of
Maj. Henry Trip (DO) exhibited that the
widow & executrix is now dec'd. Said
Owen was granted administration on his
estate, during the minority of the
children. Sureties: Hugh Eccleston,
Charles Powell.

17:86   15 April. Phillip Clarke procurator for
Arthur Wheatly vs. Mr. Robert
Gouldesborough attorney for Hugh
Sherwood (TA) executor of Judith widow &
executrix of John Brookes. Libel
exhibited.

Mr. Robert Carvill attorney for Thomas
Jones (SO) vs. Arnold Elsey.
Replication exhibited. Attachment of
contempt to said Elsey was granted.

John Gadsbuy & his wife Johanna (AA)
were granted administration on estates
of George Norman & his wife Elisabeth,
in right of the orphans. Mr. George
Ashman (BA) to administer oath.

Mr. Thomas Robins (TA) was granted
continuance.

17:87   R. Gouldesborough attorney for Henry
King (p, BA) & his wife Tabitha
(daughter of Jane Long (BA, dec'd)) vs.
Phil. Clarke attorney for Joseph Peake &
his wife Jane (daughter of said Long).
Text of libel. Mentions: said Jane

Court Session: 1698

Peake is executrix for Thomas Long (son
of said Jane Long, age 19).

17:88   Text of answer.

17:89   Text of replication. Text of rejoinder.

17:90   Ruling: legacies to be paid.

18 April. Col. Edward Lloyd (TA) one
of executors of Col. George Robotham
(TA) for self & Maj. Thomas Smithson &
Mr. John Pemberton the other executors
was granted administration on estate of
said Robotham. Maj. Thomas Smithson
petitioned

17:91   that Mr. Richard Tilghman, Capt. John
Needles, Capt. James Murphey, or Mr.
William Hemesley to prove said will.
Date: 16 April 1698.

Robert Smith, Esq. for Richard Chafe
(TA) was granted administration on
estate of John Chafe (TA). Said Smith
to administer oath.

Richard Keen (CV) petitioned for Mathew
Lewis & Thomas Jenkins as appraisers of
estate of Francis Hill (SM) & for Mr.
Samuell Watkins to administer oath.

17:92   27 April. James Chilcock & his wife
Mary executrix of Thomas Tendall (AA)
were granted administration on his
estate. Will was proved. Securities:
William Smith, James Ford. Mr. John
Tompson to administer oath.

Richard Bennett (g, TA) exhibited that
Madam Heneratta Maria Lloyde (TA) made
will, constituting her mother Ann Neale,
her 2 brothers James & Anthony Neale,
her son said Bennett & her son Phylemon
Lloyd executors. Said James Neale &
Phylemon Lloyd proved will on 2 June
last. Said Ann Neale & Anthony Neale
have renounced administration. Said
Bennett was, at that time, in ENG. Said
Bennett was granted administration on
said estate, with the others.

17:93   R. Bennett vs. estate of his father (N).
Lloyd. Caveat exhibited, against the
distribution. Date: 7 March 1698.
Petition for written instrument. Date:

Page 41

13 March 1697/8. [See f. 76.]

17:94   30 April. Nicholas Fitchsimons (BA) petitioned for Col. John Thomas to administer oath to executor & appraisers of estate of Capt. Thomas Morgan.

Mrs. Mary Denton widow of Mr. Henry Denton (Annapolis, AA) was granted administration on his estate. Sureties: MM Thomas Beale, Thomas Grunwen.

Letter from William Dent, accompanying the will of Mr. Richard Chandler. Mentions: bequest of Negro woman (now dec'd) to said Dent's wife,

17:95   Gerrard Fowke (executor). Date: 16 August 1697 at Nanjemy. Will of Richard Chandler (CH). Date: 14 October 1686. Bequests: mother Mrs. Anne Fowke Mulatto Lewis (boy) then to brother Gerard Fowke, sister Mrs. Mary Fowke Mulatto Charles (boy),

17:96   sister Elisabeth Dent Mulatto Jane (girl), Mrs. Parthania Burdett Mulatto Billey (boy, to be free after 16 years from date of will), Mrs. Anne Burford the younger, Negro Anne (woman) to be freed, John Hamilton, nephew William Chandler Negro Ellinor (girl), nephew Richard Chandler (under age 21) land, niece Jane Chandler Mulatto Betty (girl), brother Gerard Fowke. Said Gerard executor.

17:97   ...
- William Dent attorney-at-law attested before Richard Boughton (CH) that he wrote said will. Date: 16 August 1697. Said Dent questioned 26 August 1697.

17:98   ...
- Parthenia Burdit attested to will before Richard Boughton. Also Laurence Rochford had written a will which said Chandler did not approve of. Date: 16 August 1697. Said Burdit questioned 26 August 1697.

17:99   ...
- Nicholas Cooper, age 50, attested to will. He recalled a legacy to his mother Mrs. Anne Fooke of a Negro Lewis (boy), to Parthenia Burdit of

Court Session: 1698

a Negro Billy (boy) & a trunk that
belonged to her sister Mrs. Anne
Burford, Jr. Date: 26 August 1697.
Richard Boughton (CH) presented afsd
depositions, made before Mr. William
Chandler. Mentions: Gerrard Fowke
executor.

Inventory of Richard Chandler (CH).
Executor: Gerrard Fowkes. Date: 9
September 1697.
17:100 Appraisers: Jos. Manning, Samuell
Boughton.

17:101 William Dent for Gerrard Fowke (CH)
administrator of Richard Chandler (g,
CH) vs. George Brent & Ro. Carvile for
William Chandler (heir-at-law). Text of
libel. Said Richard died on 14/15
August 1697.
17:102 ...
17:103 Text of answer.
17:104 Mentions: brother & sister of the whole
blood; son & daughter of Col. William
Chandler (dec'd, only brother of dec'd).
Questions. At the request of Mr.
William Chandler (nephew & heir-at-law)
on behalf of self, his brother Richard
Chandler, & sister Jane Chandler (alias
Jane Greene), the following were
questioned: Madam Anne Fowke (widow),
Mr. Jesse Doyne, Mr. Samuell Boughton,
Mrs. Parthenia Burditt.
17:105 Mentions: marriage of his niece Mrs.
Jane Brent to Mr. Joshua Green, Mrs.
Anne Burford, Jr. has been married twice
since 1686.
17:106 ...
 • Mrs. Anne Fowke deposed that said
Chandler died 13 August last.
17:107 ...
 • Mrs. Parthania Burditt deposed.
Mentions: Negro Harrie (boy), said
Gerrard Fowke has 2 children, Maj.
William Dent as brother to said
Richard Chandler.
17:108 ...
 • Jesse Doyne deposed that Mrs. Jane
Brent married Mr. Green against the
consent of said Richard,
17:109 ...
said nephew Richard Chandler is a

Page 43

poor boy.
- Lawrence Racheford, age 63, deposed that he came from Matawon.

17:110   ...
Date: 26 August 1697.
- William Dent, age 37, attorney-at-law, deposed. Date: 26 August 1697.

William Dent procurator for Gerrard Fowke (g, CH) executor of Richard Chandler vs. George Brent procurator for William Chandler (g, CH). Date: 20 October 1697.

17:111   ...
17:112   Mentions: Lawrence Rotchford,
17:113   Laurence Rochford.
17:114   Ruling: will is valid, even though it is not signed.

Damaris Seargent, age 50, deposed on 29 January 1695, that her former husband John Ward died at his house in CH about 9 years ago on 1 October last, constituting her & his son John Ward executors. Said son renounced administration.

17:115   Citation of goods of said Ward's estate. The deponent then married Charles Shephard & then William Sergant. Before: Richard Harrison, William Stone.

17:116   ...
- Mathew Stone, age 38, deposed. Date: 29 January 1695 before: Richard Harrison, William Stone.
- John Gray, age 50, deposed. Date: 29 January 1695 before: Richard Harrison, William Stone.

17:117   William Dent procurator for Edward Millstead & his wife Elisabeth one of daughters of John Ward (CH, dec'd) vs. Charles Carroll procurator for William Sargent & his wife Dameres. Mentions 5 children of said Ward: John Ward, Thomas Ward, James Ward, Katherine Ward, Elisabeth Ward. Text of libel. Said John (son) is the son of said Damares. Said Damaris married Charles Shepard & then William Sergant.

17:118   Text of answer.
17:119   Ruling: Inventory & accounts to be

rendered. After death of said Damaris, her estate is to be divided among her 4 children.

Philip Clark procurator for John Hodges vs. Richard Mason & John Hurt. Text of libel & answer. Said Hodges is son & heir of William Hodges. Mentions: younger children of said Hodges. Said Mason & Hurt have LoA on estate of said Hodges.

17:120 Ruling: will is valid, but no executor was named. Said John is to be administrator as next-of-kin & guardian of younger children.

Samuell Wattkins procurator for Gabriell Parrott administrator of Thomas Brisco (CV) vs. John Ellsey.

17:121 Ruling: defendant to deliver books, & defendant is to receive 1/3rd of fees.

17:122 Phillip Clark procurator for Thomas Warren (CH) & Abraham Warren (CH) (sons of Humphry Warren, Sr.) vs. Robert Carvile procurator for Notly Warren (CH) executor of said Warren. Mentions: Humphrey Warren, Jr. is the son of Humphrey Warren, Sr. by a former wife. Plaintiffs' mother afterwards married Thomas Howell, & is since dec'd. Said Howell died in 1697, leaving no children of his own. Humphrey Warren their brother-in-law was granted LoA on estate of said Howell, for the use of the plaintiffs & their younger brother who is since dec'd.

17:123 Said plaintiff Thomas worked for said Humphrey until he was 21. Said plaintiff Abraham served him for 17 years at the house & another 7 years as a shoemaker. The defendant's father was administrator of said Howell's estate. Ruling: defendant to pay the plaintiffs amount of inventory of said Howell.

17:124 Phillip Clark procurator for Elisabeth & Ann Hunton (daughters of Mordeca Hunton (CV)) vs. Hugh Ellis (CV). Said Mordeca Hunton made will bequeathing to: wife Elisabeth, 3 daughters (under age): Sarah, Elisabeth, Ann. Said executrix married said Ellis. Said Elisabeth died about 3 years ago. Said orphans are of age.

17:125 Edward Wood was guardian to said orphans. Ruling: said Ellis to pay estate as per inventory to the plaintiffs.

R. Gouldesborough procurator for Henry King (p, BA) & his wife Tabitha (daughter of Jane Long (BA)) vs. Philip Clarke procurator for Joseph Peak & his wife Jane.

17:126 Text of libel. Mentions: Jane Peake (daughter of said Long) married Joseph Peak, Thomas Long (under age 19 in 1696, son of said Long). Petition that said Peak be summoned to render accounts. Text of answer.

17:127 Text of replication.

17:128 Text of rejoinder. Ruling: legacies to be paid per intent of the will. Said Peak to render accounts.

17:129 Col. John Bigger attorney for Capt. Thomas Wharton executor of Simon Wooton (CV) was granted administration on his estate, for use of the only daughter of said Wooton. Said daughter is now dec'd. LoA are revoked. John Fisher (CV), brother & next of kin, was granted administration on his estate. Said John Hodges was appointed guardian during the minority

17:130 of orphans of dec'd.

Robert Goldsborough procurator for John Fisher (p, CV) vs. Col. John Bigger (CV) administrator of Symon Wotton for use of Thomas Wharton (mariner, ENG). Said Wooten died in parts beyond the sea, bequeathing to his daughter Anne Wootton. Said Wharton was constituted executor; the will was proved in ENG.

17:131 Said Anne died long before devise in the will. Ruling: will is void. Plaintiff is to have administration.

11 May. Capt. Robert Lockwood was granted administration on estate of Gabriell Parrett, Jr. (AA), on behalf of his daughter the widow of said Gabrill.

She is very sick. Appraisers: Anthony
Smith, James Ford. Thomas Tench, Esq.
to administer oath.

12 May. Mr. Richard Bennett (TA) vs.
estate of Mr. Edward Lloyde (merchant,
London). Caveat exhibited.
17:132 Date: 8 May 1698.

John Howard (AA) was granted
administration on estate of Thomas
Smithick (AA). Securities: Thomas
Blackwell, John Dowdall. Appraisers:
John Medcalfe, Cornelius Howard. Capt.
Phillip Howard to administer oath.

13 May. Mathew Erickson (TA) on behalf
of Wenfred Harvey widow of Robert Harvey
was granted administration on his
estate. Mr. John Copage (also John
Coppedge) to administer oath.

17:133 Thomas Sparrow (Quaker, AA) was granted
administration on estate of his wife
Anne Sparrow (one of daughters of
William Burges (AA)).

16 May. Mr. William Nicholls (CV) for
self & William Coale vs. estate of
Richard Sandys (CV). Caveat exhibited.
Said Nicholls was granted administration
on his estate.

17 May. Joshua Meriken (AA) was granted
administration on estate of Hugh
Meriken. Securities: Mathew Howard,
John Ingram.

21 May. William Cromwell (BA) for self
& William Slaid (BA) was granted
administration on estate of James
Jackson (BA).
17:134 Mr. George Ashman (BA) to administer
oath.

Thomas Cockey (AA) executor of Sarah
Cockey (AA) was granted administration
on her estate.

28 May. Mr. John Riggby (AA) for self
& Mr. James Riggby (AA) was granted
administration on estate of Mrs.

Court Session: 1698

Kathern Constable (widow, AA).
Appraisers: Mr. Roger Newman, Capt.
Humphrey Boone. Capt. John Warthinton
to administer oath.

Edward Batson (CV) was sworn as
Registrar of Wills. Stephen Blatchford
was sworn as his deputy.
17:135 Signed: Kenelm Cheseldyn.

Col. John Addison & Capt. John Bean
(also John Beane) by virtue of a
commission from Court of Chancery of ENG
to examine the probate of will of
William Pawlett (Hampshire, ENG): will
produced to Nicholas Richardson & John
Lester. Mentions: Richard Pawlett, Esq.
(p) vs. Martha Pawlett. Date: 3
December 1697 at Westwood (CH).

Mr. George Ashman (BA) exhibited
inventory of George Norman & his wife
Elisabeth, by
17:136 appraisers James Murry & James Jackson.

Said Ashman also exhibited will of James
Jackson (BA) & inventory, by appraisers
James Murry & John Gardiner. Also bond
of William Slade & William Cromwell.

30 May. John Smith (AA) vs. his brother
Samuell Smith administrator of their
brother James Smith. Caveat exhibited.

31 May. Col. John Thomas exhibited
will of Capt. Thomas Morgan (BA).
Also, oath of surviving executor
Nicholas FitchSimons. Securities: John
Hayes, John Barrett. Also inventory, by
appraisers said Hayes & said Barrett.

John Boyce (TA) for self & his wife Ruth
were granted administration on estate of
Joseph Mosely (TA).
17:137 Securities: Leonard Camperson, William
Rabbetts. Mr. John Copage (TA) to
administer oath.

Letter from Mr. William Dent. Date: 7
May 1698. Petition for a copy of will
of Richard Chandler & sentence to
Gerrard Fowke. They are to be sent to

Page 48

Court Session: 1698

ENG.

Letter from Joseph Tilly. He is so sick
that he cannot ride to prove will of
Gabriell Parrett, Jr. & of his wife
Elisabeth now sick. Also, to prove will
of Francis Price. Date: 11 May 1698.
Witnesses: John Hance, Anthony Smith.

W. Bladen exhibited that John Althea (g)
is the greatest creditor to Robert
Tregellis (merchant) who died on ship
Corsellis of Colchester. Date: 4 May
1698.

17:138 Ri. Boughton (CH) exhibited a notice to
Madam Burford that copies of witnesses
to will of Mr. Burford are now available
& to come to the vestry house at Nangemy
parish church on 10 March. Copies to:
Ja. Cottrill & his wife Elisabeth,
Richard Dodd & his wife Jane, George
Plater, Esq. & his wife Ann.

John Pitt petitioned for continuance on
accounts of estate of Thomas Cooke & of
John Ashdell. Date: 10 March 1698 at
Choptank.

17:139 John Gartrill (AA) petitioned that he
married a sister of William Johnson
(AA), who died suddenly by falling
sickness, & his brother Francis Johnson
has LoA. Said William bequeathed all to
his sister Jane Gatrell. Both parties
were granted administration on 12 March
1697/8.

William Asquith (g, SM) exhibited that
the will of Richard Benton (SM),
constituting his widow Sarah Benton
executrix, has been proved. Said Sarah
is incapacitated to travel to the
Office. Said Asquith to administer
oath.
17:140 LoA granted on 27 December 1697. Said
Sarah was sworn on 10 January 1697/8.

Mr. Richard Massum deposed that 12
years ago William Rowl (CV) died &
Benjamin Evans (CV) was granted
administration on his estate.

Appraisers: Phillip Lawrence, John
Forrest. Mentions: orphan,
administrator has runaway, one of
securities is dec'd, other security
secured against the orphan & is since
dec'd & his widow refuses
administration. Said orphan, now the
wife of John Walker (PG), was granted
administration on his estate, as
greatest creditor.

17:141 Letter from Elisabeth Forrest to Mr.
Joshua Cecill (PG). Date: 2 April
1697/8. Renunciation of administration
on her husband's estate. John Walker is
greatest creditor. Witnesses: John
Wightt, Henry Dryden.

Alice Kenerly petitioned for continuance
on accounts of her husband William
Kenerly, due first to weather, then
indisposition of body. Date: 19 March
1698.

2 June. Dr. Alexander Chapell (AA) was
granted administration on estate of
Thomas Danvis (AA), as executor.
Appraisers: Thomas Hughs, Zacharia
Cadle. Capt. William Holland to
administer oath.

Exhibited bond of Mary Wallis (PG)
administratrix of her husband Richard
Wallis. Securities: James Gamblin,
Isacc Williams.

17:142 4 June. Exhibited inventory of William
Johnson (AA).

7 June. Exhibited bond of Ignatius
Craycroft administrator of Mr. John
Craycroft (PG). Securities: David
Small, Joshua Ceciell.

9 June. Capt. Ebenezar Blackston (CE)
was granted administration on estate of
Thomas Baker (AA). Security: Mr.
William Bladen, Appraisers: Lawrence
Draper, Jacob Lusby, Joseph Hill. Capt.
Richard Hill to administer oath.

11 June. Dr. Lewe de Roche Browne (TA)
administrator of Morris Hooper exhibited

Court Session: 1698

accounts.

Mr. Nathaniell Stinchcome (BA) vs.
John Gadsby & Samuell Smith
administrators of George Norman (BA).
Caveat exhibited.

17:143   Mr. John Rawlings (DO) exhibited:
- inventory of William Lewis.
  Administrator: Peter Cornelius.
  Securities: Obadia King, William
  Wargent.
- will of Humphrey Mould.
- inventory of Henry Wheeler.
  Administratrix: Susana Wheeler.
- inventory of Henry Carpenter.
  Administratrix: Mable Rose.
- inventory of John Viccory.
  Administratrix: Margarett Viccory.
- inventory of Humphrey Mould.
  Administratrix: Frances Mould.
- Mary Smith (DO) widow &
  administratrix of John Smith was
  granted administration on his
  estate. She is sickly & poor with a
  great many small children. She
  lives in the forest 20 or 30 miles
  from the water. Date: 8 June 1698.

17:144   14 June. Mr. Lawrence Draper & Capt.
Ebenezar Blackstone (CE) exhibited
inventory of Thomas Baker (AA).
Appraisers: said Draper, Jacob Lisly.

Mr. John Tompson exhibited inventory of
Thomas Tindall (AA).

Said Tompson exhibited will of John
Young (AA), proved.

16 June. John Hodges (KE) vs. Richard
Mason (KE) & John Hurt administrators of
William Hodges. Petition to render
accounts.

17 June. Thomas Heyfer & James Wood
executors of William Groves
17:145   (AA) were granted administration on his
estate. Appraisers: Thomas Hughs, John
Trundall. Capt. Holland to administer
oath.

James Lewis (AA) was granted administration on estate of Mathew Ballamy (AA). Securities: Leonard Weyman, Thomas Renolds. Nicholas Gassaway to administer oath.

21 June. Mr. Elias King (KE) was granted administration on estate of Elisabeth Kersey (KE), as greatest creditor. Mr. Phillip Hopkins to administer oath.

Said King exhibited inventory of Robert Certain (KE), by appraisers John Cheires & Robert Norrest.

Said King exhibited inventory of Richard Lowder (KE), by appraisers Charles Hinson & Thomas Record.

23 June. Francis Stevens & John Hopkins, 2 witnesses, proved will of John Young (AA).

25 June. Elisabeth Harrison widow of Edward Harrison renounced administration on his estate.

17:146 Richard Cheshire (AA) was granted administration. Thomas Tench, Esq. to administer oath.

Joshua Merrikin (AA) exhibited inventory of Richard Baley (AA), by appraisers Richard Boon & Edward Gibbs.

28 June. John Willymott (CV) was appointed Deputy Commissary (CV). Signed: Edward Batson.

Mr. Giles Bond (mariner, London) exhibited LoA granted by Archbishop of Canterbury to Ann Merrekin widow of Hugh Merekin (AA) & PoA from said Ann. Petition that LoA to Joshua Merikin be voided.

17:147 Mentions: 2 orphans. [LoA from Archbishop in Latin.] Signed: Thomas Wellham. PoA to said Bond. Date: 8 February 1698 before Thomas Lawrence (notary).

17:148 She is Ann Merrikin (Ratclife, Parish of Dunstans Stepney alias Stebonheath,

Court Session: 1698

County Midd.). Said Hugh died in said
parish of Stepney. Said Bond is from
same place.
17:149 Witnesses: Samuell Dodson, Nathaniell
Hynson.

Exhibited:
* bond of Clabern Lomax executor of
Elisabeth Smith (CV). Securities:
John Martin, John Booker, William
Sergent. Also, will of said Smith.
* bond of William Beard administrator
of John Beard (CH). Securities:
Francis Harris, John Banister.
17:150 ...
* will of Nich. Beard (CH).
* Exhibited will of Ann Browne (CH).
* bond of Patrick Mackeetas
administrator of Ann Brown.
Securities (CH): Mr. William Dent,
Thomas Jenkins.
* will of Mathew Dike (CH).
Securities: John Brooke, John
Banister.
* bond of Walter Story executor of
Thomas Burford (CH). Security: John
Theobely. Also exhibited will.
* bond of Mary Browner executrix of
Henry Browner (CH). Sureties:
Edward Till, Thomas Plunkett.
* bond of Francis Harris administrator
of Thomas Dorman. Securities:
Christopher Ford, John Banister.
* bond of Elinor Smallpage
administratrix of Robert Smallpage
(CH). Securities: Matt. Saunders,
William Elliott.
* bond of John Wilkinson administrator
of Mathew Salamstone (CH).
Security: John Wood.
* bond of Mary Dike administratrix of
Thomas Alcock (CH). Securities:
John Brookes, John Banister.
17:151 ...
* will of John Edmondson with
inventory & bond. Thomas Robins
(TA) to administer oath.
* additional accounts of Edward
Pinder.
* will of William Penn with LoA from
Metropolitan of ENG.
* bond of Eleanor Clifts

administratrix of John Clifts.
Securities (TA): William Moore,
William Rich.

- inventory of Mary Aldridge (DO).
- additional inventory of Henry
  Trueman (CV).
- accounts of John Hughes
  administrator of John Tillotson
  (KE).
- will of Daniel Clarke (AA).
- accounts of Christopher Warren & his
  wife Elisabeth administratrix of
  John Powell.
- bond of John Gadsby & his wife
  Johannah administratrix of George
  Norman. Sureties (AA): Richard
  Beard, William Bladen.
- bond of John Walker (PG)
  administrator of John Forrest.
  Surety: Richard Marsham.
- inventory of Richard Bayley (PG).

17:152 ...

- additional accounts of Gabriel
  Parrott (AA) administrator of Thomas
  Briscoe.
- accounts of Mary Pope (CE)
  administratrix of John Howell.
- bond of Samuell Duvall & his wife
  administratrix of Daniel Clerke.
  Securities (AA): Thomas Rickins,
  Gilbert Pattison.
- bond of Richard Owen administrator
  of Maj. Henry Tripp (DO).
  Securities: Hugh Eggleston, Charles
  Powell.
- will of Thomas Alcock (CH).
- accounts of Mary Floyd
  administratrix of Daniel Floyd (PG).
- accounts of Thomas Clarke
  administrator of Dennis Smith (PG).
- bond of Col. Thomas Holladay
  administrator of John Forrest.
- bond of Ignatius Craycroft
  administrator of John Craycroft.
- bond of Samuel Warren administrator
  of Henry Jones (PG).
- will of Thomas Blanford (PG).
  Administratrix: Tabitha Blanford.
- bond of Mary Hays administratrix of
  Charles Hay (PG).
- will of Thomas Hide (PG).

17:153 ...

- inventory of Nicholas Bead (CH).
- bond of Jane Doyne administratrix of Dennis Doyne (CH). Also will of said Dennis.
- bond of Dorothy Stone administratrix of John Stone. Securities: Thomas Lawson, Thomas Price.
- will of Parthenia Burditt.
- will of Charles Alleson (CH).
- will of Henry Browner (CH).
- bond of Maj. William Dent & Capt. Phillip Hoskins administrators of William Smith. Security: Benjamin Thomas.
- bond of William Smith administrator of Sarah Cooksey (CH).
- bond of Katherine Boughton administratrix of Parthenia Burditt. Securities (CH): John Bannester, John Barker.
- bond of John Kelly administrator of Charles Watson (CH). Securities: Thomas Lawson, Thomas Price.
- bond of Mathew Barnes administrator of Phillip Jones. Security (CH): John Godson.
- bond of Mathew Barnes administrator of Johann Hudson (CH). Security: John Godson.
- bond of Thomas Austin administrator of Charles Allison. Securities (CH): John Gray, John Stewart.
- bond of William Chandler administrator of Col. William Chandler (CH). Security: William Dent.

17:154 ...

- bond of John Ward administrator of John Ward (CH). Securities: John Grey, Edward Milson.
- accounts of William Hemsley (TA) administrator of Robert Noble.
- will of William Burges (AA).
- accounts of Upgatt Reeves (CH) administrator of Ignatius Causeen.
- inventory & accounts of William Hemsley (TA) administrator of Arthur Pursivall.
- inventory of John Davis (SM).
- inventory of Heugh Merrican (AA).
- inventory of Thomas Burford (CH).
- inventory of Ann Neale (CH).

Court Session: 1698

- inventory of Baker Brooke (CV).
- additional accounts of John Batty (AA) administrator of Roger Bishopp.
- accounts of Peter Harris & his wife administratrix of John Davis.
- inventory of Henry Tripp (DO).
- John Pitts (TA) administrator of (N) Cooke & administrator of (N) Ashdale was granted continuance.

17:155 ...

- inventory of Thomas Smith (AA).
- inventory of Richard Haddock.
- renunciation of Mary Ferret on her husband's estate.
- inventory of Cornelius Wilkinson (SM).
- will of Daniel Bryan.
- bond of George Hutchins administrator of Thomas Hillman (SO). Security: John White.
- inventory of Willmott Hill.
- accounts of John Leverton (SO) administrator of (N).
- accounts of John Deserton (SO) administrator of (N).
- accounts of Comfort Coston (SO) administratrix of her husband.
- bond of William Wouldhave administrator of Willmott Hill. Securities: John Webb, Walter Evans.
- inventory of John Sewell (SM). Also bond of Ann Sewell administratrix. Securities: Robert Ford, Peter Joy.
- will of Baker Brooke, by Catherine Brooke. Securities: Richard Marsham, Luke Gardiner.
- will of John Price (SM). Also bond of Joane Price. Securities: James Wood, William Williams.
- bond of Ann Roberts (alias Ann Edwards) administratrix of John Roberts. Securities: Peter William Harris, William Williams.
- bond of Ann Freeman executrix of Francis Freeman (CV). Securities: John Scott, John Kent.
- bond of Nathaniel Dare (CV) administrator of Daniel Florewood. Security: James Robinson.

17:156 ...

- bond of Margery Miles administratrix of John Miles (SM). Securities:

Page 56

William Lowry, James Baker.
- bond of Capt. Thomas Waughob administrator of Thomas Tant. Securities: Thomas Medford, William Harpam.
- bond of Ann Jarboe executrix of Peter Jarboe (SM). Securities: John Nevett, John Browne. Also will.
- bond of John Noble administrator of John Noble (SM). Securities: Lawrence Tattershall, Thomas Deakins.
- bond of name Realy John administrator of (N) MackMurry. Securities (SM): Cornelius Manly, William Bright. Also will.
- bond of Mary Swalles administratrix of Flrances Swalles. Securities: Thomas Attway, John Shanks.
- bond of Andrew Mogiah administrator of Ester Williams (SM). Security: Richard Minching.
- bond of James French (SM) administrator of (N). Securities: Patrick Farrell, William Lowry.
- bond of Patrick Farrell (SM) administrator of (N). Security: James French.
- bond of Jane Wills administratrix of Orias Wills (SM). Securities: Edward Miller, Thomas Rose.
- bond of Elisabeth Watts administratrix of (N) Watts (SM). Security: James Simons.

17:157 ...
- will of Thomas Warren (SM), by William Husbands, proved.
- bond of James Martin (SM) administrator of William Knight. Securities: Robert Sollomon, David Parsons. Also will.
- will of Thomas Warren. Also bond of Charles Daft administrator. Securities: Henry Spinke, Thomas Dant.
- will of John Cecill. Also bond of John Cecill. Securities: Henry Spinke, Thomas Dant.
- will of Richard Walker (SM). Also bond of Ann Walker.
- bond of Adam Heade administrator of Adam Head (SM). Securities: Henry

Spinke, William Sherclift.
- will of James Pattison (SM).
- bond of Ann Henington administratrix of Henry Hennington (SM). Security: Robert Tunell.
- inventory of Daniel Floorewood.
- inventory of Edward Coxnell.
- inventory of Osias Wills (SM).
- inventory of John Miles.
- inventory of William Chessum (SM).
- inventory of Arthur Keiss (SM).
- accounts of Susannah Heard administratrix of John Heard (SM).
- inventory of Robert Bayley (SM).

17:158 ...
- inventory of Charles Watts (SM).
- inventory of Hester Williams (SM).
- inventory of James Pattison (SM).
- inventory of Elias Beech (SM).
- bond of John Boye (CH) administrator of John Knight. Securities: Henry James, Henry Smith.
- bond of James Smalwood (CH) administrator of John Wincoll. Securities: Thomas Hussey, Cornelius Madox.
- bond of Robert Benson (CH) administrator of Robert Losen. Securities: Thomas Craxton, Francis Bowlery.
- bond of Gerrard Foulkes (CH) administrator of Richard Chandler. Security: William Dent.
- bond of Philip Hoskins (CH) administrator of James Bile. Securities: Thomas Taney, Richard Southerne.
- bond of Elisabeth Harbett administratrix of Richard Gosey (SM). Securities: John Burrows, William Thorne.
- bond of Elisabeth Jones administratrix of Jones Jones (SM). Security: John Moore.
- bond of Jelleom Powell administratrix of John Powell (SM). Security: John Gillens.
- bond of Ann Hartley administratrix of Joseph Hartley (SM). Security: George OKeith.

17:159 ...
- bond of Sarah Crooke administratrix

Court Session: 1698

of John Crooke (SM). Securities:
Thomas Hall, George OKeith.
- bond of Ruth Elles executrix of Hugh
Elles (CV). Securities: Daniel
Sheredine, Thomas Arnoll.
- bond of John King (CV) administrator
of Jane Stowe. Security: Thomas
Hinton.
- bond of George Wade (CV)
administrator of Robert Fisher.
Securities: Michael Catterton, John
Higer.
- bond of Margrett Kerstead
administratrix of Joachim Kerstead.
Security: Ignatius Sewall.
- bond of Elisabeth Hamond
administratrix of John Hamond (SO).
Securities: John Franklin, John
Wabbe.
- bond of Peter Cornelius
administrator of William Lewes (DO).
Securities: Obadiah King, William
Warden.
- bond of Susannah Wheeler
administratrix of Henry Wheeler
(DO). Securities: Philip Pitts,
John Whiteley.
- bond of Frances Mould administratrix
of Humphry Mould (DO). Security:
Thomas Thacker.
- bond of Mayble Rose administratrix
of Henry Carpenter (DO).
Securities: Andrew Parker, John
Haslewood.
- bond of Margrett Viccory
administratrix of John Viccous
Security: William Lawyer.
- bond of Ann Ashman administratrix of
Richard Ashman (CH). Security:
Henry Hardy.
- bond of Dinah Pew administratrix of
(N) Pew. Security: James Martin.
- bond of Thomas Craxton administrator
of Sarah Till executrix of Edward
Till (CH). Security: George Brett.
- bond of Dennis Cunnerell
administrator of William Bryan (CH).
Security: James Small, Sr. Sent
back to Mr. Dent.

17:160 ...
- will of Jane Stowe (CV).
- will of Robert Day (CV).

- will of Edward Wood (CV).
- will of Humphry Mould (DO).
- will of Richard Ashman (CH).
- will of Edward Till (CH).
- will of Cornelius Watkinson (SM).
- inventory of John Knigh (CH), by appraisers Henry Tanner & Henry Smith.
- inventory of Edward Wood, by appraisers Ignatius Sewall & Thomas Gasling.
- oath of Mr. John Fenwick & Robert Clarke, appraisers of John Miles, by Mr. James Keech.
- inventory of John Hamond (SO), by appraisers John Franklin & John Webbe.
- inventory of John Parker. John Henry & William Robinson exhibited accounts, proved before Mr. William Hopkins.
- inventory of William Lues (DO), by appraisers William Carter & John Hewes.

17:161 ...

- inventory of Henry Wheeler (<unreadable>), by appraisers Daniell Clarke & Jarvis Connter.
- inventory of Humphrey Carpenter (DO), by appraisers Thomas Dinnes & Hery <unreadable>.
- inventory of Henry Carpenter (DO), by appraisers Benjamin Hill & John Viccous.
- inventory of John Viccous (DO), by appraisers John Prois & Richard Fisher.
- inventory of Mathew Dike (CH), by appraisers Christopher Ford & Thomas Davis.
- inventory of Thomas Alcock (CH), by appraisers Christopher Ford & Thomas Davis.
- inventory of David Pew (CH), by appraisers John Barkr, & James Martin.
- inventory of William Smith (CH), by appraisers John Bookr & Lues Jones.
- inventory of Robert Lofton (CH), by appraisers Thomas Craxton & Fran. Bowlery.
- inventory of Ann Browne (CH), by

          appraisers John Clement & John
          Sangster.
- inventory of Richard Chandler (CH), by appraisers William Stone & John Craxton.
- accounts of Sarah Cooksey administratrix of Philip Cooksey (CH).
- accounts of Elisabeth Duncon on estate of (N) Duncon, proved before Mr. William Hopkins (SO).

17:162 ...
- accounts of Mary Meeke administratrix of Francis Meek (CH), proved before Mr. Richard Boughton (CH). Continuance was granted.
- accounts of Mary Hall executrix of Dr. William Hall (CH), proved before Mr. Richard Boughton.

Per request of Dr. Mordica Moore, the following depositions were taken regarding the will of William Burges (also William Burgess, AA), who died at 7 a.m. on 28 June 1698.
- John Gerrard, age 26, deposed.

17:163 ...
          Mentions: wife who is with child.
- Richard Jones, age 27, deposed. Mentions: children of Maj. Sewell.
- Said Moore deposed again.

17:164 ...
          Mentions: Capt. Hanslap.

17:165 Will [of said Burges]. Bequests: sister Susan, brother Charles, Richard Harrison 400 a., wife, Thomas Larkin, Richard Jones, John Gerrard. Executrix: wife. Date: 28 June 1698. Witnesses: M. Moore, Richard Jones, Jr., J. Gerard.

29 June. Thomas Tench, Esq. exhibited will of Gabriell Parrett & will of Elisabeth Parrett who recovered & renounced her will.

Thomas Tench, Esq. exhibited renunciation of Mary Trevors on administration of estate of her husband, recommending the greatest creditor.

Exhibited will of William Groves (AA). Witnesses: John Beech, William Hollyday,

Court Session: 1698

17:166
Nicholas White. Said White refuses to prove said will. Also Robert Smith & John Willson, Jr. were present refused to be witnesses. Thomas Heifer & James Wood executors were summoned as well as witnesses & said Smith & said Willson.

17:167
Will of Capt. William Penn (mariner, London, now Petuxent River). Bequests: 3 sisters, wife. Executrix: said wife. Date: 20 September 1696. Witnesses: Richard Marsham, John Wight, Thomas Greenfeild.
• Robert Bradly deposed on 18 November 1697 that John Bouye wrote said will. Signed: Ri. Raines. [Paragraph in Latin.] Signed: Thomas Welham.

17:168
Elisabeth Penn widow of said William appeared before Anthony Wright (notary) on 7 November 1697 & executed PoA to Thomas Greenfeild (g, PG), William Barton (g, PG), & John Wight (g, PG).

17:169
Witnesses: Henry Darnall, R. Bradly. Anthony Smith.

10 March. Henry Moore brother of Thomas Moore was granted administration on his estate, as greatest creditor. William Dent attorney for Capt. John Bayne vs. said Henry Moore. Caveat exhibited. Said Bayne is greatest creditor. Said Henry was granted administration, as brother of deceased, but refused administration.

29 March 1697. Exhibited receipt of Sarah Goddard from William Sharp executor of John Boram for land bequeathed to her. Witness: Thomas Skillington.

17:170
Exhibited receipt of Sarah Goddard (of full age) from William Sharp executor of her uncle John Boram for her legacy. Witnesses: Thomas Skillington, Ken. Skillington.

Exhibited bond of Kenelm Skillington (p, TA) to William Sharp, Sr. (merchant, TA) for legacies by John Boram bequeathed to

17:171 2 children of said Skillington:
Thomas, Penelope. Witnesses: Thomas
Skillington, William Sharp, Jr.

27 June at AA Co. Mary Trevitt widow of
Robert Trevitt (AA) exhibited her
renunciation of administration on his
estate. Witnesses: John Ratford, Thomas
Trott, Sarah Radford.

Ann Ashman widow of Richard Ashman
exhibited her renunciation of
administration on his estate.
17:172 Date: 20 June 1698. Witness: William
Hardy.

1 July. Patrick Danielly & his wife Ann
vs. Charles Powell administrator of
William Dorington. Ruling: plaintiff &
his wife were granted administration on
said estate, during the minority of the
other orphans. Mentions: William
(brother of said Ann, infant).

2 July. Thomas Heyfer executor of
William Groves petitioned for
17:173 appraisers: John Beecher, Nicholas
White. Capt. William Holland (g, AA)
to administer oath.

Edward Burges & his wife vs. estate of
their brother William Burges. Caveat
exhibited.

Mr. Charles Carroll for William Watts
vs. Capt. Gerrard Sly (SM). Petition
for attachment of defendant, issued on
16 July 1698.

Exhibited will of William Richardson
(AA), proved. No LoA were granted.

Exhibited additional inventory of
Richard Rawlins.

Exhibited accounts of Richard
ThorneBurne.

Charles Langsley who married Ann relict
& executrix of John Brasheire (CV)
exhibited accounts.

5 July. Arthur Wheateley vs. Mr. Robert Gouldesborough for Hugh Sherwood. Answer exhibited.

Mr. Joshua Merica (AA) brother & administrator of
17:174 Hugh Merica (g, AA) & Giles Bond brother & attorney for Anne widow of said Hugh agreed that said Joshua should continue as administrator. Witnesses: Giles Wigginer, W. Bladen.

7 July. Mr. Phillip Lynes (CH) was granted administration on estate of Mr. John Bouye, as greatest creditor. Sureties: William Harpam, Benjamin Inman. Appraisers: Charles Kilburne, Robert Phillips.

17:175 6 July. Capt. Edward Burges (AA) vs. estate of William Burges. Retraxett of caveat. Witnesses: Nicholas Fletham, James Methven.

Capt. Phillip Howard exhibited inventory of Thomas Smithick, by appraisers Cornelius Howard & John Meadcalfe.

8 July. Joshua Cecill for self & Katherin Willson executors of Jonathon Willson (PG) exhibited his will. Said Ceecil was granted administration. Mr. Thomas Greenfeild to prove said will & administer oath.

9 July. Mr. Thomas Greenfeild (PG) exhibited additional accounts of Mr. Richard Charlett.

17:176 10 July. Mary & John Cozens executors of John Cozens (AA) were granted administration on his estate. Sureties: Henry Wright, John Sunderland. Appraisers: Abraham Child, Henry Wright.

12 July. Mr. William Taylard for Mrs. Audry Llewellin exhibited inventory of Mr. John Llewellin. Continuance was granted.

Court Session: 1698

Said William Taylard petitioned for new
LoA on estate of John Masters.

14 July. William Elliott & Isaatt
Winchester exhibited inventory of Thomas
Fisher (KI).

17:177   15 July. Mr. Joshua Ceecill (PG)
exhibited:
- bond of Mary Falkner administratrix
  of Martin Falkener (PG).
  Securities: Hugh Ryley, Josias
  Towgood.
- bond of Annable Hooke administratrix
  of Thomas Hooke (PG). Security:
  John Dorsett.
- bond of John Launam administrator of
  Michaell Kaisly (PG). Securities:
  Samuell Westby, Henry Culver.
- bond of Elisabeth Oubeer
  administratrix of Stephen Oubeer
  (PG). Securities: James Stoddard,
  David Small.
- bond of Sarah Dunkin administratrix
  of John Dunkin (PG). Securities:
  Samuell Warner, Paule Rawlins.
- inventory of Martin Falkner (PG), by
  appraisers Thomas Sprigg & Edward
  Dawson.
- inventory of Henry Jones (PG), by
  appraisers John Joslin & Thomas
  Nellson.
- inventory of Charles Hay (PG), by
  appraisers Thomas Sprigg & Daniell
  Daniellson.
- inventory of Thomas Hyde (PG), by
  appraisers Bartholomew Goff & Joseph
  Addison.
17:178   ...
- will of John Dunkin (PG),
  constituting his widow Sarah Dunkin
  executrix.
- will of Thomas Hooke (PG).
- bond of David Small administrator of
  Charles Tracy (PG). Securities:
  James Moore, Josias Towgood.

14 July. Mr. Christopher Gregory
exhibited inventory of Parthenia Burditt
(CH), by appraisers John Banister & John
Barker.

18 July. Exhibited inventory of Joseph Moseley (TA), by appraisers George Vinson & Richard Kempston.

21 July. Mr. Richard Kilburne (Annapolis) was granted administration on estate of Stephen Blatchford (Annapolis), as greatest creditor. Securities: Charles Kilburne, John Stanley. Appraisers: MM Anthony Workman, Orlandoe Greenslade.

22 July. Mr. Joshua Ceecill (PG) exhibited inventory of Thomas Blanford (PG), by appraisers Samuell Magrooder & John Pottinger.

17:179

Mrs. Anne Burges widow of Mr. William Burges (AA) was granted administration on his estate. Securities: Thomas Larkin, Richard Jones, Jr. Appraisers: Thomas Odell, John Baldwin. Mr. James Saunders to administer oath.

25 July. Dr. Allexander Chappell executor of Thomas Dauvas (AA) exhibited inventory, by appraisers Thomas Hughs & Zacariah Cadle.

Exhibited inventory of Robert Cooper (TA), by appraisers John Coppedge & Thomas Marsh.

28 July. Maj. William Whittington (SO) for Mr. Samuell Hopkins (SO) exhibited:
- accounts of Henry Rich administrator of John Williams (SO).
- inventory of Amos Parsons (SO), by appraisers Richard Tull & William Wallace.
- bond of John Macknitt administrator of Amos Parsons. Security: John Porter.

17:180 29 July. Thomas Tench, Esq. exhibited:
- renunciation of Elisabeth Parrett (AA) of her will. She is relict of Gabriell Parrett, Jr. Witnesses: Thomas Tench, Robert Lockwood, Gilbert Winterford.
- bond of Elisabeth Parrett (AA) on estate of her husband. Securities:

Court Session: 1698

Robert Lockwood, John Blackmore.

Thomas Cockey (AA) executor of Sarah
Cockey (AA) exhibited inventory, by
appraisers Mathew Howard & Richard
Morss.

17:181 1 August. Mr. Thomas Nichols (CV)
exhibited accounts on estate of Joseph
Fary (CV). Continuance was granted.

6 August. Charles Kilburne one of
appraisers of John Bouye (AA) exhibited
inventory, by appraisers said Kilburne &
Robert Phillips.

Dr. Allexander Chappell one of
executors of Thomas Davis (also Thomas
Dauvas, AA) exhibited renunciation of
Francis West the other executor. Date:
27 June 1698. Witnesses: Richard
Deavor, Charles Scott.

17:182 Mr. John Willymott (CV) exhibited:
• will of Mr. Francis Hutchins (g,
CV), constituting his widow
Elisabeth Hutchins executrix. She
is a Quaker. Said Elisabeth was
granted administration.
• will of Ailse Smith (CV), proved by
Thomas & Nathan Smith her executors.
Also exhibited inventory, by
appraisers George Cole & Richard
Evans.
• will of John Lawrence (CV),
constituting his widow Margerett
executrix. Also exhibited
inventory, by appraisers John Hunt &
Henry Cox.
• will of Timothy Gunton (CV),
constituting his widow Elisabeth
Gunton executrix. Also exhibited
inventory, by appraisers George
Spice & Thomas Kingcroft.
• letter of caveat by Mr. John Elsey
(CV) on behalf of his wife that none
may administer on estate of her
brother Lewis German (BA). Said
Gorman died at house of Mr. Gibson.

17:183 ...
There are no kindred, but said
Elsey's wife. Said Lewis Jarman

Page 67

died 1 June 1698. To: Mr. Edward
Batson (Annapolis).

10 August. Mrs. Elisabeth Gassaway
(AA) widow of John Gassaway (AA) was
granted administration on his estate.
Securities: MM Richard Galloway, William
Richardson. Appraisers: John Chappell,
John Gaile. Mr. John Merriton to
administer oath.

15 August. William Edmondson on behalf
of rest of the executors & William Sharp
one of the creditors of John Edmondson
(TA) petitioned for appraisers: Nicholas
Lowe, John Dorson. Thomas Robins (TA)
to administer oath.

Mr. Robert Gouldesborough exhibited
inventory of John Robins (TA), by
appraisers Thomas Robins Jr., William
Curtis.

17:184 Said Gouldesborough exhibited inventory
of Col. George Robotham (TA), by
appraisers John Emerson & William
Clarke.

7 August. Mr. Michaell Taney executor
of William Morse (CV) exhibited
accounts.

27 August. Mr. Robert Carvile
procurator for Col. Henry Lowe (SM) &
his wife Susanah vs. Col. Henry
Darnall. Demurrer exhibited against the
replication of said Darnall.

24 August. Exhibited release by Solomon
Sparrow & William Richardson for their
wives' legacy from Thomas & Nathan Smith
executors of Alice Smith (widow, CV).
Witness: Ger. Hopkins.

Exhibited verbal will of Peter Clarke
(KE). Bequests to: James Williams.
17:185 Proved before Robert Smith. Said
Williams is to have LoA, but Edward
Sweatnam was granted administration.
Ruling: coroner (KE) to summon said
Sweatnam.

James Pattison deposed that he witnessed Stephen Walton make his will on 22 February last. Said Pattison was too sick to travel.

John Hammond deposed that he witnessed the will of John Atkins on 20 February last & is now too sick to travel. Date: 2 March 1697.

17:186 Exhibited renunciation of William Harbert executor of Stephen Walton. Other executor is Thomas Haddock. Date: 2 March 1697.

Administration bonds from PG:
- Richard Lancaster administrator of Thomas Edmundson. Security: John Boyd. Date: 23 July 1698.
- Henry Dryden administrator of Robert Biggs. Securities: Thomas Bridges, Timothy Maghall. Date: 2 June 1698.
- Elisabeth Gambling executrix of James Gambling. Securities: Samuell Copeland, Hugh Williams. Date: 27 August 1698.
- John Chapman executor of James Williams. Security: David Small. Date: 17 July 1698.
- Hannah Emmett executrix of John Emett. Security: David Small. Date: 17 July 1698.
- Katherine Willson & name Cecill Josuah executors of (N). Securities: David Small, James Moore. Date: 23 July 1698.
- Mary Prather executrix of George Prather. Security: Edward Ball. Date: 29 June 1698.

Administration bonds from BA:
- Sarah Heath executrix of Thomas Heath. Security: Francis Dallahide. Date: 10 July 1698.
- John Rouse administrator of Richard Thompson. Securities: Joseph Strawbridge, John Seale. Date: 30 June 1698.
- Thomas Hedge, Jr. administrator of Thomas Hedge, Sr. Securities: Samuell Sicklemore, Thomas Smith. Date: 16 July 1698.

17:187 Administration bonds from CH:
- Philip Lynes administrator of Edward Dwyer. Security: William Harpham.
- Maurice Mankin administrator of Stephen Mankin. Securities: John Wood, John Wilkinson.
- Conier Clark executor of John Clark. Securities: Ralph Shaw, John Bacon.
- Elisabeth Marshall administratrix of William Marshall. Securities: Walter Story, Edward Philpot.
- Henry Moor administrator of Thomas Moor. Security: Thomas Chapman.
- Mary Martin administratrix of John Martin. Securities: Robert Benson, John Godshall.
- Sarah Key administratrix of Henry Key. Securities: Ignatius Wheeler, Mathew Barns.
- Francis Coffer administratrix of Thomas Coffer. Securities: John Allen, Henry Barnes.
- John Wood & Michaell Martin administrators of Francis Butterie. Securities: Milenex Ratcliff, John Wilkinson.
- John Bayne administrator of Notley Warren. Securities: John Wilder, Thomas Whichaley.
- James Waggen & Joseph Ward executors of Philip Allen. Securities: Thomas Lawson, Thomas Hagan.
- Anne Hutchinson administratrix of Thomas Hutchinson. Securities: Richard Sotheron, Jacob Mereton.
- Dorothy Gates executrix of Robert Gates. Securities: Edward Cole, Richard Jenkins.
- Mary Mathews executrix of Isaac Mathews. Securities: William Thompson, John Doyne.
- Richard Jenkins administrator of William Williams. Securities: Thomas Taney, William Smith.
- Thomas Stone executor of John Stone. Securities: William Stone, Joseph Manning.
- Elenor Stone executrix of John Stone. Securities: William Stone, John Maning.

Court Session: 1698

Administration bonds from CV:
- Sarah Roberts administratrix of Robert Roberts. Security: Elisabeth Bearne.
- Anne Shorte administratrix of John Short. Securities: John Willimott, John Elsey.
- Elisha Hall administratrix of William Hall. Security: Henry Cox.
- Sarah Dickinson administratrix of Edward Dickinson. Security: Samuell Scott.
- John Davies administrator of Nathaniell Cranford. Securities: William Turner, John Willimott.

Administration bonds from SO:
- James Wallice administrator of William Wallice. Security: John Macknitt.
- Isaack Horsey administrator of John Atkin. Security: John West. Date: 29 June 1698.

17:188 ...
- Rachell Huitt administratrix of John Huitt (minister). Securities: James Dashiell, George Megee. Date: 10 June 1698.
- Thomas Wilson administrator of Col. David Brown. Securities: Samuell Hopkins, Sr., Samuell Worthington. Date: 17 September 1697.
- John Booth executor of John Booth. Securities: Philip Askue, James Spence. Date: 10 June 1698.

Administration bonds from TA:
- Mary Grafton administratrix of Robert Grafton. Securities: William Sharp, Edward Clark. Date: 12 June 1698.
- William Swift & his wife administrators of Richard Eubanks. Securities: John Hunam, John Swift. Date: 23 August 1698.
- Francis Sayer executrix of Jacob Seth. Security: Charles Black. Date: 7 April 1698.
- William Scott administrator of Richard Pott (merchant). Securities: James Scott, Ambros Kinimont. Date: 20 August 1698.

- William Sharp administrator of Obadiah Judkin. Securities: William Edmundson, Samuell Abott. Date: 12 July 1698.
- Philemon Lloyd one of executors of Madam Henretta Maria Lloyd. Securities: Edward Sweatnam, Edward Batson. Date: 5 September 1698.
- Sarah, James, William, & Thomas Edmundson executors of John Edmundson. Security: Abraham Morgan.
- Robert Blunt administrator of Mr. Robert Cooper. Securities: Isaack Winchester, Stephen Thomas. Date: 18 May 1698.
- Elisabeth Farmer administratrix of Samuell Farmer. Securities: Fra. Neale, James Ragles. Date: 14 June 1698.
- Thomas Yowle executor of Sarah Yowle (TA). Securities: Henry Costin, Henry Pratt.
- Nath. Scott, James Meens, & William Scott administrators of John Pinnard. Date: 9 April 1698.

Administration bonds from SM:
- Thomeson Heyden administratrix of Francis Heyden. Security: John Bap. Carbery. Date: 12 October 1697.

Administration bonds from CE:
- Elisabeth Wheeler administratrix of John Wheeler. Securities: William Boyer, Samuell Hill. Date: 6 August 1698.

17:189 ...

- John Brockson & wife administrators of Thomas Moor. Security: William Brockson. Date: 25 July 1698.
- Thomas Thranstone & Philip Reason administrators of (N). Securities: William Pearce, Henry Eldersley. Date: 15 July 1698.
- Charles James administrator of Charles James. Securities: Humphrey Tilton, Darby Hely. Date: 19 May 1698.
- George Biston administrator of James Taylor. Securities: John Hutchinson, Charles Bermont. Date:

Court Session: 1698

16 May 1698.
- Henry Guilder administrator of John Guilder. Securities: Hugh Fout, Richard Barker. Date: 23 April 1698.
- Joane Lindsey administratrix of Thomas Lindsey. Securities: Thomas Pearce, Thomas Cox. Date: 17 April 1698.
- Owen Hewes executor of Edward Johnson. Securities: John Cesing, Henry Benning, Sr. Date: 17 April 1698.

Administration bonds from DO:
- Elisabeth Ladmore executrix of George Ladmore. Security: John Alford, Jr. Date: 5 April 1698.
- Susannah Washfield administratrix of Robert Washfield. Security: Henry Whiteaker.

Administration bonds from KE:
- Edward Sweatnam administrator of Peter Clark. Security: Elias King. Date: 30 August 1698.

Administration bonds from SM:
- Sarah Hulse administratrix of Robert Harrison. Security: Philip Lock. Date: 23 August 1698.
- Mary Hodgeson administratrix of William Hodgeson. Security: John Smith. Date: 14 June 1698.
- Audrey Llewelyn administratrix of John Llewelyn. Securities: Thomas Waughop, William Taylard. Date: 18 June 1698.
- Richard Berckhead executor of Charles Goff. Security: Cornelius Manly.
- Elinor Long executrix of John Long. Securities: Samuell Cookery, Ralph Foster. Date: 2 May 1698.
- William Gwither administrator of Thomas Gwither. Securities: Owen Gwither, Allexander Dehiniossia. Date: 31 August 1698.

17:190 31 September. Richard Boughton (CH) exhibited:
- will of John Stone (CH),

Page 73

constituting his widow Ellinor Stone & his son John Stone executors.

- inventory of Daniell Simons, by appraisers Robert Shephard & William Hutchins. Date: 14 May 1698.
- inventory of John Stone, by appraisers John Hanson & John Addison. Date: 15 December 1697.
- accounts of Christopher Williamson administrator of Nathaniell Buttons. Date: 1 September 1698.
- Robert Doyne list of debts received of William Chandler in 1685.
- inventory of Philip Joans, by appraisers George Godfrey & Samuell Wheeler. Date: 1 August 1698.
- inventory of Charles Watts, by appraisers Thomas Lawson & Thomas Prise. Date: 8 April 1698.
- inventory of John Ward, by appraisers Henry Moor & John Clement. Date: 15 May 1698.
- will of Ignatius Mathews, constituting Mary Mathews executrix. Date: 19 February 1697.
- will of William Marshall, constituting his son William Marshall executor, proved by Hugh Tears & Joseph Marshall. Date: 2 November 1697.
- inventory of Edmond Dwyer, by appraisers Thomas Blackwell & Thomas Orrell. Date: 13 September 1698.
- accounts of John Wood administrator of James Regon. Date: 1 April 1698.
- will of William Whittam, constituting Richard Jenkins executor, proved by John Evans, Margrett Sape, & Francis Long. Date: 13 May 1698.

17:191 ...

- inventory of Thomas Dorman, by appraisers Christopher Ford & John Bannester. Date: 30 June 1698.
- inventory of Charles Allison, by appraisers John Gray & Peter Mackmillion.
- inventory of James Boyle, by appraisers Jesse Doyne & Mathew Barns. Date: 9 August 1698.
- inventory of William Whitom, by appraisers William Smith & William

Norris.
- inventory of Gates Robert [!], by appraisers William Boarman, Jr. & William Norris.
- inventory of Johanna Hudson, by appraisers George Godfrey & Ignatius Wheeler. Date: 1 August 1698.
- inventory of William Marshall, by appraisers Walter Story & Edward Philpott. Date: 25 August 1698.
- will of Francis Colory, proved by John Wood & Doroty Former. Date: 17 March 1698.
- inventory of Dennis Doyn, by appraisers Richard Harrison & William Thompson. Date: 4 June 1698.
- inventory of Sarah Cookesey, by appraisers John Hunt & Thomas Price. Date: 26 April 1698.
- will of Robert Gates, constituting Dorithy Gates executrix, proved by Richard Edlen, James Connell, & James Hagen. Date: 5 February 1694/5.
- inventory of Ashman Richard [!], by appraisers Walter Story & Edward Phillpott. Date: 22 June 1698.
- inventory of John Stone (cooper), by appraisers Thomas Lawson & Thomas Price. Date: 22 June 1698.

17:192 ...
- accounts of Magdelen Taylor administratrix of William Taylor. Date: 20 May 1697.

Exhibited:
- inventory of Adam Head, by appraisers Joshua Guibert & James French. Date: 14 July 1698.
- inventory of Thomas Barker, by appraisers Henry Lowe & Richard Southerne. Date: 25 April 1698.
- inventory of William Hinington, by appraisers John Nutthall, Sr. & John Nutthall, Jr. Date: 25 June 1698.
- inventory of William Meren, by appraisers Richard Newman & Henry Spink. Date: 20 June 1698.
- inventory of John Powell, by appraisers Nathaniell Vivers & George Aketh. Date: 19 April 1698.

- inventory of Capt. Thomas Peare, by appraisers Thomas Hebb & Edward Haleid. Date: 1 August.
- inventory of Bartholomew Morry, by appraisers Peter Peake & William Bannester. Date: 30 August 1698.
- inventory of Thomas Shank, by appraisers Samuell Chamberline & David Parsons. Date: 12 May 1698.
- inventory of Christopher Gwinn, by appraisers Sollomon Joanes & William Morgan. Date: 4 June 1698.

17:193 ...

- inventory of John Bayle, by appraisers Thomas Kertley & Richard Vowles. Date: 11 December 1698.
- accounts of Sarah Crook executrix of John Crook. Date: 8 August 1698.
- inventory of Francis Swaile, by appraisers Joshua Houldsworth & John Smith. Date: 23 July 1698.
- inventory of Thomas Warren, by appraisers Richard Newman & Henry Spinke. Date: 25 June 1698.
- accounts of Ann Abell executrix of Samuell Abell. Date: 25 July 1698.
- inventory of William Spinke, by appraisers Richard Newman & John Jarboe. Date: 20 June 1698.
- inventory of Walter Taylor, by appraisers John Miller & Daniell Bell. Continuance was granted.
- inventory of Thomas Tole, by appraisers John Cowly & William Hollon. Date: 21 June 1698.
- inventory of Richard Walker, by appraisers Henry Spinke & William Sheircliffe. Date: 20 July 1698.
- inventory of William Medley, by appraisers Stephen Gough & John Tant. Date: 17 March 1697/8.
- inventory of John Joans, by appraisers John Gawdard & Cornelius Dunevan. Date: 6 April 1698.
- inventory of John Murphey, by appraisers John Gawdard & Lewis Hazlon. Date: 27 July 1698.
- inventory of John Miles, by appraisers Ro. Clarke & John Fenwick. Date: 4 April 1698.

17:194 ...

- inventory of Elisabeth Brimmer, by

Court Session: 1698

appraisers Thomas Reeves & Abraham
Brooke. Date: 6 June 1698.
- inventory of William Knight, by
  appraisers Richard Newman &
  Christopher Norris. Date: 8 August
  1698.
- inventory of Thomas Keirkley, by
  appraisers James Greenwell & Stephen
  Gough. Date: 26 March 1698.
- inventory of Samuell Abell, by
  appraisers John Fenwick & Richard
  Newman. Date: 12 April 1698.
- inventory of Sollomon Rottee, by
  appraisers Richard Attwood & Thomas
  Haddock. Date: 18 June 1698.
- accounts of Thomas Gwither
  administrator of Nicholas Coates.
  Date: 30 August 1698.
- accounts of John Powell. Date: 6
  August 1698.
- accounts of William Morgan & his
  wife Elisabeth administrators of
  Robert Large. Date: 29 July 1698.
- inventory of John Sissill, by
  appraisers Henry Spink & James
  French. Date: 6 July 1698.
- inventory of John Crook, by
  appraisers Thomas Hall & George
  Keeth. Date: 6 July 1698.
- inventory of Peter Jarboe, by
  appraisers Stephen Gough & James
  Greenwell. Date: 13 April 1698.

17:195 ...
- will of William Hodgson,
  constituting Mary Hodgson executrix,
  proved by Thomas Annis, John Ubgat,
  & John Smith. Date: 10 June 1698.
- will of Samuell Abell, constituting
  his widow Ann Abell executrix,
  proved by Edward Coale, Luke
  Gardiner, & Charles Carles. Date: 8
  January 1697.
- will of Charles Brooke, constituting
  Leonard Brooke executor, proved by
  Henry Lowe, Luke Gardiner, Roger
  Brooke, Jr., & Edward Cole. Date:
  13 February 1697/8.

31 August. Mr. Jossuah Cecill (PG)
exhibited:
- additional accounts of John White
  administrator of Thomas Gannt.

Court Session: 1698

Date: 22 April 1698.

- will of George Prather, constituting Mary Prather executrix, proved by William Prater, John Prater, & Henry Butler. Date: 3 May 1698.
- will of John Emmett, constituting Hannah Emmett executrix, proved by William Tannehill, James Beale, & Francis Prisly. Date: 13 April 1695.
- will of James Gambling, constituting his widow Elisabeth Gambling executrix, proved by Henry Pope, William Hill, & Thomas Davies. Date: 3 July 1698.
- will of James Williams, constituting John Chapman executor, proved by James Watts, Daniell Hirst, & John Bennett. Date: 14 May 1698.
- will of Jonathon Willson, constituting Katherine Willson & Josuah Cecill executors, proved by Henry Glover, John Withers, & Thomas Waters. Date: 7 May 1698.
- accounts of Sarah Dunkin administratrix of JOhn Dunkin. Date: 9 August 1698.

17:196 ...

- inventory of Charles Tracey, by appraisers James Stoddart & Josuah Hall. Date: 20 May 1696.

Mr. John Willimot (CV) exhibited:
- will of Hugh Ellis, constituting his widow Ruth & her child executors, proved by George Gray & John Bigger. Date: 1 January 1697/8.
- inventory of William Harris, by appraisers John Leach, Jr. & James Heigh. Date: 23 July 1698.
- will of Daniell Simmons, constituting his widow & John Groves, Jr. executors, proved by John Groves, William Wilkison, Robert Groves, & Joan Groves. Date: 10 December 1697.
- will of John Smith, constituting his widow Joan executrix, proved by John Turner, Thomas Brickenden, James Dawkins, & Richard Willis. Date: 19 April 1698.
- will of John Holloway, constituting

Court Session: 1698

his widow Mathew Holloway executrix,
proved by John Smith, Robert Day,
William Hutchins, & Thomas Simmons.
Date: 2 November 1697.
- will of John Short, constituting his
widow executrix, proved by Elisabeth
Evans, Edward Hull, Ann Hall, &
Joseph Owen. Date: 27 June 1698.
- inventory of Hugh Ellis, by
appraisers John Manyng & Robert
Skinner. Date: 29 August 1698.
- inventory of Jochem Keristed, by
appraisers John Taney & Peter
Sewell. Date: 15 August 1698.
- inventory of Robert Fisher, by
appraisers Edward Wenman & Thomas
Edmans. Date: 25 April 1698.
- inventory of William Head, by
appraisers John Godsgrace & Robert
Skinner. Date: 15 June 1698.

17:197 ...

- inventory of Edward Dickenson, by
appraisers Henry Esterling & Evan
Rice. Date: 6 August 1698.
- inventory of Richard Sands, by
appraisers William Derrumple & John
Ford. Date: 8 June 1698.
- accounts of Elisabeth Jones
administratrix of John Jones. Date:
8 August 1698.
- inventory of John Holloway, by
appraisers Samuell Scott & William
Hutchins. Date: 4 November 1698.
- accounts of Peter Sewell executor of
Walter Gellett. Date: 31 August
1698.
- accounts of Mr. Aaron Hall & his
wife administrators of Joseph
Edwards. Date: 30 August 1698.
- additional accounts of John Manyng &
his wife Ruth executrix of Hugh
Ellis who married Elisabeth Hunton
executrix of Mordecai. Hunton.
- accounts of John Bigger
administrator of William Head.
Date: 7 September 1698.

Maj. Smithson (TA) exhibited:
- will of Jacobus Seth, constituting
Madam Anne Swyer executrix, proved
by William Fitzgerald, Edmund
Fitzgerald, Francis Osen, Susannah

Neale, Mery Steward, & William
Denton. Date: 22 December 1699.
- accounts of William Edmondson one of
  executors of John Edmondson. Date:
  1 September 1698.
- accounts of Daniell Toas executor of
  Daniell Toas. Date: 1 September
  1698. Continuance was granted.
- accounts of John Coppedge executor
  of Allen Smith. Date: 2 September
  1698.
- accounts of Thomas Smithson, Edward
  Loyde, & John Pemberton executors of
  Col. George Robothem. Date: 1
  September 1698.

17:198 ...

- accounts of John Pitt administrator
  of John Estall. Date: 1 September
  1698.
- will of Thomas Clements, dated 10
  March 1698, constituting his widow
  Elisabeth executrix, proved by
  Lawrence Knowles, James Benson,
  James Sewell, & Samuell Junett on 14
  June 1698.
- accounts of John Hacker
  administrator of Edward Smith,
  proved before Maj. Smithson.
- inventory of Jacobus Seth, by
  appraisers William Coursey &
  Phillimon Hemsley. Date: 19 April
  1698.
- will of Obediah Judkin, constituting
  William Sharp executor, proved by
  Jeffy Hardman, William Dixon, Mary
  Morton, Robert Spring, & Robert
  Register. Date: 3 May 1698.
- accounts of Thomas Robins executor
  of George Robins. Date: 8 September
  1698.
- accounts of John Bartlett
  administrator of Sarah Bartlett.
  Date: 8 September 1698.
- additional accounts of William Carr
  administrator of Joseph Wiggott.
  Date: 8 September 1698.
- will of John Sargent, constituting
  his widow Mary Sargent executrix,
  proved by William Coursey, Vincent
  Hemsley, & Peter Jolly. Date: 4 May
  1698.

17:199 ...

- accounts of John Pitt administrator of Thomas Cooke. Date: 8 September 1698.
- accounts of John Glover administrator of Henry Boston. Date: 8 September 1698.
- will of John Pickard, constituting Juliana Young executrix, proved by James Meende, Nathaniell Scott, & John Gwinn. Date: 25 November 1697.
- accounts of Thomas Hopkins & his wife Elisabeth administratrix of Jacob Abrams. Date: 8 September 1698.
- accounts of namec Hopkins Thomas Sr. administrator of Clement Hopkins. Date: September 1698.
- accounts of Jane Boone administratrix of John Boone. Date: September 1698.
- will of John Wright, constituting Maj. Thomas Smithson executor, proved by John Jay & John Ludingham. Date: 9 May 1698.
- inventory of Capt. Richard Sweatnam (TA), by appraisers Thomas Smithson & William Coursey. Date: 6 August 1697.
- inventory of John Edmondson, by appraisers Nicholas Lowe & John Dorson. Date: 26 August 1698.
- inventory of John Wright, by appraisers John Nunan & Thomas Eubanks. Date: 30 August 1698.
- inventory of Samuell Farmer, by appraisers John Swallow & John Glover. Date: 16 July 1698.

17:200 ...

- inventory of Obediah Judgkins, by appraisers Thomas Hopkins & Thomas Eubanks. Date: 25 July 1698.
- accounts of John Sargent administrator of William Gibson. Date: 19 April 1698.
- inventory of John Swaine, by appraisers Michaell Earle & Christopher Denny. Date: 14 October 1697. Continuance was granted.
- inventory of Thomas Blackenden, by appraisers Thomas Smithson & William Coursey Date: 28 June 1698.
- additional inventory of John Swaine,

by appraisers Michaell Earle &
Christopher Denny. Date: 26 June
1698.
- will of Sarah Yewell, constituting
Thomas Yewell executor, proved by
William Hemsley, William Clayton, &
Henry Coston. Date: 23 August 1698.

Col. John Thompson (CE) exhibited:
- will of Thomas Linsey, constituting
Joane Linsey executrix, proved by
Thomas Peirce, Mathias Hendrixson, &
Thomas Cox. Date: 18 March 1697/8.
- will of Edward Johnson, constituting
Owen Hews, Sr. executor, proved by
John Consene, Elisabeth Consene,
Peter Mainardoe, & Joa. Lewis.
Date: 18 October 1697. Also
accounts, dated 8 September 1698.

17:201 ...
- accounts of Abraham Redgrave
administrator of John Morris. Date:
8 September 1698.
- inventory of James Taylor, by
appraisers Cornelius Herkin & Thomas
Parker.
- inventory of Thomas Linsey, by
appraisers Thomas Tarry & Mathias
Hendrixon.
- inventory of Charles James, by
appraisers Robert Gibson & Richard
Kennard. Date: 17 June 1698.
- accounts of William Brockson & his
wife Elisabeth executrix of Thomas
Nicholson. Date: 20 July 1698.
- inventory of John Gilders, by
appraisers Richard Franklin & Thomas
Parker.
- accounts of William Elmes
administrator of Ezakell Jackson.
Date: September 1698.

John Rawlings (DO) exhibited:
- will of George Ladmor, constituting
Elisabeth Ladmore executrix, proved
by John Alford & John Nicholls.
Date: 6 January 1697/8.
- accounts of Walter Cambell
administrator of Mary Aldridge.
Date: 5 September 1698.
- inventory of George Ladmor, by
appraisers John Nicholls & Mathias

Court Session: 1698

Allford. Date: 20 June 1698.
- inventory of Robert Washfield, by appraisers John Nicholls & John Wade. Date: 5 September 1698.
- inventory of Benjamin Hunt, by appraisers John Kirke & Charles Powell. Date: 26 April 1698.
- accounts of Charles Powell administrator of William Dorrington. Date: 8 September 1698.

17:202 Mr. John Hall (BA) exhibited:
- will of Richard Thompson, constituting Henry Thompson executor, proved by Joseph Strawbridge, Sarah Strawbridge, Nicholas Fitzsymons, & Alce Sutton. Date: 30 March 1698.
- will of Thomas Heath, constituting Sarah Heath executrix, proved by Edmond Hensley, William Horn, Catherine Lomax, Susannah Richardson, & Anne Richardson. Date: 15 May 1698.
- inventory of Richard Thompson, by appraisers Joseph Strawbridge & John Coale. Date: 30 (N) 1698.
- additional accounts of William Barker & his wife Mary administrators of Francis Watkins. Date: 1 September 1698.
- accounts of Joseph Peake executor of Mrs. Jane Long. Date: 10 September 1698.
- inventory of Thomas Hedge, by appraisers Thomas Smith & Daniell Sicklemore. Date: 16 May 1698.
- accounts of Nicholas Fitzsymons administrator of Capt. Thomas Morgan. Date: 1 September 1698.

Mr. Samuell Hopkins (SO) exhibited:
- will of John Booth, constituting John Booth, Jr. executor, proved by William Kible, James Spence, & Thomas Horsman. Date: 16 May 1698.
- accounts of John West surviving executor of Capt. John King.

17:203 ...
- inventory of William Wallass, Sr., by appraisers John Gray & James Caldwell. Date: 25 July 1698.

- inventory of William Venables, by appraisers Ben. Collman & Thomas Horsman. Date: 28 May 1698.
- inventory of Capt. John King, per Mr. John West.
- accounts of James Dashiell executor of James Dashiell. Date: 10 August 1698.
- inventory of John Atkins, by appraisers William Coulbourne & John Roach, Jr. Date: 20 June 1698.
- inventory of John Booth, by appraisers Benjamin Collman & Thomas Horsman.
- inventory of Col. David Brown, by appraisers Richard Chambers & Samuell Worthington.
- inventory of John Hewitt (minister), by appraisers James Dashiell & Nicholas Evans.

Mr. Elias King (KE) exhibited:
- will of John Hollinsworth, constituting George Vanderford, William Hynson, & William Brewerton executors. Exhibited renunciation of George Vanderford (TA). Date: 3 May 1698. Witnesses: Charles Vanderford, John Vanderford.

17:204 ...

Exhibited renunciation of William Hynson (TA) & William Brewarton (TA). Date: 27 May 1698. Witnesses: Nathaniell Wright, Robert Norrest.
- will of Thomas Collens, constituting Barbara Collens executrix, proved by Edward Offley, Frances Ambross, & Nicholas Clouds. Date: 23 April 1698.
- inventory of John Percifull, by appraisers Walter Toley, Sr. & Michaell Miller, Jr. Date: 12 July 1697.
- inventory of Peter Clark, by appraisers John Chaires & George Smith. Date: 26 August 1698.
- inventory of William Hodges, by appraisers Charles Hynson & William Glanvell. Date: 17 August 1698.
- accounts of William Osburn & his wife Hannah executrix of Edward

Court Session: 1698

Owen.   Date: 29 (N) 1698.

Exhibited from AA:
- accounts of Alice Collier administratrix of Samuell Austin. Date: 1 September 1698.

17:205 ...
inventory of William Burges, by appraisers John Baldwin & Thomas Odell. Date: 16 September 1698.
- inventory of William Groves, by appraisers Thomas Hughs & John Trundell. Also list of debts. Date: 29 August 1698.
- inventory of John Cozens, by appraisers Abraham Child & Henry Wright. Date: 18 July 1698.
- accounts of Margrett Steward administratrix of David Steward. Date: 1 September 1698.
- will of Calleb Chew, constituting Samuell Chew executor, proved by Roger Crudgentone, Ann Quin, & Mary Smith. Date: 5 September 1698.

17:206   30 August. Robert Gouldesborough procurator for Patrick Dannelly (DO) & his wife Ann (daughter of William Dorrington (dec'd)) vs. Phillip Clarke procurator for Charles Powell administrator of said Dorrington. Text of libel filed on 12 March 1697/8. Said Patrick married said Ann after administration was granted to said Powell. Text of answer. Said Patrick married said Ann when she was 14, and took her from the custody of the administrator.
17:207   Ruling: plaintiff to find security for the other orphan. Plaintiff was granted administration on said estate. Said Powell to render accounts.

Arthur Wheatley (DO) administrator of William Worgane (DO) unadministered by John Brooke (TA, dec'd) vs. Hugh Sherwood executor of Judith Brooke executrix of said John. Libel filed on 15 April 1696. Mentions: plaintiff married Sarah daughter of said Brooke, Charles Wheeler married Mary another daughter. Said Wheeler assigned his

Page 85

Court Session: 1698

17:208
17:209
rights to said Wheatley.
Ruling: said Sherwood to pay plaintiff
based on the mutual agreement between
the parties.

Samuell Smith vs. Charles Carroll
procurator for John Gadsby (BA). Libed
filed on 21 April 1698 by Robert
Gouldesbury procurator for John Smith
(AA). Mentions: George Norman married
Elisabeth Smith a sister of plaintiff &
had 2 children. She died shortly after
he died. Plaintiff is her only brother.
Said Gadsby was granted administration
on said estate. Answer. Mentions: said
Gadsby married mother of said Norman.
Ruling: for defendant.

17:210
Dr. Alexander Chappell one of executors
of Thomas Danvis (also Thomas Danvies,
AA) exhibited renunciation of Francis
West the other executor.
Date: 27 June 1698. Witnesses: Richard
Deaver, Charles Scott.

John Willymott (CV) for Mr. John Elsey
on behalf of his wife vs. estate of her
brother Lewis Jarman (BA). Caveat
exhibited. Said Jarman died on 1 June
last. Date: 6 August 1698.

Robert Carvile procurator for Col.
Henry Lowe (SM) & his wife Susannah vs.
Col. Henry Darnall. Demurrer exhibited
against the replication. Date: 27
August 1698.

William & Elisabeth Richardson were
granted administration on estate of
William Richardson (AA). Securities:
Garrett Stepkin, Joseph Richardson. Dr.
Zachariah Allen to administer oath.

17:211
Mr. John Carvill (CE) administrator of
John Cane (alias Black Jack a Negro,
dec'd)
deposed that he had not received
anything from the estate.

1 September. Col. Edward Loyd (TA)
petitioned for new appraisers for the
estate of his father Col. Philomon Loyd

Page 86

(TA), because one of the appraisers is
dec'd.

8 September. Robert Smith, Esq. (KE)
was granted administration on estate of
John Glandering (KE). Appraisers: James
Williams, George Smith. Mr. Robert
Martin to administer oath to appraisers.
Capt. John Harris to administer oath to
administrator.

Said Robert Smith for Nicholas Massey
was granted administration on estate of
(N) Carsey administrator of James
Carsey. Appraisers: John Powell, John
Parsons. Said Smith to administer oath
to appraisers. Capt. John Hawkins to
administer oath to administrator.

9 September. Edward Laddimore was
appointed an appraiser of estate of Col.
Casp. Harman (CE), in place of James
Gray (incapacitated). Col. John
Thompson to administer oath.

14 September. Thomas Tench, Esq. for
Hannah Powell executrix of William
Powell (p, AA) exhibited his will.
Capt. William Holland to prove said
will. Said Hannah was granted
administration.

Samuell Magruder, age 38, deposed on 2
September 1698 that on 27 January last
he was in PG with Thomas Hillory (dec'd)
& James Barrott & that they
17:212 agreed to certain bills of exchange.
Before: Edward Battson.

William Harbert renounced administration
on estate of Stephen Walton. Date: 2
March 1697/8.

17 October. Mary Jarvice widow of
Humphry Jarvice (butcher, AA) was
granted administration on his estate.
Securities: Richard Jones, Manus
Danverin. Appraisers: Capt.
<unreadable> Burgiss, Mr. Benjamin
Bond. Capt. Nicholas Gassaway to
administer oath.

Court Session: 1698

23 October. Mrs. Elisabeth Hanslopp widow of Capt. Henry Hanslap (AA) exhibited his will. Said Elisabeth was granted administration. Securities: Joseph Chew, Joseph Hanslopp. Appraisers: MM James Saunder, John Gresham. Capt. Nicholas Gassaway to administer oath.

17:213 26 October. Mr. Haunce Hanson (CE) for his daughter Mary relict & executrix of Thomas Francis (AA) was granted administration on his estate. Mr. Elazar King (KE) to administer oath.

15 September. Mr. William Bladen for Mr. Garrett Vanswearingen (SM) was granted administration on estate of Mr. William Massey. Securities: said Bladen, Christopher Grigory. Appraisers: Mr. John Freeman, John Dowdell.

16 September. Ann Marke (AA) widow of William Marke (AA) was granted administration on his estate. Securities: John Stanley, John Newton. Appraisers: William Lewis, William Merriday. Capt. John Worthington to administer oath.

25 September. Robert Francklyn for his sister Sarah Herne widow of William Herne (AA) was granted administration on his estate. Securities: Richard Gott, Robert Franklyn. Appraisers: John Chappell, John Trundell. Thomas Tench, Esq. to administer oath.

3 November. John Gill (p, AA) who married a sister of William Bates (AA) was granted administration on his estate. Securities: Peter Bond, Stephen Hancock. Appraisers: Francis Mead, Mathew Howard. Capt. John Worthington to administer oath.

17:214 4 November. Sarah Perry widow of John Perry (Annapolis) was granted administration on his estate. Securities: MM William Bladen, John Murray. Appraisers: Evan Thomas, John

Court Session: 1698

Newman.

5 November. Katherine Harman was
granted administration on estate of
Robert Sowright, as greatest creditor.
Capt. John Moll (Chief Justice, CE) to
administer oath. Date: 6 November 1698.

10 November. William Pennington (AA)
was granted administration on estate of
Will. Martin (AA). Securities: John
Hurst, William Hawkins. Appraisers:
Joseph Moss, Joseph Conneway. Mr. John
Worthington to administer oath.

11 November. Isabella Wyatt renounced
administration on estate of William
Collier (AA). Robert Wyott, husband of
said Isabella, was granted
administration on said estate, as
greatest creditor.
17:215 Securities: George Burgiss, Thomas Oram.
Appraisers: William Brewer, Stephen
Warman. Capt. Nicholas Gassaway to
administer oath.

15 November. Maj. Thomas Smithson
executor of John Wright (TA) was granted
administration on his estate.
Securities: Thomas Collier, John
Lambert. Appraisers: John Newham,
Thomas Eubanc. Mr. William Hemsley to
administer oath.

Lewis Jones landlord of Morgan Cook (AA)
was granted administration on his
estate, as greatest creditor. [Said
Jones would bring in his wife's
renunciation tomorrow.] Securities: John
Harbottle, George Groomlight.
Appraisers: Henry Chappell, Thomas
Ryder. Administrator is poor & blind.

Mr. John Hall (BA) exhibited:
* bond of Anthony Drue administrator
  of Daniell Palmer. Securities:
  Marke Richardson, James Phillips.
  Date: 12 May 1698.
* bond of Andrew Anderson
  administrator of Michaell Connworth.
  Securities: Christopher Bembridge,
  Christopher Shaw. Date: 6 September

1698.
- will of Anthony Phillips, dated 19 April 1698, constituting his mother Susannah Arnall executrix, proved by John Hall, George Smith, Aquilla Paca, & Jane Gunnell. Date: 6 June 1698.
- additional accounts of Thomas Staly & Robert Olesse administrators of Mary Warfoot. Date: 22 October 1698.

17:216 ...
- inventory of Lewis German, by appraisers Roger Mathews & Henry Jackson. Date: 17 September 1698.
- additional accounts of Joseph Peake administrator of Mrs. Jane Long. Date: 2 October 1698.
- inventory of Thomas Heath, by appraisers Francis Dallahide & William Horne. Date: 18 June 1698.
- bond of John Watson administrator of Richard Bensher. Securities: Francis Robinson, John Eweings. Date: 6 September 1698.
- bond of Thomas Smith administrator of Humphry Day. Securities: John Lekmes, William Farfar. Date: 3 August 1698.
- bond of Elisabeth Gibson administratrix of Lewis Jerman. Securities: James Phillips, Garrett Garruttson. Date: 29 August 1698.
- bond of Simon Person administrator of Richard Askue. Security: Samuell Brown. Date: 20 July 1698.

17:217 Maj. Thomas Smithson (TA) exhibited:
- bond of John Salter administrator of Samuell Newton. Securities: James Benson, John Dawson. Date: 31 August 1698.
- bond of Thomas Evans administrator of Zorababell Wells, unadministered by his wife Katherine (dec'd). Securities: Robert Smith, John Hawkins. Date: 5 November 1698.
- bond of Thomas Smithson executor of John Wright. Securities: John Lamberty, Thomas Collier. Date: 15 November 1698.
- bond of Isabell Rogers

Court Session: 1698

administratrix of David Rogers.
Securities: John Emerson, John
Sides.   Date: 22 September 1698.
- bond of Robert Robertson & his wife
Margret administrators of Jacobus
Seth. Securities: David Blany,
Thomas Thomas. Date: 20 September
1698.
- renunciation of George Lumley on
estate of Samuell Newton.

17:218 ...

Date: 28 August 1698. Said Lumley
is second cousin to said Newton.
Said Lumley recommends Mr. John
Salter as administrator, as greatest
creditor.
- bond of Elisabeth Harney
administratrix of Mortaugh Harney.
Securities: Joseph Newnam, William
Dixon. Date: 23 August 1698.
- inventory of Col. Peter Sayers, by
appraisers William Coursey &
Lawrence Knowles. Date: 9 March
1697/8.
- inventory of Richard Ewbanks, by
appraisers Samuell Hambleton &
Daniell Newnam. Date: 10 October
1698.
- accounts of William Gwinn & his wife
Sarah administratrix of William
Anderson. Date: 15 November 1698.
- accounts of Ann Fisher
administratrix of Thomas Fisher.
Date: 6 November 1698.

17:219 ...
- inventory of Mortaugh Horney, by
appraisers Samuell Hambleton &
Robert Voss. Date: 29 August 1698.
- accounts of William Moore & his wife
Hannah administratrix of Christopher
Batson.

18 November. Mr. Edward Sweatnam
deposed that he was principle creditor
to estate of Peter Clarke, on accounts
due to Capt. Richard Sweatnam.

22 October. Capt. James Keech (SM)
exhibited:
- inventory of Joshua Doyne, by
appraisers Joshua Guibert & Nicholas
Power.

- inventory of John Askins, by appraisers John Doxey & John Maning. Date: 14 March 1697/8.
- inventory of Joseph Hartley, by appraisers Nathaniell Vivers & Thomas Hall. Date: 25 April 1698.

17:220 ...

- accounts of John Tant administrator of Ignatius Warren. Date: 22 October 1698.
- inventory of Edward Sissons, by appraisers John Woodward & Edward Morgan. Date: 9 April 1698.
- accounts of Ann Hartly administratrix of Joseph Hartly. Date: 28 June 1698.
- bond of Joseph Waters administrator of Patience Burket. Securities: John Chevirell, William Wherrett. Date: 26 September 1698.
- inventory of John Grubb, by appraisers John Slye & Francis Swaile. Date: 4 March 1697/8.
- accounts of John Ryley administrator of Bartholomew Murry. Date: 15 November 1698.
- bond of Priscilla Sly executrix of Robert Sly. Securities: Luke Gardiner, Richard Clouds. Date: 12 October 1698.

17:221 ...

- bond of Jane Doyne executrix of Joshua Doyn. Securities: Clement Hill, Luke Gardiner. Date: 16 August 1698.
- bond of Elinor Long administratrix of Clement Healey. Securities: Samuell Cooksey, Ralph Foster. Date: 2 May 1698.
- bond of Mary Sanner administratrix of John Sanner. Securities: John Price, John Cooper. Date: 26 September 1698.
- bond of Thomas Blackman administrator of Daniell Richman. Securities: John Bright, William Stone. Date: 25 September 1698.
- bond of Thomas Sykes administrator of Edward Baly. Securities: Barthollomew Shephard, Francis Swaile. Date: 30 April 1696.
- bond of Christopher Williamson

administrator of Nathaniell Button. Security: Thomas Williams. Date: 18 November 1695.
- bond of Olive Sisson administratrix of Edward Sisson. Securities: James Bland, Robert Trumell. Date: 20 March 1697.

17:222 15 November. Col. John Thompson (CE) exhibited:
- will of Sutton Queeney, constituting his widow Joce Queeney executrix, proved by Edward Beck, Nicholas Smith, Joseph Hall, William Hopkins, John Rayos, & John Carvile. Date: 5 August 1697.
- inventory of Dan. Vanderhay, by appraisers Robert Randall & Hugh Douch. Date: 19 November 1695.
- will of John Ricketts, constituting his widow Penelope Ricketts executrix, proved by Mary Beck, Edward Beck, & John Beck. Date: 4 June 1698.
- inventory of Thomas Moore, by appraisers William Perce & John Touson. Date: 29 July 1698.
- bond of Penelope Ricketts executrix of John Ricketts. Securities: John Beck, John Ellis. Date: 4 October 1698.
- inventory of Edward Jones, by appraisers John Vesey & Owen Hewes. Date: 1697.

17:223 ...
- bond of James Cannon administrator of Robert Seuerwright. Securities: John Eldridge, Thomas Hitchcock. Date: 17 October.
- bond of Joce Queeney executrix of Sutton Queeney. Securities: John Carvile, Edward Beck. Date: 4 October 1698.
- inventory of Col. Casparus Harman, by appraisers Edward Lademore & Thomas Killton. Date: 1698.
- accounts of Michaell Higgens administrator of John Guyatt. Date: 31 August 1698.
- accounts of Seaborne Tucker & his wife Dorothy administrators of Charles Harrington. Date: 15

Court Session: 1698

November 1698.

Mr. John Willymott (CV) exhibited:
- accounts of Robert Sumner administrator of John Sunderland. Date: 15 November 1698.
- bond of Robert Blinkhorne administrator of Robert Blinkhorne. Securities: Robert Hobes, William Harbent. Date: 24 September 1698.

17:224 ...
- bond of Elisabeth Hunton executrix of Thomas Hunton. Securities: John Willymott, John Howes. Date: 19 July 1698.
- bond of Thomas Seagar & his wife Margrett executors of John Lawrence. Securities: Thomas Seagar, Thomas Hinton. Date: 9 September 1698.
- discharge of James Martin to William Gilley administrator of Francis Higham. Witnesses: Samuell Warner, Robert Blinckhorne, Jr. Thomas Howe. Date: 17 November 1698.
- additional accounts of George Lingan administrator of John Abington. Date: 11 November 1698.

20 October. Exhibited from AA:
- inventory of John Gassaway, by appraisers John Chappell, & John Gaile. Date: 1698.
- inventory of Henry Francis, by appraisers Edward Fuller & William Pennington. Date: 7 May 1698.

17:225 ...
- accounts of Lewis Jones administrator of Morgan Cooke. Date: 21 October 1698. Also inventory, by appraisers Henry Chappell & Thomas Rider. Date: 17 November 1698.
- inventory of Col. Nicholas Greenberry, by appraisers Roger Newman & Humfrey Boone. Date: 13 June 1698.
- bond of Thomas Tench, Esq. administrator of Benjamin Scrivener. Security: Roger Newman. Date: 23 November 1698.
- bond of Ann Marke administratrix of William Marke. Securities: John

Court Session: 1698

Newton, John Stanley. Date: 16
September 1698.
- bond of Robert Wiatt administrator
of William Colliar. Securities:
George Burges, Thomas Oram. Date:
12 November 1698.
- bond of Lewis Jones administrator of
Morgan Cooke. Securities: John
Harbotle, George Groomelight. Date:
15 November 1698.
- bond of William Richardson & his
wife Elisabeth executors of William
Richardson. Securities: Gerratt
Hopkins, Joseph Richardson. Date:
30 August 1698.

17:226 ...
- bond of Mary Jarvis administratrix
of Humphry Jarvis. Securities:
Manus Devorriland, Richard Jones.
Date: 17 October 1698.
- bond of Elisabeth Hanslop executrix
of Henry Hanslop. Securities:
Joseph Chew, Joseph Hanslap. Date:
23 October 1698.
- bond of John Gill administrator of
William Bates. Securities: Peter
Bond, Stephen Handcock. Date: 3
November 1698.
- bond of Sarah Horne administratrix
of William Horne. Securities:
Richard Gott, Robert Franklin.
Date: 10 October 1698.
- bond of Sarah Perry administratrix
of John Perry. Securities: William
Bladen, John Morrough. Date: 4
November 1698.

18 November. Mr. Elias King (KE)
exhibited:
- accounts of Henry Hosier executor of
Henry Hosier. Date: 18 November
1698. Edward Batson is charged with
the fees.

17:227 ...
- accounts of Edward Walwin & his wife
Susanah executors of Phillip Davis
(KE). Date: 1 October 1698.

Exhibited:
- will of Francis Heydon (SM),
constituting his widow Thomasin
Heyden executrix, proved by John

Page 95

Bta. Carbery, John Merritt, & Henry
Newton. Date: 30 April 1697.

- will of David Rogers, constituting
David Blaney & John Thrift overseers
& to assist wife. Date: 27 August
1698.
- will of John Belt (AA), constituting
his widow Elisabeth Belt executrix,
proved by John Tidings, Charity
Jordan, Ann Smith, & Thomas Hoges.
Date: 13 May 1697.
- will of James Browne (SM),
constituting John Synnott & Thomas
Grunwin executors, proved by William
Guyther, John Fisher, & William
Ruarke. Date: 7 September 1698.
- will of John Grubb (SM),
constituting his widow Ann Grubb
executrix, proved by Samuell
Cooksey, Thomas Toynes, Joseph
Jesup, & David Parsons. Date: 14
April 1695.
- will of John Browne (TA),
constituting his widow Elisabeth
Browne executrix, proved by Isaac
Winchester, Thomas Marsh, Elisabeth
Hood, & Edward Stevenson. Date: 8
November 1696.

17:228 11 November. Exhibited will of Madam
Frances Sayers, constituting her niece
Mrs. Elisabeth Rousbey executrix,
proved by Robert Johnson, Rhoda Bruff, &
Lawrence Knowles. Date: 26 May 1698.

Exhibited will of Thomas Francis (AA),
constituting his widow Frances Francis
executrix, proved by Samuell Young, Hans
Hanson, & John Gerard. Date: 7 August
1698.

Exhibited will of Henry Hanslap (AA),
constituting his widow Elisabeth Hanslap
executrix, proved by John Gressam,
Edward Burgis, Stephen Warman, & Robert
Hopper. Date: 1697.

Exhibited will of Joshua Doyne (SM),
constituting his widow Jane Doyne
executrix, proved by John Clarke,
Cornelius Braunan, Peter Johnson, &
Thomas Melton, Jr. Date: 10 March

1697/8. Further proved by: Francis Gallampton, William Hunter, Luke Gardiner.

17:229   20 October. Mr. Richard Boughton (CH) exhibited:
- inventory of Thomas Coffer, by appraisers John Allen & Henry Barnes. Date: 1698.
- inventory of Matthusalem Stone, by appraisers John Wood & Garrett Sinnett. Date: 1698.
- inventory of Henry Kee, by appraisers Ignatius Wheeler & Mathew Barnes. Date: 1698.
- additional accounts of James Thompson administrator of Andrew Clark. Date: 20 October 1698.
- inventory of Richard Hubert, by appraisers John Bowling & Richard Edelen. Date: 1698.
- inventory of Thomas Taylor, by appraisers William Timothy & Thomas Dixon Date: 15 October 1698.

Mr. Samuell Hopkins (SO) exhibited:
- accounts of William Richardson executor of David Richardson. Date: 15 November 1698.
- accounts of John Macknitt administrator of Amos Parsons. Date: 15 November 1698.
- inventory of John Townsand, by appraisers John Porter & John Outen. Date: 8 October 1698.

17:230   ...
- inventory of Richard Wharton, by appraisers Francis Thoroughgood & Peirce Bray. Date: 31 August 1698.
- accounts of Thomas Killam administrator of George Hutchins. Date: 25 October 1698.
- accounts of Richard Davis administrator of Richard Davis. Date: 15 November 1698.
- bond of Francis Jenkins administrator of Richard Wharton. Security: Samuell Hopkins. Date: 19 July 1698.
- bond of Elisabeth Townsdend administratrix of John Townsend. Security: John Porter. Date: last

September 1698.
- accounts of John Booth executor of John Booth. Date: 29 October 1696.
- accounts of Isaac Horsey administrator of John Attkins. Date: 28 October.

17:231 ...
- accounts of Katherine Lawes administratrix of John Lawes. Date: 26 October 1698.
- accounts of Margrett Layton administratrix of Henry Layton. Date: 28 October 1698.

15 November. Mr. Joshua Cecill (PG) exhibited:
- bond of John Watkins administrator of Katherine Watkins. Securities: William Clarke, Robert Clarke. Date: 3 October 1698.
- bond of William Hutchison executor of William Atchison. Security: William Tanyhill. Date: 4 August 1698.
- bond of Sarah Willson administratrix of William Willson. Securities: Thomas Paggett, John Anderson. Date: 6 October 1698.
- accounts of Richard Marsham & his wife Ann relict & administratrix of Henry Brent. Date: 10 November 1698.
- inventory of Jonathon Willson, by appraisers Robert Bradley & James Stoddert. Date: 22 October 1698.

17:232 ...
- accounts of John Chapman administrator of James Williams. Date: 15 November 1698.
- inventory of John Emmett, by appraisers Daniell Ellett & William Tannehill. Date: 30 January 1698.
- inventory of James Williams, by appraisers John Joyce & Martha Mogbee. Date: 17 November 1698.
- inventory of Katherine Watkins, by appraisers Daniell Connell & Phillip Leven. Date: 7 November 1698.
- accounts of Henry Darnall administrator of Mary Darnall. Date: 10 November 1698.
- inventory of James Gamblin, by

appraisers George Nailer & Robert
Done. Date: 30 November 1698.
- inventory of Thomas Edmundson, by
appraisers Francis Collier & Abraham
Clarke. Date: 17 October 1698.

17:233 Audry Llewellin widow & administratrix
of John Llewellin was granted
continuance.

William Gaskin (alias William Geskin)
exhibited his release of Simon Nicholls
administrator of William Smith. Date:
25 June 1698.

17:234 Petition of Coniers Clark relict &
executrix of John Clark (CH). Mentions:
estate to be divided amongst his
children. Petition for her 1/3rds.
17:235 She is poor, with small children.
Petition granted. Date: 10 November
1698.

16 November. Jane Cooke widow of Morgan
Cooke (AA) exhibited her renunciation of
administration on his estate. She
empowers Lewis Jones (p, AA) as
administrator. Witnesses: Henry
Chappell, John Harbottle, Thomas Redar.

17:236 Lawrence Knowles deposed that Capt.
Edward Sweatnam executor of Capt.
Richard Sweatnam came to the deponent's
house on 8 October last. Mentions: Maj.
Thomas Smithson (appraiser), Mr.
William Coursey (appraiser). Said
Smithson exhibited that he could not do
the appraisal. Said Coursey did not
come. Date: 2 November 1698.
17:237 Said Coursey was pre-engaged with the
appraisal of estate of Madam Henrietta
Maria Lloyd. The next time, he had to
go to Annapolis. The third time he had
to attend Mrs. Elisabeth Coursey, who
is dangerously sick.

Kympton Mabbott vs. Mr. Richard Owen.
Date: 18 October 1698.
17:238 Hu. Eccleston (DO) exhibited
depositions.

10 November. Col. Henry Darnall vs. Mr. Charles Carroll procurator for Mr. Henry Lowe & his wife. Answer exhibited.

William Pennington (AA) was granted administration on estate of William Martin (AA). Securities: John Hurst, William Hawkins. Appraisers: Joseph Moss, Joseph Conneway. Capt. John Worthington to administer oath.

17:239 Thomas Jones vs. Arnold Elsey. Continuance was granted. Summons to Mr. Arnold Elsey & Sarah Luff regarding the estate of Mr. Ballard.

23 November. Thomas Tench, Esq. (AA) was granted administration on estate of Benjamin Scrivener (AA), as next of kin. Security: Roger Newman. Appraisers: Thomas Hughs, Nicholas Roads. Capt. William Holland to administer oath.

16 December. Col. Thomas Hollyday (PG) & Joshua Cecill (PG) exhibited will of Capt. Richard Brightwell (PG), proved. Also exhibited renunciation of Thomas Greenfeild & William Watson as executors.

17:240 Date: 23 November 1698. Said Hollyday & Cecill were granted administration on said estate. Mr. Robert Bradly to administer oath.

30 November. Mrs. Rachell Kilburn widow of Richard Kilburne (AA) vs. his estate. Caveat exhibited.

17:241 Before: Mr. Edward Batson, Henry Loftus.

20 December. Said Rachell was granted administration. Securities: Richard Beard, Edward Batson. Appraisers: Richard Jones, Manus Dworen. Orlando Greenslade to administer oath.

Docket:
* (N) Carvile for Col. Henry Lowe, Esq. vs. (N) Carroll for Henry Darnall, Esq.

17:242 ...

- (N) Carvile for Allexander Forbes vs. William Taylard.
- (N) Dent for (N) Hoskins & (N) Dent administrators of (N) Smith vs. (N) Carroll for Cleb. Lomax.
- (N) Carroll for William Watts vs. (N) Clark for Gerrard Slye.
- (N) Carroll for Henry Darnall, Jr. vs. Henry Lowe & his wife administrators of John Darnall.
- (N) Goulds. for Edward Lloyd vs. executors of Hen. Maria Lloyd.
- (N) Goulds. for Elisabeth Rousby vs. administrators of (N) Seth.
- (N) Clark for Thomas Jones vs. Arnold Elsey.
- William Hemsley vs. Edward Sweatnam.

17:243 Charles Carroll for petitioned for Maj. Nicholas Sewell & Dr. Mordica Moore on behalf of their children legatees of William Burgess. Mentions: Ann Burgess (widow) was granted administration on said estate, without a will being proved. Ruling: said Ann to process said will.

17:244 22 November. Depositions of witnesses to will of William Burges read by Mr. Carroll. Former administration is revoked. New appraisement appointed according to law: in presence of two legatees & 2 creditors. Widow to take out LoA.

17:245 Mr. William Dent for Ann Burgess widow exhibited reasons why the will should not be annexed to the new administration.

29 December. Dr. Joakim Kersteed (now dec'd), with Col. John Bigger, was security to Thomas Tany & Michaell Taney for use of Margrett Taney daughter of Michaell & Margrett Tany.

17:246 Mentions: Edward Miles. Margrett widow of said Kersteed administered his estate. Col. John Bigger for self & said daughter enters a caveat against the accounts of said Kersteed's estate. Signed: William Dent, John Bigger.

7 January. John Hall (g, BA) to prove accounts of Mary Frizell (BA) executrix of William Yorke (BA).

9 January. Mr. William Sharp executor of Obada Judkins (TA) exhibited accounts.

17:247   Said Sharp (Quaker) on behalf of Mary Gressum administratrix of Robert Gressum (TA) exhibited inventory, by appraisers John Dawson & William Scott. Also exhibited accounts.

Edward Batson (Registrar, Annapolis) is going abroad & empowers Henry Loftus (Deputy) to grant LoA. Date: 23 January 1698.

17:248   30 January. Jonathon Neale & Henry Merriday securities to Christopher Green administrator of Edward Jones (AA) exhibited caveat against John Harebottle who married Ann relict of said Jones who is also relict of Christopher Green.

Margrett Messer (AA) widow of John Messer (AA) was granted administration on his estate. Securities: Thomas Harding, Edward Batson. Appraisers: John Baldwin, Edward Rumney. Mr. Samuell Young to administer oath.

Mr. Joseph Hanslap exhibited inventory of his father Henry Hanslap (AA), by appraisers James Sanders & John Gresham.

Mr. Robert Gouldesborough for Mr. Charles Greenberry administrator of William Fuller vs.
17:249   estate of John Bennett (AA). Caveat exhibited.

20 January. Exhibited from CV:
* accounts of George Johnson.
* inventory of William Meares, by appraisers Robert Shephard & William Hutchins. Date: 18 November 1698.
* inventory of Robert Day, by appraisers Thomas Clegett & Nathaniell Dare. Date: 9 June 1698.
* accounts of Robert Gott.

- will of Richard Brightwell, constituting Thomas Greenfeild, Sr. & William Watson executors, proved by William Mills, Elisabeth Mills, & George Naylor. Date: 21 August 1698.

Exhibited:
- inventory of Robert Harvy (TA), by appraisers Mathew Eareckson & George Vinson. Date: 26 July 1698.
- inventory of William Richardson, Sr., by appraisers John Chappell & John Meriton. Date: 21 October 1698.

17:250 ...

- inventory of Samuell Newton (TA), by appraisers Benjamin Peck & Anthony Rumball. Date: 22 November 1698.
- inventory of Mathew Bellamy (AA), by appraisers Lenard Wayman & Walter Phelpes. Date: 30 November 1698.
- inventory of Humphry Jarvis (AA), by appraisers Edward Burgiss & Benjamin Bond. Date: 12 December 1698.
- inventory of William Marke (AA), by appraisers Henry Meryday & William Lewis. Date: 6 October 1698.
- accounts of Nicholas Terrett (AA).
- bond of Elisabeth Browne executrix of John Browne (TA). Securities: Thomas Emerson, Thomas Winchester, William Scott. Date: 22 September 1698. Also inventory, by appraisers John Emerson & David Blaney. Date: 6 November 1698.

17:251 ...

- bond of Daniell Sherwood administrator of James Bell. Securities: James Auld, John Hatton. Date: 16 December 1698.
- bond of Daniell Sherwood administrator of William Kersey (TA). Securities: James Auld, John Hatton. Date: 16 September 1698.
- bond of Mary Hadaway administratrix of Peter Hadaway. Securities: Ralph Nixon, Enionn Williams. Date: 12 November 1698.
- bond of Richard Clark administrator of Richard Harris. Securities: William Fuller, James Scott. Date:

26 November 1698.

- bond of George Hadaway administrator of Stephen Benson. Securities: William Webb, Enion Williams. Date: 23 November 1698.

2 February. Mr. Samuell Chew (AA) for his wife Ann Chew executrix of Dr. Alexander Chappell (AA) was granted administration on his estate. Capt. William Holland to take said Ann's renunciation & the renunciation of Elisabeth Chappell relict of said Alexander & to prove said will.

17:252 3 February. James Lewis (AA) was granted administration on estate of Nicholas Groce (AA), on behalf of children, as principle creditor. Securities: MM Richard Beard, Thomas Renolds. Appraisers: Thomas Simpson, William Disney. Capt. Nicholas Gassaway to administer oath.

5 February. Exhibited accounts of Robert Proctor (AA).

Exhibited will of Jarvis Morgin, constituting William Roper, Sr. executor, proved by James Chrichley, Henry Coles, & Charles Harrison. Date: 10 January 1698.

6 February. William Roper (AA) proved will of said Morgin, and was granted administration on his estate. Securities: Charles Harrison, Lewis Duvall.
17:253 Appraisers: Leonard Wayman, richard Snoden, Jr. Henry Ridgley to administer oath.

Exhibited inventory of Mr. John Perry, by appraisers George Jackson & Thomas Grunwin. Date: 14 November 1698.

Exhibited will of Alexander Chappell (AA), constituting Ann Chew executrix, proved by Moses Wilson & Daniell Lyon. George Symons (cooper, AA) & his wife Elisabeth widow of said Chappell renounced administration. Witness:

Margarett Birkhead. Samuell Chew (merchant, AA) & his wife Ann executrix of said Chappell renounced administration. Witnesses: William Holland, Margarett Birkhead.

17:254 28 February. Thomas Blackwell vs. estate of John Newton (Annapolis) or his wife Elisabeth (Annapolis). Caveat exhibited.

Exhibited:
- will of William Harris (CV), constituting his widow Elisabeth Harris & his eldest son Richard Harris & his second son George Harris executors, proved by Dorothy Oliver, William Norris, & Nathaniell Dare. Date: 25 March 1697.
- will of Francis Leaf (CV), constituting Ann Leaf executrix, proved by George Cole, Richard Swann, & Edward Ball. Date: 16 April 1698.
- will of William Shrive (CV), constituting his widow Jane Shrive executrix, proved by Jonathon Goosey, Ann Jenkins, & Robert Dove. Date: 20 February 1697/8.
- will of Thomas Dickson (CV), constituting Elisabeth Gunton wife of Timothy Gunton executrix, proved by Thomas Kingcart & Nicholas Fountaine. Date: 30 May 1698.
- will of Thomas Sedwick (CV), constituting his son Joshua Sedwick executor, proved by Roger Brooke, Jr., John Grover, & John Willson. Date: 11 January 1698.

17:255 ...
- will of Samuell Scott (CV), constituting William Dawkins executor, proved by Benjamin Hill, Edmund Hungerford, & John Easterling. Date: 19 January 1698.
- will of Richard Jackson (CV), constituting his daughter-in-law Mary Jackson executrix, proved by William Wadsworth, Absolom Kent, Elisabeth Wadsworth, & Fra. Smith. Date: 23 January 1697.
- inventory of Nathaniell Cranford

Court Session: 1698

(CV), by appraisers William
Williams, Sr. & Joseph Baker. Date:
6 May 1698.
- inventory of Thomas Dickson (CV), by
appraisers Thomas Kingcart & George
Spicer. Date: 6 May 1698.
- inventory of John Taylor (CV), by
appraisers John Jenkins & George
Odaham. Date: 3 January 1698.
- inventory of William Howard (CV), by
appraisers Daniell Sherdne &
Ignatius Samuell. Date: 3 January
1698.
- renunciation of George Symons
(cooper, AA) & his wife Elisabeth
widow of Allexander Chappell
(chirurgeon, AA) of administration
on his estate.

17:256 ...

Date: 7 February 1698. Witnesses:
William Holland, Margatt Birckhead.

Rebecca Nicholson vs. estate of Symon
Fenox. Caveat exhibited. Date: 17
February 1698/9 at South River.
Witness: Charles Kilbourn.

23 February. Elisabeth Nicholson
executrix of John Nicholson (AA) was
granted administration on his estate.
Capt. John Worthington to prove said
will.

15 March. Mrs. Anne Jones, now wife of
Richard Jones, relict of Mr. William
Burges (AA) exhibited her renunciation
of her former administration &
petitioned that she & her husband be
granted administration. Signed: Ann
Jones, Richard Jones, Jr. Witness: J.
Cranford.

17:257 MM Thomas Grunwin & John Sinnott
renounced administration on estate of
Mr. James Brown (SM) before Kenelm
Cheseldyn. Date: 11 December 1698.
Mrs. Francis Browne widow of said James
was granted administration.

Mr. Ralph Foster (SM) exhibited oath of
Thomas Nickolls & William Maddox,
appraisers of John Johnson (SM).

William Allen (VA) son of John Allen (dec'd) petitioned that Mr. Phillip Lynes (CH) be granted administration on his father's estate. Date: 16 December 1698. Witness: John Leake.

17:258 Hon. Charles Hutchins, Esq. to His Excellency Francis Nicholson, Esq.: Mentions: letter from Col. Jowles, plantation of Maj. Trip, Mr. Mabbott, Mr. Owen, Richard Owen, Mrs. Mabbot, children, servants. Date: 13 August 1698 at Nanticoke River.

17:259 Petition of Phillip Griffin who married Jane relict & administratrix of Richard Rawlings (AA). Mentions: children of said Richard & Jane, said Jane is recently dec'd, Mr. John Taylor (merchant), Capt. Phillips. Ruling: copy of estate sent.

17:260 Mr. James Heath (KE), who bought of Thomas Hackett heir of Theophilus Hackett (AA) all of his estate, was granted administration on estate of said Theophilus. Securities: MM James Cullen, John Taylor.

Mary Barner (AA) widow of Thomas Barner (AA) was granted administration on his estate. Securities: Edward Lunn, James Carr. Appraisers: Robert Eagle, Jonathon Neale. Capt. John Worthington to administer oath.

Mary Rabitts (TA) widow of William Rabbitts (TA) was granted administration on his estate. Securities: Nicholas Keely, William Osborne. Appraisers: Mathew Errickson, Francis Stevens. Mr. John Coppage to administer oath.

17:261 William Osborne (TA) executor of Thomas Denew (TA) was granted administration on his estate. Mr. John Coppage (TA) to prove said will & administer oath.

Elisabeth North executrix of John North (BA) was granted administration on his estate. Securities: James Floyd, Thomas Earp. Appraisers: Thomas Knightson,

Court Session: 1698

William Williamforeman.

Robert Lockwood (AA) for Edward Price
(AA) petitioned for Thomas Tench, Esq.
to prove will of Robert Phillips (AA).

James Homewood (AA) executor of George
Robinson (AA) was granted administration
on his estate. Securities: John Floyd,
William Foreman. Appraisers: Edward
Gibbs, Samuell Smith.

William Penington (AA) executor of
Edmond Duncalfe (AA)
17:262 was granted administration on his
estate. Securities: William Moot, John
Kendall. Appraisers: Thomas Dawson,
Ralph Moss. Capt. John Worthington to
administer oath.

1 March. Joshua Cecill (PG) exhibited:
* inventory of William Atheson, by
  appraisers Daniell Elliott & William
  Tannehill. Date: 26 September 1698.
* inventory of Gavin Hamilton, by
  appraisers Daniell Elliott &
  Michaell Ashford. Date: 2 March
  1698/9.
* inventory of William Kersey, by
  appraisers Thomas Dickson & William
  Hunter. Date: 2 November 1698.
* will of Edward Whellock,
  constituting his widow Ann Whellock
  executrix, proved by Edward Smith,
  Benjamin Smith, & James Floyd.
  Date: 23 August 1697.

17:263 Exhibited:
* will of Robert Phillips (AA),
  constituting Francis Price executor,
  proved by John Crane, Ann Waterman,
  George Hartshorne, & Nicholas
  Waterman. Date: 17 April 1686.
* will of Thomas Danvis (AA),
  constituting Allexander Chappell
  executor. Date: 1 May 1698.
* will of Jeremiah Eldridge (CV),
  constituting Mr. Walter Smith
  overseer. Date: 5 December 1698.
* [Entry crossed out] inventory of
  Thomas Dixon (CV), by appraisers
  Thomas Kingcart & George Spicer.

Court Session: 1698

- inventory of Newman Barber, by appraisers John Floyde & Nicholas Fountaine.
- inventory of Edward Armstrong, by appraisers Thomas Howe & Thomas Arterby. Date: 14 January 1698.
- inventory of Charles Brooke, by appraisers Francis Knott & Edward Cole.
- inventory of John Short, by appraisers George Cole & Edmond Ball. Date: 26 August 1698.

17:264 ...

- accounts of Cornelius Watkinson. Date: 12 March 1698.
- will of Samuell Scott, constituting William Dakins executor, proved by Benjamin Hill, Edmond Hungerford, & John Easterling. Date: 19 January 1698.
- will of Edmond Duncalfe (AA), constituting William Pennington executor, proved by William Moate, John Kendall, & Jonathon Sanders. Date: 16 February 1698.
- will of George Robinson, constituting James Homewood (AA) executor. Date: 20 September 1698.
- will of John North, constituting Elisabeth North executrix. Date: 13 December 1698.
- will of Abraham Bird (CV), constituting John Feanly & James Ford overseers. Date: 7 January 1698.
- will of Edward Armstrong, constituting Darby Hernley executor, proved by David Hellen, Joseph Dawkins, & Thomas Howe. Date: 20 October 1698.
- inventory of Robert Blinkhorne, by appraisers David Bole & John MackDowell. Date: 13 February 1698/9.

17:265 ...

- inventory of Richard Jackson, by appraisers Richard Polley & Hugh Pinton. Date: March 1698.
- inventory of William Martin (AA), by appraisers Richard Moss & Joseph Conneway. Date: 11 November 1698.
- inventory of William Hudson (SM), by

Page 109

appraisers Ralph Foster & John
Smith. Date: 29 October 1698.
- inventory of William Willson (PG),
by appraisers John Josling & Phillip
Tatersall. Date: 15 December 1698.

9 March. Ann Whellock widow & executrix
of Edward Whellock (AA) exhibited his
will, proved by Edward Smith, Benjamin
Smith, & James Floyd. Said Ann was
granted administration. Securities:
James Floyd, Edward Smith. Appraisers:
James Homewood, John Peeckley.

Amy Skidmore widow & administratrix of
Samuell Skidmore (AA) was granted
administration on his estate.
Securities: Joseph Connoway, Mathew
Neale. Appraisers: Humphry Boone,
Robert Eagle. Mr. John Worthington to
administer oath.

17:266   11 March. Elias King (KE) exhibited
will of Edward Sweatnam (KE). Maj.
Thomas Smith (KE) to prove said will.
Said King was granted administration, as
surviving executor. Said Smith to
administer oath.

16 March. Richard Jones, Jr. (AA) & his
wife Ann were granted administration on
estate of William Burgess (AA).
Securities: Thomas Blake, David Small.
Appraisers: James Rigby, John Baldwyn.
Mr. James Sanders to administer oath.

Mr. William Bladen (AA) was granted
administration on estate of Dr.
Alexander Chappell (AA), for His Majesty
& self as principle creditor. Mentions:
Ann Chew executrix & her renunciation,
Elisabeth relict & her renunciation.
17:267   Securities: Edward Batson, Evan Thomas.

17 March. Robert Lockwood exhibited
commission to Mr. Tench to prove will of
Robert Phillips (AA). Edward Price (AA)
is nearest of kin & only brother to
Francis Price, legatee of said Phillips.
Said Edward was granted administration.
Securities: Robert Lockwood, Samuell
Manthorpe. Appraisers: John Willowby,

John Watters. Esq. Tench to administer oath.

Mary Whitchell vs. estate of Thomas Standbauck. Caveat exhibited. She is greatest creditor. Date: 8 March 1698/9.

Mary Rockhold vs. estate of Nat Dotton. Caveat exhibited. Date: 25 January 1698.

17:268 Exhibited:
- inventory of Ignatius Mathews (CH), by appraisers Jesse Doyne & John Sanders. Date: 10 August 1698.
- inventory of Edward Whellock, by appraisers James Homewood & John Peasly. Date: 23 March 1698/9.
- will of Gawham Hamilton (PG).
- will of William Selby (PG), constituting Mary Selby executrix. Securities: Paul Busey, Jo. Cecill.
- bond on estate of Thomas Kemston (PG). Securities: Edward Ball, William Conley.
- bond on estate of Gawham Hamilton. Securities: David Small, James Watts.
- bond of James Beale administrator of Thomas Sheppard. Security: Samuell Magrooder.
- will of John Hume (CV), proved before Mr. William Nicholls.
- inventory of Abraham Bird, by appraisers Richard Samesberry & Darby Sulevant.

Mr. John Willymott (CV) exhibited:
- bond of Martha Howard executrix of William Howard. Securities: Joshua Cecill, John Willymott.

17:269 ...
- bond of Elisabeth Gunton executrix of Thomas Dixon. Securities: John Meads, Nicholas Fountaine.
- bond of Thomas Kincraft administrator of Newman Barber. Securities: George Spicer, John Willymott.
- bond of Joshua Sedgwick executor of Thomas Sedgwick. Securities: John

Court Session: 1698

Chittham, William Bradley.
- bond of Mary Jackson executrix of Richard Jackson. Securities: Richard Rowlin, John Willymott.
- bond of James Ford executor of Abraham Bird. Securities: John Ellsey, John Harris.
- bond of Hercules Humes executor of John Humes. Security: Francis Malden.
- bond of Darby Hernley administrator of Edward Armestrong. Securities: Joseph Dawkins, John Willymott.
- bond of Elisabeth Hutchins executrix of Francis Hutchins. Security: Thomas Tench, Esq.
- bond of William Dawkins executor of Samuell Scott. Securities: John Turner, James Dawkins.
- bond of Mary Taylor administratrix of John Taylor. Securities: Richard Wattkins, John Robinson.
- bond of Bridgett Hedger administratrix of John Hedger. Securities: James Sawell, Ignatius Sawell.
- bond of John Landerkin administrator of Stephen Barber. Securities: Thomas Tillsley, John Willymott.

Exhibited:
- inventory of John North (BA), by appraisers William Foreman & Thomas Knightsmith.
- bond of Madam Kathern Harman administratrix of Robert Sherwight. Securities: William Parson, Samuell Manthrop.
- bond of Elias King executor of Edward Swettnam. Securities: Michaell Miller, John Salter.

17:270 ...
- accounts of William Nicholls administrator of Richard Sandys (CV).
- bond of Richard Jones (AA) & his wife Ann administrators of William Burges. Securities: David Small, Thomas Blake.
- bond of Nathaniell Dalton (AA). Securities: Richard Jones, Edward Hall.

Court Session: 1698

Capt. William Holland exhibited his commissions of 2 February & 16 September 1698. On back of will of James Browne (SM), because one of the witnesses lives in CV, is endorsed: John Fisher attested to will of said Browne. Date: 14 April 1699.

17:271 Letter from Richard Boughton. Mentions: Maj. Dent, James Hagan & Joseph Ward administrators of Mull Allen, Murphy Ward (grandfather), Mary Brawner, estate of Mr. John Stone, will of Henry Brawner, Jane Saunders relict of Edward Saunders.

17:272 20 March. Mr. James Saunders for Ann relict of Nicholas Gassaway (g, AA) was granted administration on his estate. Said Saunders to administer oath.

Dr. Mordicay Moore & his wife Ursula executors of Col. William Burges (AA) exhibited inventory, by appraisers Thomas Knighton Marreen Divall, &
17:273 Henry Wriogley. Also exhibited accounts. Continuance was granted.

Court Session: 1699

24 March. Mary Rockhold relict & executrix of John Rockhold (AA) exhibited his will. Said Mary was granted administration. Securities: Lancellott Todd, John Howard. Appraisers: John Howard, Jr., Thomas Blackwell. Capt. Phillip Howard to administer oath.

29 March. Thomas Blackwell & his wife Sarah (AA) executors of Elisabeth Newton widow of John Newton (AA) were granted administration on estate of said John. Securities: Cornelius Howard, John Dowdall. Appraisers: Richard Jones, Robert Phillips. Said John died a short time before said Elisabeth.

17:274 Capt. William Holland (AA) executor of Mary Gill (widow, AA) exhibited her will. Mr. Seth Biggs to prove said

Page 113

will. Said Holland was granted
administration. Securities: Seth Biggs,
James Saunders.

John Hurst (AA) for self & the orphan &
only child of James Harrington (AA) was
granted administration on his estate.
Securities: Alexander Gardner, John
Floyd. Appraisers: Francis Maude,
Thomas Dauson. Capt. John Worthington
to administer oath.

17:275 Exhibited from SM:
- will of John Davis, proved before
  John Baptista Carbery.
- will of Dr. William Lowry,
  constituting Thomas Grunwyn
  executor, proved.
- inventory of Robert Sly (SM), by
  appraisers James Swan & John Rose.
- inventory of Daniell Moy (SM), by
  appraisers William Asquith & John
  Horne.
- inventory of John Johnson, Jr., by
  appraisers Thomas Nickolls & William
  Mattax.
- will of Gerrard Vansweringen,
  constituting his widow & his son
  Joseph executors, proved by 3
  witnesses.
- inventory of Robert Foster, by
  appraisers John Smith & Nottley
  Warren.
- will of Robert Sly, constituting his
  widow Priscilla Sly executrix,
  proved by 2 witnesses.
- bond of Edward Miller administrator
  of Daniell Moy. Securities: Daniell
  Bell, John Sauage.
- bond of Elisabeth Hall
  administratrix of Thomas Hall.
  Security: Ralph Howard.
- bond of Alice Johnson administratrix
  of John Johnson. Securities: Robert
  Lowe, Thomas Carvill.
- bond of Mary widow & executrix of
  Garrett Vansweringen. Securities:
  Thomas Grunwyn, Cecill Buttler,
  William Taylard.
17:276 ...
- bond of John Evans administrator of
  Anthony Evans. Securities: William

Taylard, William Aisquith.
- accounts of Thomas Ennis.
- accounts of Arthur Keife.
- accounts of Thomas Miles.
- accounts of John Noble.
- accounts of Robert Bayley.
- Mr. Luke Gardiner (SM) was granted administration on estate of Thomas Tole (SM), as no one would take said administration. Appraisers: John Coley, William Hotten. Also exhibited inventory & accounts.
- additional accounts of Thomas Mooney. Estate is overpaid.
- accounts of William Boswell.
- accounts of John Curry.
- accounts of Elias Beach.
- accounts of Phillip Hoskins & his wife Ann & Thomas Mudd executors of Thomas Mudd (CH).

17:277 ...
- additional inventory of Thomas Mudd.
- will of Patience Burkett, constituting Joseph Waters executor, proved by 3 witnesses before Mr. Jacob Moreland. Said will is null until Proomce Burrill (in ENG) arrives in the Province. Also exhibited inventory, by appraisers John Bright & Lawrence Tettersall. Said Burrell was granted administration & LoA to said Waters revoked.
- accounts of Mr. Notley Rozier on estate of Col. Edward Pye.
- accounts of Thomas Shanks.

1 April. Mr. William Harris (CE) for Sarah Simms relict & executrix of Allexander Simes (CE) was granted administration on his estate. Mr. John Carvill to prove said will. Appraisers: John Jordan, John Read. Said Carvill to administer oath.

17:278 4 April. Ralph Rawlings (AA) brother-in-law on his mother's side to John Cumberland (AA) was granted administration on his estate. Securities: Hugh Merriday, Richard Jones. Appraisers: William Lewis, Jonathon Neall. Capt. John Worthington to administer oath.

5 April. Maj. Thomas Smith exhibited commission to take bond of Elias King executor of Edward Sweatnam. Also citation for said King to answer suit of Francis Williams executor of Peter Clarke.

6 April. Edmond Goodman executor of Alexander Toulson (TA) was granted administration on his estate. Mr. John Cobbage to prove said will. Securities: Harbert Morgan, James Williston. Appraisers: Isaack & Thomas Marsh.

7 April. Elisabeth Bennett (AA) widow of John Bennett (AA) was granted administration on his estate. Securities: William Holland, Alexander Gardner. Capt. John Worthington or Mr. Hamond to administer oath.

17:279   11 April. Rose Bruce widow of George Bruce (AA) was granted administration on his estate. Securities: Leonard Wayman, Robert Hopper. Appraisers: John Gather, Leonard Wayman. Edward Batson to administer oath.

19 April. Col. Ridgley (AA) vs. estate of William Browne (AA). Caveat exhibited. Date: 18 April 1699. Mentions: widow. Signed: Henry Wridgley, Sr.

22 April. Amy Doland (TA) widow of William Doland petitioned for Mr. John Cobbage to prove his will. Appraisers: Isaack Wells, Edward Browne. Said Cobbage to administer oath.

Mary Doyne (TA) widow of John Doyne was granted administration on his estate. Securities: Mr. George Jackson, Amy Doland. Appraisers: Valentine Carter, Mathew Erickson. Mr. John Coppage to administer oath.

17:280   23 April. Ann Pattison widow of Mr. Gilbert Pattison (AA) was granted administration on his estate.

Court Session: 1699

Securities: Lawrence Draper, John
Devall. Appraisers: Robert Hopper,
Leonard Wayman. Mr. James Saunders to
administer oath.

24 April. Mr. William Dent for self &
Mr. Phillip Hoskins administrators of
William Smith, by letter dated 21st
instant, vs. Cleborne Lomax executor of
Elisabeth Smith. Appeal exhibited by
said Dent from a sentence. Security:
Mr. Christopher Gregory.

Ralph Hawkins brother & executor of
William Coventry (BA) exhibited his
will. Said Hawkins was granted
administration. Securities: John
Downes, Charles Turner. Appraisers:
Jonathon Neale, William Lewis. Mr.
Edward Batson to administer oath.

26 April. Mary Garey widow of Lawrence
Garey (AA) was granted administration on
his estate. Securities: Manus Devorin,
Nicholas Fleathear. Appraisers: Richard
Jones, William Jelf. Mr. Edward Batson
to administer oath.

17:281   28 April. Elisabeth Plumer executrix of
Thomas Plummer (AA) exhibited inventory
& accounts. Continuance was granted.

29 April. Exhibited renunciation of
Jane Browne widow of William Browne
(BA). Date: 22 April 1699. Witnesses:
Henry Ridgly, Jr., Charles Ridgley,
George Main. Henry Ridgley, Sr.
attested to said renunciation. Date: 27
April 1699.

1 May. Col. Henry Ridgley (AA) was
granted administration on estate of
William Browne (AA), as greatest
creditor. Securities: Charles
Greenbury, Richard Jones, Jr.
Appraisers: Leonard Weyman, Richard
Duckett.

17:282   Mrs. Ann Pettibone relict & executrix
of Joseph Pettibone (AA) was granted
administration on his estate.
Securities: Thomas Homewood, John

Page 117

Ingram. Appraisers: Robert Eagle,
Humphrey Boone. Capt. John Worthington
to administer oath.

Roger Newman administrator of Thomas
Nollett (AA) exhibited accounts.
Mentions: William Clarke executor.

Exhibited inventory of John Hume (CV),
by appraisers John Hollett & James
Height.

Mr. John Gressam administrator of
Edward Selbey (AA) exhibited that no
estate was to be found.

William Mole administrator of John Smart
exhibited accounts.

10 May. Alice Kenerly administratrix of
William Kenerly (DO) exhibited accounts.

Daniell Ingram who married Seth relict
of Henry Pratt (TA) exhibited additional
accounts. Estate is overpaid.

Ralph Hawkins & Margarett Downes (AA)
executors of Florah Kile (AA) exhibited
her will.
17:283 Said Hawkins & Downes were granted
administration. Securities: John
Ingram, James Homewood. Appraisers:
William Lewis, Jonathon Neale. Edward
Batson to administer oath.

Exhibited inventory of Ralph Smith (CH),
by appraisers Cleborne Lomax & Walter
Storey.

Mr. James Wroth (CE) administrator of
William Nowell (CE) exhibited that Mr.
Richard Bennett (CE) has taken away said
estate. Petition for dismissal.

Elias King executor of Edward Sweatname
(KE) exhibited his will.

Ann Smith executrix of James Smith (AA)
exhibited that all debts are paid & she
is sole legatee.

Court Session: 1699

Benjamin Capell (AA) on behalf of
Elisabeth Selbey only daughter & heiress
of Mathew Selbey (AA) was granted
administration on his estate.
Securities: Richard Jones, Jr., Edward
Parrish. Appraisers: John Chappell,
Christopher Meckley. James Rigbey to
administer oath.

Exhibited:
- additional accounts of Col.
  Nehemiah Blackiston. Also exhibited
  additional inventory

17:284 ...
  & further additional inventory.
- inventory of Robert Phillips (AA),
  by appraisers John Waters & John
  Willought.
- additional accounts & additional
  inventory of Charles Williams
  administrator of Michaell Taylor.
- additional accounts of John Wight
  (PG) who married Ann relict &
  executrix of Thomas Gaunt.
- inventory of John Smith (CV), by
  appraisers John Turner & David
  Hellen.
- inventory of John Cornelius (CV), by
  appraisers John Turner & David
  Hellen.
- additional accounts of Richard
  Gressam (TA).

Mr. Jacob Reigneir procurator for
Thomas Jones (SO) vs. Mr. Carvil for
Arnold Elsey. Petition for hearing.

12 May. Mr. William Edmondson one of
executors of John Edmondson (TA)
exhibited additional accounts.

17:285 Attachment of contempt against (N)
Miller (KE) to answer exceptions of
Elisabeth Bourne to accounts of James
Boly.

William Roper administrator of Jarvis
Morgan (AA) exhibited inventory, by
appraisers Leonard Weyman & Richard
Snowden.

Major Bell (PG) to receive LAC on estate of Richard Chaffee until administration is granted.

Robert Blunt (TA) administrator of Robert Cooper (TA) exhibited accounts. Estate is overpaid.

15 May. Col. Henry Ridgley (AA) who married Mary executrix of Mareen Duvall (AA) exhibited additional accounts. Legatees to be paid as they come of age.

Mr. Phillip Lynes (CH) vs. Daniele Towes executor of Daniell Toes (KE). Caveat exhibited.

16 May. Alexander Furbush vs. William Taylor. Libel & answer exhibited. Continuance was granted.

Mr. Richard Bennett (CE) one of executors of Madam Hen. Marya Loyd (CV) exhibited further account on estate of Col. Phillemon Loyd (TA).

Henry Tripp son of Henry Tripp (DO) was granted administration on his estate, unadministered by the widow Elisabeth now dec'd. Securities: William Mackeel, John Harwood. Appraisers: John Lecount, John Brannock. Mr. Walter Cambell to administer oath.

17:286 Mr. Notley Rozier administrator of Col. Edward Pye (CH) petitioned for Mr. Clement Hill & Josh. Guybert to deliver books, etc.

Mr. Phillip Hoskins who married Ann relict & one of executors of Thomas Mudd (CH) petitioned for allowance for his wife out of additional accounts.

Mr. Phillip Hoskins (CH) was granted administration on estate of John Hall & Mary Hall (executrix of said John, now dec'd), on behalf of orphans. Securities: Edward Batson, Thomas Jones. Appraisers: George Britt, Richard Nelson.

Mr. Henry Fernley (CV) who married
Winnifred relict & executrix of John
Broome (CV) exhibited that there are
debts due to persons in ENG.
Continuance was granted.

Richard Owen (DO) former administrator
of Henry Tripp (DO) exhibited additional
inventory & accounts.

17:287 Elias King one of executors of Charles
Tilden (KE) exhibited will. Said King
for self & other executor petitioned
that Mr. Michaell Miller, Sr. (KE)
prove said will.

Said Elias King executor of Edward
Sweatnam (KE) executor of Richard
Sweatnam (TA) was granted administration
dbn on estate of said Richard.
Securities: Mathew Exerkson, James
Wroth.

Exhibited inventory of William Rabett
(TA).

Exhibited inventory of Lawrence Garey
(AA).

Exhibited inventory of John Vines (TA),
by appraisers Valentine Carter & Mathew
Ereckson.

Robert Hinwood (AA) administrator of
Richard Rawlings (AA) petitioned that
his administration be revoked. Phillip
Griffin was granted administration on
said estate, on behalf of children.

Thomas Jones vs. Arnold Elsey. Ruling:
(1) plaintiff to have 1/3rds; (2)
accounts to be produced; (3) said Elsey
(SO) & Sarah Luff (SO) were summoned
17:288 to show validity of receipts on estate
of Mr. Ballard.

Edward Loid vs. executors of Madam Loyd.
Exhibited were accounts of Mr. Richard
Bennett one of executors. Ruling: Judge
to decide by next court where legacy out
of estate of Col. Phillemon Loyd to
said Bennett from his father Richard

Bennett to be paid.

Per John Sweatnam (KE), Mr. Michaell Miller (KE) to examine witnesses to will of Edward Sweatnam.

Christopher Beanes (PG) obtained the liberty of having administration bond for estate of Thomas Cosden (CV) put in suit for relief of Alfonso Cosden, etc. Note to His Excellency Nathaniell Blakiston, Esq. Capt. General & Governor in Chief. Petition of Christopher Beane guardian of Alphonso Cosden orphans of Alphonso Cosden (CV). William Parker (CV) & Francis Hutchins (CV) were security for George Parker & Mordecay Hunton administrators of Mr. Thomas Cosden (CV).

17:289 Ordered that bond be delivered to Attorney General. Signed: N. Blakiston. Bond received by William Dent.

Francis Collyer who married Sarah administratrix of John Evans (CV) exhibited additional accounts. Mentions: 2 orphans.

Cleborne Lomax executor of Elisabeth Smith executrix of Archibald Waughop (CH) was granted continuance.

20 May. Sarah Fuller widow of Edward Fuller (AA) was granted administration on his estate. Securities: Edward Gibbs, Philemon Smith. Appraisers: John Hurst, William Pound. Capt. John Worthington to administer oath.

Phillip Griffin (AA) was granted administration on estate of Richard Rawlings, unadministered by his wife Jane. Securities: William Griffin, John Carter. Appraisers: Thomas Bland, Theophilus Kitten. Mr. Phillip Howard to administer oath.

Katherine Cullen widow of James Cullen (Annapolis, AA) was granted administration on his estate. Securities: Thomas Grunwyn, William Guyther, John Lecount. Appraisers: MM

Court Session: 1699

Thomas Blackwell, Richard Jones. Mr.
William Bladen to administer oath.

17:290   19 May. Alexander Deliniosa (AA) eldest
brother of Mary Deliniosa was granted
administration on her estate.
Securities: William Guither, Thomas
Grunwyn. Appraisers: William Collyer,
James Purnall. Mr. James Saunders to
administer oath.

Exhibited:
- inventory of Alexander Toulson (TA),
  by appraisers John Winchester &
  Thomas Marsh.
- inventory of Nathaniell Dolons (TA),
  by appraisers Charles Stevens &
  Thomas Browne.
- inventory of Samuell Withers (TA),
  by appraisers Lawrence Knowles &
  Ralph Dawson.
- accounts of Mrs. Audery Llewellin
  relict & administratrix of John
  Llewellin (SM), by William Taylard.

20 May. Exhibited:
- will of Edward Fuller (AA), proved
  by Edward Gibbs, John Hurst, & Mary
  Gardner.
- accounts of Thomas Attwood & James
  Wood executors of William Groves
  (AA).
- Col. Ninian Beale (PG) was granted
  LAC on estate of Richard Chaffee
  (PG).
- accounts of John Manning & his wife
  Rachel executrix of Hugh Ellis (CV).
  Continuance was granted.

17:291   ...
- accounts of Benjamin Hunt (DO).
- accounts of Thomas Greenfeild
  administrator of Richard Charlett
  (PG). Continuance was granted.
- inventory of Stephen Owns (PG), by
  appraisers Thomas Bridges & William
  Cooley.
- inventory of Thomas Denew (TA), by
  appraisers Mathew Erickson & Francis
  Steevens.
- bond of Mr. William Taylard
  administrator of James Paws (SM).
  Securities: John Bapt. Carbury,

Page 123

George Burch.
- list of debts due estate of Col. Nehemiah Blakiston (SM).
- additional inventory of Walter Powell (SO), by appraisers John Cornish & Peter Dent.
- examination of papers of Col. Edward Pye (g, CH), by MM Clement Hill & Joshua Guybert
- accounts of Col. John Bigger first administrator of Symon Wooten.
- accounts of Mr. Phillip Hoskins who managed affairs of widow of Dennis Dayne (SM).

Edward Batson (Annapolis) vs. estate of Richard Keene (CV). Caveat exhibited.

17:292 Exhibited from BA:
- inventory of Humphrey Daniell, by appraisers John Ferry & Robuck Linch.
- accounts of Joseph Guyston.
- inventory of Isaack Masheell, by appraisers William Farfar & Daniell Swindell.
- will of Edward Boothbey, constituting his widow executrix, proved by 3 witnesses.
- inventory of Anthony Phillips, by appraisers George Smith & Samuell Browne.
- bond of Joseph Peake administrator of Francis Robinson. Securities: Thomas Richardson, Thomas Scaley. Also inventory, by appraisers John Gray & Joseph Bridge.
- bond of Isbell Davidson administratrix of Patrick Davison. Security: Thomas Ruston. Also inventory, by appraisers William Elders & John Webster.
- will of Mr. John Ferry, constituting Charles Merriman executor, proved.
- depositions regarding estate of Lewis Jarman.
- bond of Rosemond widow & administratrix of Ambross Powell. Securities: Abraham Taylor, Robert Olwis.
- bond of Mary Bown administratrix of

William Bown. Securities: John Kimball, John Shield.
- bond of Elisabeth Smith administratrix of Thomas Smith. Securities: Thomas Teton, William Hicks.
- will of Jonas Bowers, proved.
- inventory of Michaell Conwith, by appraisers Christopher Bembridge & Christopher Shaw.
- inventory of Moses Groome, by appraisers Mr. Thomas Staley & William Puckett.

17:293 ...
- inventory of Thomas Smith, by appraisers John Rawlings & Samuell Landiferr.

Exhibited from SM:
- receipt of Thomas Holdsworth of Mr. Michaell Curtiss executor of Capt. Justinian Gerrard.
- will of Charles Egerton (SM), constituting his widow Ann & son Charles & son John executors, proved by 3 witnesses.
- inventory of Mr. James Browne (SM), by appraisers John Evans & Charles Egerton. Also inventory at his Quarter in CH, by appraisers Luke Gardner & Cornelius Branham.
- bond of James Bowles administrator LAC of Capt. Anthony Bowles. Securities: Col. Henry Muschett, Thomas Johnson.
- bond of Ann Duckworth administratrix of John Duckworth (SM). Securities: Richard Hopewell, Joseph Hopewell.
- will of James Cheason, constituting his widow Ann Cheason executrix, proved.
- inventory of John Duckworth (SM), by appraisers John Wiseman & William Aisquith.
- bond of Ann Ceason executrix of James Ceason (SM). Securities: Richard Attwood, Thomas Rose.
- bond of William Guyther administrator of Thomas Guyther. Securities: Zachar. Vansweringen, Thomas.
- bond of Elisabeth Tennison

Court Session: 1699

administratrix of Justinian
Tennison. Securities: John Shankes,
Daniell Henly.

- bond of Francis Browne
administratrix of James Browne.
Securities: John Pope, John Synodd,
William Taylard, Thomas Grunwyn.

17:294   ...

- bond of Charles & John Egerton
executors of Charles Egerton.
Securities: Thomas Grunwyn, John
Synnodd.
- bond of Margarett Winchen
administratrix of John Winchen.
Securities: John Doxey, Andrew
Magra.
- bond of Elisabeth Greenhall
administratrix of Edward
Greenhaulgh. Securities: Thomas
Haddock, William Frisdell.
- inventory of Stephen Walton, by
appraisers John Doxey & John
Manning. Also accounts by Thomas
Haddock.
- will of John Sheppard, constituting
his widow Mary executrix, proved
before Mr. William Husbands by
Elisabeth Jarboe.

Exhibited from TA:
- inventory of John Bowdell, by
appraisers Joseph James & Richard
Moore.
- inventory of Richard Harris, by
appraisers William Webb & John
Lomax.
- inventory of John Sargent, by
appraisers William Coursey & Vincent
Hemsley.
- inventory of Stephen Benson, by
appraisers John Lowe & Thomas Unky.
- inventory of John Richards, by
appraisers John Sargoon & Edward
Tomlin.
- bond of Michaell Russell
administrator of Samuell Stanes.
Securities: Anthony Rumball, James
Scott.
- will of Charles Hemsley,
constituting Vincent Hemsley
executor. Securities: Phillomen
Hemsley, Thomas Braff.

Court Session: 1699

17:295 ...

- renunciation of Elisabeth BroadWay (TA) widow & administratrix of Robert Broadway.

   Date: 22 March 1698. Witnesses: Da. Blaney, John Hawkins, Jr. Securities: Vincent Hemsley, Phil. Hemsley, Thomas Bruff.
- bond of John Jones administrator of John Muckgiver. Securities: Richard Daniell, Henry Maunaur.
- will of John Sydes, constituting his widow Bridget executrix, proved by 3 witnesses. Securities: Vincent Hemsley, Thomas Bruff.
- inventory of Peter Haddaway, by appraisers William Webb & John Lowe.
- bond of Edward Loyd & Richard Tilghman administrators of William Garey. Security: Thomas Thomas.
- bond of Henry Frith & his wife administrators of Thomas Clements. Securities: Robert Harrison, Thomas Hopkins.
- will of Richard Chafe, constituting Richard Hinson & Richard Morris executors, proved.
- inventory of Mr. Richard Potts, by appraisers Anthony Rumball & Andrew Kinemount.
- inventory of Edward Smith, by appraisers William Hatfield & Peter Evans.
- inventory of Christopher Botton, by appraiser John Cape.

17:296 Exhibited from CH:
- bond of Constance Fry administratrix of John Fry. Securities: Francis Goodrick, Randolph Garland.
- bond of Grace Adams administratrix of Francis Adams. Securities: George Godfrey, John Paine.
- bond of Ann Taylor administratrix of Thomas Taylor. Securities: Joseph Willson, Ralph Smith.
- bond of Isabella Thompson administratrix of Henry Thomson. Securities: Edward Rockwood, Mathew Land.
- bond of Jane Saunders executrix of Edward Saunders. Securities: John

Page 127

Saunders, Samuell Luckett.

- bond of Rando. Brent, Jr. executor of Richard Hubbard. Securities: William Holland, Jr., Cleborne Lomax.
- bond of Rando. Brent, Jr. executor of Rando. Brent, Sr. Securities: William Hatton, Jr., Cleborne Lomax.
- bond of Edward Rockhold & his wife Mary executors of John Nelson. Securities: William Moss, Mathew Saunders.
- bond of Sarah Smith executrix of Ralph Smith. Securities: Cleborne Lomax, Walter Storey.
- bond of Phillip Lewis administrator of John Allen. Securities: William Harpham, Thomas Vaughop.
- will of John Nelson, constituting his widow Mary & Griffin Davis executors, proved by 2 witnesses.
- accounts of John Stone.
- inventory of John Battery, by appraisers John Wilkinson & Mathew Ratclyff.
- will of namec Smith Ralph constituting his widow Sarah Smith executrix, proved.
- will of William Coventry, constituting Ralph Coventry executor, proved.

17:297 ...

- will of George Delahay, constituting Susannah Delahay executrix, proved.
- accounts of James Byles.
- inventory of Francis Addams, by appraisers George Godfrey & John Paine.
- inventory of Stephen Mankin, by appraisers John Wood & John Wilkinson.
- inventory of John Clerk, by appraisers Ralph Shaw & John Barton.
- inventory of Phillip Allen, by appraisers Thomas Lawson & Thomas Hagan.
- will of Rando. Brent, constituting his son Rando. Brent executor, proved by 3 witnesses.
- inventory of James Smallpage, by appraisers Mathew Saunders & William Ellit.

- inventory of Sarah Till, by appraisers George Brett & Francis Frampton.
- inventory of Henry Brawner, by appraisers Francis Frampton & Thomas Stone.
- inventory of Thomas Hutchinson, by appraisers Jacob Moreland & John Sotheron.
- accounts of Thomas Craxon administrator of Sarah Till.
- accounts of Robert Benson administrator of Robert Loften.
- accounts of Barbara Gouerly administratrix of John Gourley.
- accounts of Martha Cornish relict & executrix of John Cornish.
- accounts of John Watson administrator of Robert Hill.
- accounts of John Boy & his wife Jennett administrators of John Knight.
- inventory of William Chandler, by appraisers James Smallwood & John Hatton.

17:298 Exhibited from CV:
- accounts of Nathaniell Cranford. Estate is overpaid.
- bond of Walter Smith administrator of Jeremiah Eldridge. Securities: Henry Butler, John Willmott.
- bond of Edward Reynolds administrator of Timothy Hickman. Securities: Thomas Tench, Esq., Thomas Blake.
- accounts of Mathew Gardner administrator of James Gardner.
- accounts of Mary Taylor administrator of John Taylor.
- [?] of Mary Pearce administratrix of John Pearce (CV).
- inventory of William Shrine, by appraisers William Harbert & William Bradley.

Exhibited from CE:
- will of John James, proved.
- accounts of James Taylor.
- accounts of John Brockson & his wife Bridget administratrix of Thomas Moore.

Court Session: 1699

- inventory of Robert Scromingk, by appraisers Alexander Cambell, & James Gray.
- accounts of Richard Thornson. Also inventory, by appraisers Thomas Windell & Peter Cale.
- inventory of Peter Soforon, by appraisers Henry Eldersley & John Stoop.
- will of Peter Soforon, proved by 2 witnesses.
- bond of John Atkins & his wife Mary executrix of Peter Soforon. Securities: Mathias Vanderheyden, Edward Ladimore.

17:299 ...

- bond on estate of Arnoldus DelaGeorge. Securities: Charles Bass, Edward Blay, John Carvill.
- inventory of Thomas Thackstone, by appraisers Robert Gibson & Richard Ginrood.
- will of Arnoldus DelaGeorge.

Exhibited from DO:
- will of Mary Aldridge, proved. Also renunciation of John Brittaine. Date: 10 December 1697. Signed: John Britten. Witness: John Rawlings.
- will of Phillip Pitt, constituting Ann Pitt executrix, proved. Securities: William Meshew, Thomas Shankam. Also inventory of Phillip Pitts, by appraisers Francis Mayward & Edward Stevens.
- accounts of John Smith.
- bond of Ann Hunt administratrix of Benjamin Hunt. Securities: John Taylor, Hugh Erickson.
- bond of Patrick Danelly & his wife Ann executors of William Dorrington. Securities: John Keene, William Cattrell. Also inventory, by appraisers John Hazelwood & John Richardson.
- bond of Charles Powell administrator of Clary Gray. Securities: Hugh Erickson, William Markes. Also inventory, by appraisers John Haselwood & Humphrey Hubbard.
- bond of Mary Russell administratrix

Page 130

of John Russell. Securities: John
Russell, Peter Cornish. Also
inventory, by appraisers Anguish
Morrow & William Fisher.

17:300   ...
- will of John Winsmore, proved.
  Elisabeth Winsmore executrix was
  granted administration on his
  estate. Securities: William Meshew,
  Arthur Wheatley.
- inventory of John Winslow, by
  appraisers Thomas Vickers & Peter
  Stoakes.

Exhibited from CH:
- bond of Susannah Delahay executrix
  of George Delahay. Securities:
  Edward Mang, Joseph Harrison. Also
  inventory, by appraisers Richard
  Harrison & Joseph Harrison.
- bond of Rando. Brent administrator
  of Edward Fitzgarrett. Securities:
  John Theobalds, Richard Morris.
  Also inventory, by appraisers
  William Hawton, Sr. & Anthony Neale.
- will of Rando. Henson, proved by 3
  witnesses. Barbara Henson executrix
  was granted administration on his
  estate. Securities: Richard
  Harrison, Richard Wade.
- inventory of John Martin, by
  appraisers John Godshall & Robert
  Benson.
- inventory of Rando. Brent, by
  appraisers William Houghton, Sr. &
  Anthony Neale.
- accounts of Henry Brawner.
- accounts of John Ward.
- accounts of John Dooman.
- bond of Elenor Leet administratrix
  of George Leet. Security: Walter
  Poor.
- accounts of Stephen Mankin.
- accounts of Edward Saunders.

17:301   ...
- will of Edward Saunders, proved by 3
  witnesses.

Exhibited accounts of Charles Walson.

Exhibited inventory of John Bennett
(AA), by appraisers John Hurst & Joseph

Court Session: 1699

Connoway. Also accounts.

Exhibited accounts of Thomas Pennington.

Thomas Homewood (AA) exhibited will of John Bennett (AA), constituting him executor. Said Homewood was granted administration. Securities: Jonathon Neale, James Homewood. Appraisers: Robert Eagle, Capt. Humply Boone. Capt. John Worthington to administer oath.

30 May. Joseph Hawkins (AA) who married Elisabeth relict & administratrix of Christopher Rowles (AA) exhibited additional accounts.

Mrs. Katherine Cullen administratrix of James Cullen (Annapolis) exhibited that his estate is in SM. New appraisers: MM Thomas Grunwyn, Thomas Haddock. Mr. William Taylor to administer oath.

Ann Wallis widow of Richard Wallis (KE) was granted administration on his estate. Securities: Benjamin Bond, Ann Davenish. Appraisers: Benjamin Bond, Richard Daniell. Mr. Benjamin Frisbey to administer oath.

Ann Davenish widow of Robert Davenish (KE) was granted administration on his estate. Securities: Benjamin Bond, Ann Wallis. Appraisers: Benjamin Bond, Richard Daniell. Mr. Benjamin Frisbey to administer oath.

31 May. James Homewood (AA) administrator of George Robinson (AA) was granted continuance.

17:302   2 June. Thomas Hutchins (Annapolis) vs. estate of Henry Loftus (Annapolis). Caveat exhibited, as greatest creditor. Said Hutchins was granted administration. Appraisers: Joell Perry, Nicholas Auger. Mr. Thomas Collier to administer oath.

23 June. Exhibited inventory of George Robinson (AA), by appraisers Edward

Gibbs & Samuell.

<u>24 June.</u> Sarah Whitehead widow &
executrix of Charles Whitehead (AA) was
granted administration on his estate.
Security: Capt. Richard Hill.
Appraisers: Richard Garrett, Jacob
Harniss. Mr. Orlandoe Greenslade (AA)
to administer oath.

17:303   <u>28 June.</u> Mr. Richard Boughton (CH)
exhibited:
- accounts of Francis Adams.
- accounts of Henry Brawner.
- accounts of Francis Buttery.
- accounts of Henry Kee.
- accounts of John Martin.
- inventory of John Nelson, by
  appraisers Mathew Saunders & William
  Moss.
- inventory of Henry Tompson, by
  appraisers Mathew Saunders & Edward
  Rookwood.
- additional inventory of Edward Till,
  by appraisers John Allen & Robert
  Taylor.

Mr. Robert Bradley (PG) exhibited bond
of Thomas Hollyday & Joshua Cecill
administrators of Richard Brightwell
(PG). Securities: Edward Willett,
Joshua Hall.

Exhibited inventory of John Rockhold
(AA), by appraisers John Howard & Thomas
Blackwell.

<u>29 June.</u> Thomas Tally executor of
Walter Tally (KE) petitioned for Mr.
William Frisbey to prove said will.
Said Thomas was granted administration.
Securities: Hance Hanson, Lawrence
Draper. Appraisers: John Wade, William
Glanfeild. Mr. William Frisby to
administer oath.

17:304   Exhibited from SM:
- inventory of Charles Egerton, by
  appraisers John Evans & Thomas
  Haddock.
- additional inventory of William
  Knight, by appraisers Richard Newman

& Christopher Horrell. Also further
additional inventory. Also
accounts.
- accounts of John Sewell.
- inventory of Richard Mutchin, by
  appraisers Charles Smith & James
  Tompson.
- accounts of John Askin. Estate is
  overpaid.

Exhibited will of Andrew Magrow,
constituting Margarett Mitchen
executrix, proved by Charles Smith &
Patrick Buckley. Said Mitchen renounced
administration. Abraham Roades &
Charles Roades trustees of said dec'd
were granted administration on his
estate. Securities: William Harbert,
James Thompson. Appraisers: William
Harbert, James Tompson. Edward Batson
to administer oath.

17:305 Margaret Camperson widow of Leonard
Camperson (TA) was granted
administration on his estate.
Securities: Harbert Morgan, Nathaniell
Hull. Appraisers: Richard Kempton,
George Vincent. Mr. John Coppage to
administer oath.

Exhibited inventory of Robert Davenish
(KE), by appraisers William Smith &
Thomas Tolley.

Exhibited inventory of Richard Wallis
(KE), by appraisers Richard Daniell &
Benjamin Bond.

30 June. Exhibited inventory of Thomas
Pennington, by appraisers Thomas
Greenfeild & Robert Orme.

Maj. Thomas Smithson (TA) exhibited:
- Robert Munday, age 22, deposed on 10
  June 1699 that William Garey stated
  after he had signed his will, that
  there was a gift to Daniell Walker.
- Daniell Norman deposed the same on
  27 June.
- will of Nicholas Millbourne, proved
  by Thomas Grundy, James Benson, &
  Benjamin Peck. Robert Grundy &

Robert Ungle executors were granted administration on his estate. Date: 13 June.

- oath of James administrator of William Hornely. Date: 24 April 1699. Securities: Charles Neall, Edward Harris, Bryan Canelly.
- will of Robert Macklyn, proved by John Lillingstone & Thomas Bullock. Date: 24 April 1699.

17:306 ...

- will of Daniell Glover, proved by Richard Macklyn & Robert Sales. Ann Moore (also Ann More) was granted administration on his estate. Security: John Hadly. Appraisers: William Hynson, John Davis. Mr. Tillgman to administer oath. Date: 27 April.
- oath of Richard Hynson & Richard Moore executors of Richard Chaffee. Securities: Richard Jones, Sr., Mathew Reed. Appraisers: Richard Jones, Jr., John Johnson.
- will of Arthur Emery, proved by George Vanderford, Arthur Emery, Jr., & Thomas Evans. Katherine Emery was granted administration on his estate. Security: Arthur Emery. Appraisers: Thomas Evans, John Symons. Date: 26 April.
- David Fairbanck & Thomas Lurtey were granted administration on estate of Thomas Lurtey. The relict had renounced administration. Appraisers: Hugh Frith, John Hunt. Mr. Hugh Sherrwood to administer oath. Date: 2 May 1699.
- Nicholas Lowe was granted administration on estate of Will. Korry who married a daughter. His will was proved by 2 witnesses. Appraisers: John Cape, Thomas Tate. Date: 5 May.

17:307 ...

- Nicholas Lowe exhibited will of Mary Whittaker, constituting him executor, proved by 2 witnesses. Said Lowe was granted administration. Appraisers: John Cape, Thomas Tate. Date: 5 May.
- Nicholas Lowe exhibited will of John

Lee, who died at (N) Williams &
lived in DO, constituting Mary
Whittaker executrix, proved. Said
Lowe was granted administration.
Date: 5 May.

- will of William Hemsley, proved.
- will of Daniell Blaney, constituting
  Katherine Blaney executrix, proved.
  Said Katherine was granted
  administration. Securities: William
  Ringold, Thomas Thomas. Appraisers:
  William Clayton, John King.
- oath of Richard Tillgman (also
  Richard Tillman) one of executors of
  Robert Macklyn. The other executor
  Mr. Edward Loyd renounced
  administration. Security: Phillip
  Hemsley. Date: 30 May 1699.
- nuncupative will of Susannah Vahan,
  proved by Thomas Robins, Sr. & Lydia
  Bryant. Thomas Robins, Jr. was
  granted administration on his
  estate. Security: Thomas Robins,
  Sr. Appraisers: Thomas Robins, Sr.,
  John Robinson. Date: 30 May 1699.

13 June. Ellioner wife of Arthur Rigby
& relict of Andrew Oram was granted
administration on his estate.
Securities: Arthur Rigby, Peter
Anderson. Appraisers: Thomas Barnett,
Thomas Smith.

17:308 Exhibited oath of John Emerson & William
Clayton executors of Robert Macklyn,
sworn by Edward Loyd. Date: 4 June.

20 June. Exhibited will of James
Murphey, proved.

Exhibited will of Thomas Skilleton,
proved by Thomas Donelson.

Exhibited will of Henry Snowden, proved
by William Ringold, Martha Ringold, &
Daniell Ingerson. The relict renounced
administration. Henry Clayton was
granted administration on his estate.
Securities: Moses Harris, John Hacker.
Appraisers: William Clayton, Edward
Harris.

25 June. Ralph Moone (TA) was granted administration on estate of Katherine Catterson. Securities: William Alderne, Daniell Kerwyn. Appraisers: Thomas Burnett, Peter Anderson. Thomas Smithson administered oath.

Samuell Hopkins (SO) exhibited:
* bond of Robert King. Securities: Samuell Watkins, William Bosman.

17:309 ...
* Also inventory, by appraisers Peter Dent & Ephraim Willson.
* inventory of Samuell Showell, by appraisers Thomas Powell & Thomas Morris.
* inventory of Col. John Winder, by appraisers James Dasheill & Thomas Dasheill. Securities: Samuell Hopkins, Sr., Samuell Hopkins, Jr. Also will, constituting John Winder executor, proved.
* accounts of John Conner.
* accounts of John Hammon.

30 June. Exhibited inventory of William Karsey, by appraisers Henry Frith & Robert Harrison. Martha Kersey widow renounced administration. Witnesses: Thomas Smithson, Mary Smithson.

17:310 Exhibited from SO: heirs & legatees of our father Mr. James Dasheill attested to will. Date: 25 August 1697. Signed: James Dasheill, Thomas Dasheill, George Dasheill, Robert Dasheill, Robert Collier, William Jones, John Smith.

John Wiggins for his wife renounced administration on estate of John Miller or Willhm Miller. Date: 1 April 1699. Witnesses: Ja. Saywell, Joyce Stafford.

Exhibited from SO:
* Richard Plunkett was granted administration on estate of Michaell Harrison, as greatest creditor. Archibald Smith renounced administration. Date: 15 June 1699 at SO. Witnesses: Robert Perrey, John Taylor.

17:311 ...

- inventory of Thomas Johnson, by appraisers Samuell Hewley & Nicholas Evans. Security: Samuel Shinsllin.
- inventory of Edward Day, by appraisers Thomas Foreman & Benjamin Cattae. Also bond of Mary Day administratrix. Securities: Walter Lane, William Scott.
- inventory of William Wright, by appraisers John Jones & John Panter. Also bond of Francis Wright administratrix. Securities: Stephen Cannon, Julian Messick.
- inventory of Allexander Price, by appraisers Nicholas Evans & Thomas Foreman. Also bond of Rebbeca Price administratrix. Security: Samuell Hopkins, Sr.
- will of Will Owens, constituting his widow executrix, proved. Also bond of Ann Owens administratrix. Security: Archibald Smith.
- inventory of William Wheatly, by appraisers Robert Givan & John Winder.
- inventory of William Owens, by appraisers Peter Churbey & Eph. Willson.

Mr. John Coppage exhibited:
- will of Thomas Denro, proved by 3 witnesses. Also bond of William Osbourne. Securities: Robert Blunt, John Blare.

17:312 ...
- will of Allexander Toulson, constituting Edmond Goodman executor, proved.
- will of William Doland, constituting Amy Doland executrix, proved. Securities: John Mullen, Ralph Diston. Also inventory, by appraisers John Wells & Edward Brown.
- inventory of William Carter, by appraisers Edward Tench & Anguish Marrow.
- will of John Sharpe, constituting John Makett executor, proved.
- inventory of Edward Wooland, by appraisers William Robinson, Jr. & David Mackeele. Also accounts.

Court Session: 1699

Securities: William Robinson, Sr., William Robinson, Jr.
- accounts of John Powell.
- inventory of John Sharp, by appraisers William Gray & Thomas Gray.

Exhibited:
- inventory of William Burges (AA), by appraisers James Rigby & John Baldwyn.
- accounts of Thomas Lewes (PG).
- bond of John Robinson. Securities: Richard Beard, John Gray. Appraisers: John Sellman, Richard Duccat. Mr. Odeell administered the oath.

17:313 ...
- bond of Moses Groome. Securities: Stephen Johnson, Richard Isaack.
- bond of Martha Bowen administratrix of Jonas Bowen. Securities: Jonas Bowen, John Thomas, Nathaniell Ruxton.
- bond of Joane Chatham administratrix of Francis Chatham. Security: Henry Jackson.
- bond of Sarah Whitehed administratrix of Charles Whitehead. Security: Capt. Richard Hill.
- bond of Henry Smallwood administrator of John Ives. Securities: Thomas Coard, Thomas Greenfeild.
- will of Nathaniell Andrew, constituting Thomas Capell executor. Securities: James Jones, Samuell Jackson.
- will of Henry Haselwood, constituting James Hues executor, proved.
- bond of Ann Baker administratrix of Samuell Baker.
- bond of Susannah Arnold administratrix of Anthony Phillips. Security: James Phillips.
- inventory of John Weales, by appraisers William Wilkinson & Roebuck Lynch.
- inventory of Daniell Palmer, by appraisers William Holland & Henry Jackson.

Court Session: 1699

- inventory of Jonas Bowen, by appraisers George Ashman & William Wilkinson.
- inventory of William Powell, by appraisers John Deaver & Thomas Hews.
- inventory of Gilbert Pattison (AA), by appraisers Leonard Wayman & Robert Hopper.

17:314 ...

- additional inventory of Col. Nicholas Greenbury, by appraisers Humphry Boone & Roger Newman.
- accounts of Samuell Greenwood.
- bond of Jane Carter administratrix of William Carter. Security: Walter Cambell.
- bond of John Nicholls administrator of John Sharpe.
- will of Sarah Strawbridge, constituting Nicholas Neale executor, proved.
- inventory of Mary Vine, by appraisers Lawrence Taylor & George Smith.
- bond of Elenor Wells administratrix of John Wells. Security: Tobias Scanbrough.

1 July. Sarah Peddow widow of Lazarus Peddoe (TA) was granted administration on his estate. Securities: Michaell Fleasham, John Boyce. Appraisers: Alexander Walters, Lewis Merriday. Mr. John Coppage to administer oath.

Dorothy George was granted administration on estate of James George (TA). Securities: John Boyce, Nicholas Keeley. Appraisers: Lewes Merriday, John Houlton. Mr. John Coppage to administer oath.

17:315 5 July. Jacob Moreland (merchant, CV) administrator of Thomas Barker (mariner, SM) exhibited accounts. Receipts from: George Plater, Esq. & Amos Garrett (merchant) attorneys for Mary Barker relict & administratrix in ENG of said Thomas. Date: 3 July 1699. Witnesses: E. Batson, Thomas Jones. Receipt from: George Plater & Amos Garrett of Mr.

Jacob Moreland. Mentions: bill of
exchange on Mr. Thomas Wharton
(merchant, London) payable to Mr.
Benjamin Braine. Date: 6 July 1699.
Witness: Charles Butler.

Exhibited will of Nathaniell Andrew
(BA), proved by 3 witnesses.

17:316 Honorable Coats for Sarah Smith
administratrix of Ralph Smith (CH)
petitioned for said Coats to examine
accounts.

8 July. Thomas Hill proved will of Mary
Yate (AA).

10 July. Mr. Cleborne Lomax appraiser
of estate of Henry Hawkins (CH)
exhibited inventory. Other appraiser is
William Barton, Sr.

Dr. Mordicay Moore executor of John
Swawell (PG) exhibited accounts. Estate
is overpaid.

17:317 Mr. Michaell Miller (KE) exhibited
interviews regarding proof of will of
Edward Swettnam (KE):
• interviewed Mr. Nathaniell Hinson &
Geoffery Power who are departing the
Province.
• John Sweettnam the plaintiff desired
Mr. Nathaniell Hynson to attest to
validity of said will.
• Dr. Coker was physician in
attendance.
17:318 ...
• Said Sweettnam also desired Jeoffry
Power to attest to validity of will.
Signed: Geffery Power. Date: 24 May
1699.

17:319 Exhibited will of Francis Hill (SM),
constituting his daughter Elisabeth
Hopewell afterwards wife of Richard
Keene executrix. Afterwards, on 10 July
1697, Richard Keen (CV) & Elisabeth
Smithson his wife were granted
administration. Then said Richard died.
Then Elisabeth Keen was granted
administration. Securities: William

Taylard, Edward Batson. Mr. Samuell
Watkins to administer oath. Said
Elisabeth was granted continuance.

Mary Bagg administratrix of Thomas Bagg
exhibited additional accounts. "Quietus
est" was granted.

Thomas Reaves (also Thomas Reeves) one
of witnesses to will of Robert Sly (SM)
proved his will. Date: 11 July 1699.

17:320   John Boules & his wife Crout relict &
administratrix of George Hardesty (CV)
exhibited accounts.

Jacob Regneir procurator for John Athe
(also John Athey, AA) vs. estate of
Robert Trigellis. Caveat exhibited.
Said dec'd died on the ship Corsellis.
Exhibited nuncupative will.
- Elisabeth Fletcher, age 22, deposed
  on 17 May 1698 that Robert Tregelly
  was on board the ship Corsellis,
  Capt. Giles Wigganer commander.
  Before: Robert Smith.
- Joseph Davis, age 23, deposed on 25
  May 1698 regarding a passenger from
  ENG who mentioned Joseph Roswell.

17:321   ...
- Francis Bean, age 20, deposed on 25
  May 1698 regarding Robert Trigellis
  & John Athea.

Exhibited will of Francis Hill (SM),
constituting his daughter Elisabeth
Hopewell afterwards wife of Richard Keen
executrix. On 10 July 1697, said
Elisabeth & Richard were granted
administration on said estate. Said
Richard died before an appraisal. Said
Elisabeth was granted administration.
Securities: William Taylard, Edward
Batson. Appraisers: Mathew Lewis,
William Hume. Mr. Samuell Watkins to
administer oath.

17:322   Said Elisabeth Keen widow of Richard
Keen (CV) was granted continuance.

Mary Bagg administratrix of Thomas Bagg
(TA) exhibited additional accounts.
"Quietus est" was granted.

Thomas Reeves one of witnesses to will
of Robert Sly (SM) proved said will.
John Reeves [sic] attested before Edward
Batson. Date: 11 July 1699.

John Bowles for his wife Cicllia relict
of George Hardistey (CV) exhibited
accounts.

17:323 Edward Ball (CV) who married Pricilla
widow & administratrix of William Lisle
(CV) exhibited accounts. Mentions: bill
of Col. Beale.
- Ninian Beale (PG) deposed that he
  sold William Lisle 500 a. & there
  was still payment due which was paid
  by said Ball.
- distribution to: orphans.

Mr. Charles Blake (TA) surviving
executor of Col. Peter Sayer (TA)
petitioned for exemplification.

17:324 12 July. Capt. Phillip Hoskins
administrator of Mary Hall (CV)
exhibited inventory, by appraisers
George Britt & Richard Nelson.

William Respeer executor of Jarvis
Morgan (AA) exhibited accounts.

William Gwyn administrator of William
Anderson (TA) exhibited additional
accounts.

Samuell Warren who married Sarah relict
& administratrix of John Crooke (SM)
exhibited additional accounts.

Exhibited inventory of Charles Whitehead
(AA), by appraisers Jacob Harniss &
Richard Garrett.

13 July. William Smith (PG) proved will
of John Bennett (AA).

17:325 Joshua Cecill one of executors of
Jonathon Wilson exhibited accounts.
Continuance was granted.

14 July. Elisha Hall for self & Capt.
William Holland the greatest creditor &

Court Session: 1699

executors of Mr. James Cranford (CV)
vs. said estate. Caveat exhibited.

Levin Denwood (SO) was summoned to show
cause why he took possession of the
estate of George Knight (CV). Mr.
Worthington attorney exhibited a letter
from George Knight (merchant, London).
- Date: 18 February 1698/8. Notice
  from George Gray citing the death of
  said George Gray. Mentions: goods
  consigned to John Tooney, Thomas
  Church & Co., John Toovey
  (Bartholomew Crose, London),
  Ezekiell Woolsey who ordered rum
  from NY, John Askew (Philadelphia),

17:326 ...

George Gray (who lives on the
Spott). Signed: John Toovey, John
Knight, Ezekiell Wooley, Joshua Gee,
Thomas Church.

15 July. John Sweatnam (KE) vs. Elias
King surviving executor of Edward
Sweatnam (KE). Libel & 2 depositions
exhibited.

Mary Duglass administratrix of Robert
Duglass (CH) & administratrix of Richard
Beaumond (CH) was summoned to render
accounts. Charles Jones, neighbor,
petitioned that there is no estate.

17:327 Capt. Phillip Hoskins who married
relict of Thomas Mudd (CH) vs. Mr.
William Boreman (CH) & Thomas Mudd (CH)
executors of said Mudd. Said Boreman &
Mudd were summoned. Continuance due to
inability to travel so far.

John Sweatnam (KE) kinsman & nephew of
Capt. Edward Sweatnam (KE) petitioned
for Mr. Michaell Miller to take
depositions of witnesses to will of said
Edward. Executor: Mr. Elias King.

Walter Smith administrator of Henry
Taylor (CV) exhibited statement before
Mr. John Bojo (former Registrar) of
bill due to Mr. Peter Pagan & Co. Said
Smith was factor. Estate is overpaid.

Stephen Johnson & his wife vs. executor of Thomas Hedge (BA). Mr. Charles Carroll exhibited summons to executor to answer libel of said Johnson.

Benjamin Capell administrator of Mathias Eley (AA) exhibited inventory, by appraisers John Chapell & Christopher Mitley.

17:328 18 July. Manus Devoren (Annapolis) executor of Stephen Francis (AA) exhibited his will, proved by 3 witness. Said Devoren was granted administration. Securities: William Taylard, George Slacon. Appraisers: John Freeman, Thomas Hutchins. Mr. Orlando Greenslad to administer oath.

Mr. Elisha Hall one of executors of Mr. James Cranford (CV). vs. Capt. William Holland (now in ENG) the other executor. Caveat exhibited.

20 July. Mr. William Harris one of executors of Thomas Parker (KE) exhibited additional inventory & accounts. Continuance was granted.

17:329 20 March 1699. Phillip Hoskins & William Dent administrators of William Smith (CH) for children of Adam Smith (Berkshire, ENG) vs. Charles Carroll procurator for Cleborne Lomax executor of Elisabeth Smith (CH). Mentions: William Smith son of Adam Smith (clothier), Adam Smith eldest brother of dec'd & his sister, Martin Lind
17:330 (since dec'd),
17:331 said Elisabeth was executrix of her first husband (N) Wahop.
17:332 Ruling: plaintiff.
17:333 Said Hoskins & Dent were granted administration on his estate. Executor of said Elisabeth to dispose of effects from estate of Archibald Wauhop.

Mr. Eli Hall one of executors of Mr. James Cranford (CV) exhibited his will. Said Hall was granted administration on said estate, with Capt. Holland who is out of the Province. Securities: Walter

Court Session: 1699

Smith, Benjamin Hall.

17:334 John Hall (BA) for Mrs. Susannah Arnold administratrix of Anthony Phillips (BA) petitioned for accounts to be examined. Date: 20 June.

21 July. Mr. John Tompson (AA) for Mary Trundell relict & executrix of John Trundell (AA) to administer oath to said Mary & appraisers.

Richard Johns for Elisabeth Bourne administratrix of Samuell Bourne vs. Michaell Miller (KE) administrator of James Boulay (CV). Agreement exhibited.

17:335 Thomas Luckett executor of Mary Yate (AA) was granted administration on her estate. Securities: John Nutthall, Mareen Duvall. Appraisers: Mr. James Saunders, Sr., Phillip Odell. Mr. James Rigbey to administer oath.

Mr. Thomas Blackwell & his wife exhibited accounts on estate of Stephen Francis.

Rebbecca Nicholson executrix of Symon Fenoe (AA) was granted administration on his estate. Securities: John Gather, Robert Hopper. Appraisers: John Jacob, William Danee. Mr. Thomas Odell to administer oath.

22 July. Alexander Browne one of executors of Col. David Browne (SO)
17:336 was granted administration on his estate, for self & his wife Margarett Browne (alias Margarett Ereckson) & her sister Mary Ereckson. The 2 other joint executors are in ENG. Security: Mr. Samuell Worthington.

24 July. Exhibited:
- accounts of Cleborne Lomax executor of Elisabeth Smith (CH) executrix of Archibald Wauhop.
- Cleborne Lomax for Elisabeth Hawkins executrix of Henry Hawkins (CH) administrator of Henry Reynolds (CH) exhibited that there are no

Court Session: 1699

accounts.
- Robert Blinkhorne executor of Robert Blinkhorne (CV) was granted continuance.
- Exhibited inventory & accounts of Jonah Winfield. Estate is overpaid.

17:337 ...
- additional inventory & additional accounts of Thomas Harman.

Exhibited accounts of Col. Benjamin Rozier.
- accounts of Ann Fisher.
- additional accounts of Cornelius Johnson.
- bond of Nicholas Haile. Securities: William Wilkison, Robuck Lynch.
- inventory of Joseph Strawbridge (BA).
- additional accounts of Edward Beedle.
- bond of Rebecca Nicholson administratrix of Symon Fenoe. Securities: John Gather, Robert Hopper.
- inventory of Ambross Hogg (BA).
- inventory of Capt. Nicholas Gassaway, by appraisers James Lewis & John Baldwyn.

28 July. Elisabeth Bourne vs. Michaell Miller administrator of James Boulay. Objections to accounts exhibited.

Exhibited:
- bond of Elisha Hall executor of James Cranford. Securities: Walter Smith, Benjamin Hall.
- inventory of Edward Wooler, by appraisers John Hurst & Francis Meade.
- inventory of Stephen Francis (AA), by appraisers John Freeman & Thomas Hutchins.

17:338 ...
- additional inventory of Charles Tracey, by appraiser James Stoddard.
- inventory of Timothy Wickman, by appraisers John Hurst & Richard Fido.
- inventory of Bryan Conely (TA), by appraisers James Benson & Daniell

Page 147

Sherwood.
- inventory of Joseph Pettibone (AA), by appraisers Robert Eagle & Humphrey Boone.
- accounts of Thomas Edmondson (PG).
- inventory of John Harrington, by appraisers Francis Meade & Thomas Dawson.

27 July. William Richardson one of executors of William Richardson (AA) exhibited accounts. Also receipt from Elisabeth Talbott for legacies to her 3 children from their grandfather said William: Edward, John, Elisabeth. Date: 23 July 1699.

17:339 Also receipt by heirs of full age & release of William Richardson & Elisabeth Richardson executors. Signed: Daniell Richardson, Joseph Richardson, Thomas Sparrow for his wife, Sophia (daughter). Witnesses: Samuell Galloway, Samuell Thomas, Richard Galloway. Date: 24 July 1699.

1 August. Mary Burnett (AA) spinster vs. Thomas Freeborne surviving executor of

17:340 Elisabeth Burnett (widow, AA). Said Freeborne summoned to render accounts.

Robert Tyler attorney for Richard Lancaster administrator of Thomas Edmondson exhibited accounts.

Exhibited additional accounts of Cornelius Johnson (SO).

Elisha Hall (CV) who married Sarah relict & administratrix of Jonathon Winfeild (CV) exhibited accounts. Estate is overpaid.

John Hurst administrator of James Harrison (AA) exhibited accounts.

Joshua Cecill (PG) exhibited:
- accounts of Henry Jones (PG).
- bond of Mary Beven executrix of Charles Beven. Securities: Richard Marsham, William Barton. Also will, proved by 3 witnesses.

17:341 ...

- inventory of Thomas Hooks by appraisers Joseph Harrison & James Watts.
- inventory of Thomas Sheppard, by appraisers Thomas Sprigg & William Offitt.
- accounts of William Willson.
- bond of Christopher Beanes administrator of Ann Cosden. Security: James Brooke.
- Col. Ninian Beale (PG) was granted LAC on estate of Richard Chaffee. Mentions: will, constituting his widow Ann Chaffee executrix. She unwillingly renounced administration,

17:342 ...

recommending Thomas Box. Date: 26 May 1699. Witnesses: Edward Willett, John Bennett. Said Box was granted administration, as greatest creditor. Security: Edward Willett.

John Willmott (CV) exhibited:
- accounts of Edward Wood. Estate is overpaid.
- inventory of Daniell Buckmaster, by appraisers Clarke Skynner & Thomas Harvey.
- will of John Blackner, constituting his widow Elisabeth executrix. Securities: John Hunt, Nicholas Scarff.
- inventory of Thomas Sedgewick, by appraisers George Young & Hezekiah Bussey.
- bond of Robert Brothers. Securities: Daniell Browne, Robert Wood.
- bond of John Brookes administrator of James Bray.

17:343 ...

- inventory of Joseph Shimey, by appraisers John Mead & James Berry.
- inventory of Francis Leaff, by appraisers Jeremiah Eldridge & John Underwood.
- inventory of William Smith, by appraisers Henry Buttler & Robert Sumner.
- inventory of John Hedger, by

appraisers John Arnold & John
Glover.

John Thompson exhibited, dated 18 June
1699:
- Elisabeth Wheeler (CE)
  administratrix of John Wheeler
  exhibited inventory. Date: 1 June
  1699.
- Penellope Ricketts (CE) widow &
  executrix of John Ricketts (CE)
  exhibited inventory. Date: 1 June
  1699.
- Joyce Quinney (CE) widow & executrix
  of Sutton Quinney (CE) exhibited
  inventory. Date: 14 June 1699.

17:344 ...
- Joseph Porter (CE) son of Giles
  Porter exhibited his will,
  constituting him executor, proved.
  Said Joseph was granted
  administration. Securities: John
  James, Darby Haley. Appraisers:
  Richard Kinnard, Humphrey Tilton.
- Ann James (CE) widow of John James
  exhibited his will, constituting his
  son-in-law Humphry Tilton executor,
  proved. Said Tilton renounced
  administration. Date: 13 May 1699.
  Said Ann was granted administration.
  Securities: Mathias Mathiason,
  Gerrardus Wessells. Appraisers:
  Richard Kinnerly, Darby Haley.

17:345 John Rawlings (DO) exhibited:
- bond of John Snelson administrator
  of Ann Pitt. Securities: Richard
  Owen, Thomas Skinner. Also
  inventory of William Pitt, by
  appraisers William Meshew & Peter
  Swakes
- bond of Elisabeth King
  administratrix of Obediah King.
  Securities: Edward Williams, Anthony
  Rawlings. Also inventory, by
  appraisers Hugh Eccleston & Fer.
  Makey.
- bond of John Russell administrator
  of Mary Russell. Securities: Petter
  Cornoly, John Anderson. Also
  inventory, by appraisers William
  Wargent & Roger Hurley.

Court Session: 1699

- accounts of Philladelphia Gray
  executrix of Andrew Gray.

17:346 Exhibited:
- inventory of William Battes (AA), by
  appraisers Francis Maud & Mathew
  Howard.
- inventory of John Bennett (AA), by
  appraisers Robert Eagle & Humphry
  Boone.
- accounts of James Meaney (CV).
- accounts of Col. Edward Pye (CV).
- additional accounts of John Abington
  (CV).
- additional accounts of Henry Brent
  (CV).
- accounts of John Wright (TA).
- inventory of Robert Roberts (CV), by
  appraisers Isaack Baker & William
  Masters.

Ann Walker executrix of Richard Walker
(SM) was granted continuance.

Mr. Richard Boughton (CH) exhibited:
- bond of executor of Robert Marston
  (CH). Security: Richard Edgar.
  Also will, proved by 2 witnesses.

17:347 ...
- accounts of William Spickman (CH).
- inventory of Charles Leet (CH), by
  appraisers John Tompson & Richard
  Edgar.
- will of Justinian Tennis (CH),
  proved by 3 witnesses. Executrix:
  Katherine Tennis. Securities:
  Thomas Claxon, Thomas Simson.
- bond of Elisabeth Peunis
  administratrix of James Peunis.
  Securities: Richard Edgar, Thomas
  Johnson.
- bond of Thomas How & his wife
  Elisabeth administratrix of Francis
  Fraughton. Securities: Mathew
  Sanders, Sr., Mathew Sanders, Jr.
- bond of Constant Fry administratrix
  of John Fry (CH). Securities:
  Francis Goodwick, Randall Garland.
- William Taylor for Audery Llewellin
  exhibited accounts on estate of John
  Llewellin. Continuance was granted.
- accounts of Mr. William Boreman,

Page 151

Jr. (CH) executor of Elisabeth Young.

- accounts of Prisilla Sly executrix of Robert Sly (CH). Estate is overpaid.

Exhibited:
- additional accounts of James Pargrave (SM).

17:348 ...
- further additional accounts of Col. Nehemiah Blackiston (SM).
- bond of Elisabeth Meares administratrix of William Meares (CV). Securities: Robert Shepard, John Webb.
- will of Thomas Purnall (CV), constituting his widow executrix, proved by 2 witnesses. Other witness is in ENG. Executrix: Elisabeth Purnall. Securities: John Dixon, James Dixon.
- will of James Cranford (CV), proved by 2 witnesses before Mr. John Willymott (CV).
- will of Robert Brothers (CV), constituting Elish Sedgwick executor, proved by 3 witnesses.
- inventory of John Blacketter (CV), by appraisers Thomas Hinton & William Meads.
- inventory of John Debbs (TA), by appraisers Mathew Errickson & James Ringold.
- inventory of Capt. Edward Greenhalch (SM), by appraisers William Harbert & Henry Smith.

17:349 ...
- accounts of William Richardson (AA).
- additional accounts of William Head (CV). Administrator: John Bigger.

Jane Hemesley relict & one of executors of William Hemesley (TA) was granted administration on his estate. Securities: William Alden, John Tidings. Col. Edward Lloyd to administer oath.

Court Session: <no date>

18A:0 "A list of books and records belonging to the Prerogative Court or Office for

Court Session: <no date>

Probatt of Wills etc. & according to
their numbers as followeth:

All manner of Testamentary Proceedings:
1. Anno 1637, 1638, 1639, 1640.
2. Anno 1657.
3. Anno 1658, 1659.
4. Anno 1660 & 1661.
5. Anno 1662, 1663.
6. Part 1665.
7. Part 1665, 1666 part.
8. Part 1666, 1667, part 1668.
9. 1668, 1669.
10. 1671, 1672, 1673, part 1674.
11. Part 1674, part 1675.
12. Citations 1676 to 1678.
13. Testamentary causes 1675.
14. Ditto 1676.
15. Ditto 1677.
16. Ditto 1678.
17. Ditto 1679.
18. Ditto 1680.
19 & 20. Ditto containing 3 books to
1682.
21. Part 1682, 1683, 1684, 1685, 1686,
part 1687.
22. Part 1687, 1688 from fol. 1 to 157.
Ditto Book L from fol. 1 to 15 1692.
23. Part 1693, 1694 (KC).
24. 1695, 1696, part 1697 (KC).
25. Part 1697, 1698, 169 (KC).

Inventorys and Accounts:

I. Anno 1674, 1675.
II. Anno 1676.
III. Anno part 1676, 1677.
IV. Anno 1677.
V. Anno 1678.
VI. Anno 1679.
VII. Anno 1680 part torne first leafe.
VIII. Anno 1681.
IX. Anno 1682.
X. 1683, 1684, 1685, 1686.
XI. Part 1686, 1687.
XII. 1688, part 1689. Ditto Book L
1692, part 1693.
XIII. Part 1693, 1694.
XIIII. Part 1694, part 1695.
XV. Part 1695, part 1696.
XVI. 1696, part 1697.
XVII. 1697, part 1698.

Court Session: <no date>

Wills and Inventorys:

A. 1670.
B. part 1670, 1671, 1672, part 1673.
C. PC. Part 1673, 1674, 1675.

Wills and Testaments:

A. Anno 1676, 1677.
B. Anno 1678.
C. Anno 1679.
D. Anno 1680.
E. Anno 1681.
F. Anno 1682.
G. 1682 to 1687.
H. 1688, part 1689. Ditto L fo. 1 to 52
1692.

KC

I. 1693, 1694.
K. 1695, 1696. 1697, 1698. In Lib: No.
H, as above more 1698 & 1699.

KC Inventorys and Accompts.

XVIII. 1698.
XIX. 1698.
XX. 1698, part 1699.
XXI. 1699.

Signed: Kenelm Cheseldyn.

Records of County Courts kept by the Clerk
in Testamentary Causes

This 7 are in the Office:
1. St. Mary's County - in a Book.
2. Charles County - in a Book.
3. Calvert County - in a Book.
4. Ann Arundel County.
5. Cecill County - in papers.
6. Kent County - in papers and a Book.
7. Somerset County - in a Book.

Dorchester County - returned in papers.
Talbott County - returned.
Baltemore County - not returned.

October 1697
Signed: Kenelm Cheseldyn

Court Session: <no date>

August the 14th 1699.
Then received of the Honorable Kenelm
Cheseldyn, Esq. late Com. Generall of
the Province of Maryland these following
bundles of bonds:
1. 28 bundles from the year 1661 to
    year 1689.
2. 2 bundles of bonds for the years
    1692/3, one of which was found in
    the Councill Room at St. Mary's.
3. 1 bundle qt. 14 bonds from Mr.
    Bonner's papers.
4. 1 bundle qt. 178 bonds is from
    Calvert County for the years 1693 &
    1694.
5. 2 bundles qt. 193 & 18 bonds for
    1695, 1696 & pt. 1696/7.
6. 1 bundle qt. 152 bonds for 1697.
7. 1 bundle qt. 216 bonds for 1698.
8. 1 bundle qt. 142 bonds 1698/8 and
    1699.
9. 1 bundle qt. 32 bonds which want to
    be renewed.

August the 18 1699.

Then delivered to W. Bladen, Esq. of the
Court of Probate of Wills etc. the above
bundles of bonds.
Signed: Ken. Cheseldyn."

Court Session: 1699

18A:1   12 August. John Addison, John Court, &
         Thomas Brooke, Esq. appointed Judges of
         Probate.
18A:2   Signed: Nathaniel Blakiston, Esq. Capt.
         General & Governor. Said Addison &
         Brooke sworn.
18A:3   William Bladen (g, Annapolis) appointed
         Registrar. Evan Thomas sworn as
         Assistant Registrar.

18A:4   15 August. Thomas Tench, Esq. executor
         of Benjamin Scrivener (AA) exhibited
         inventory.

         Said Tench for Joseph Saunders
         administrator of John Trouton (AA)
         exhibited inventory.

Capt. Robert Lockwood (AA) for Francis Price administrator of Robert Philips (BA) petitioned for Mr. John Hall to take depositions regarding will of said Philips.

Richard Jones, Jr. & his wife Ann administrators of William Burgess (AA) exhibited accounts.

17 August. Mr. John Thompson (AA) for Mary Trundell executrix of John Trundell exhibited his will, proved. Appraisers: John Attwood, John Gale. Also exhibited inventory.

Said Thompson for Martha Carr widow of Walter Carr, Jr. was granted administration on his estate. Said Martha was also granted administration on estate of Walter Carr, Sr.

19 August. Capt. Ebenezar Blakiston exhibited accounts of Thomas Baker (AA).

Thomas Hutchins exhibited inventory of Henry Loftus (AA).

18A:5 21 August. Thomas Blackwell exhibited inventory of Elisabeth Newton (AA).

25 August. William Edmundson for Elisabeth Sharp executrix of William Sharp (TA) petitioned for Thomas Robins, Jr. to prove said will. Said Elisabeth was granted administration on his estate. Appraisers: Nicholas Lowe, Robert Ungle.

Exhibited inventory of James Pery (CH).

30 August. Maj. William Dent exhibited will of Christopher Gregory (AA). Said Dent was granted administration on his estate.

Exhibited inventory of William Horne, Jr.

7 September. Mary Barnett for Ralph Hawkins exhibited inventory of William Coventry (BA) & inventory of Flora Kiles

Court Session: 1699

(BA).

13 September. Mr. Robert Hopper
petitioned to examine accounts of Rose
Bruse administratrix of George Bruce
(AA).

Exhibited inventory of James George
(TA).

20 September. Mr. John Thompson for
Martha Carr administratrix of Walter
Carr exhibited inventory of Walter Carr,
Sr. (AA) & inventory of Walter Carr, Jr.
(AA).

18A:6   Said Thompson exhibited bond of Mary
Trundell administratrix of John
Trundell.

Said Thompson to administer oath to
Susan Heiford administratrix of Thomas
Heiford (AA).

23 September. Exhibited inventory of
William Selby (PG).

24 September. Exhibited will of William
Sharp (TA), constituting Elisabeth Sharp
executrix. Thomas Robins to prove said
will. Said Elisabeth was granted
administration on his estate.
Securities: William Stephens, William
Edmundson.

26 September. Exhibited will of Andrew
Insly (DO). Michaell Todd was granted
administration on his estate.
Securities: John Meredith, James Foxon.
Also exhibited inventory.

28 September. Exhibited accounts of
John Nichols executor of John Sharp
(DO).

Exhibited will of John Gouty, Jr. (DO).
John Wille, Jr. was granted
administration on his estate.
Securities: Robert Pope, James Cannon.
Also exhibited inventory.

Court Session: 1699

Exhibited inventory of Richard Raulings (DO).

18A:7 29 September. Exhibited:
- will of Alexander Chappell (AA).
- will of Ignatius Wheeler.
- inventory of Francis Frampton.
- bond of Frances Wheeler administratrix of Ignatius Wheeler. Securities: Math. Barnes, Evan Jones.
- accounts of Thomas Coffer (PG).
- accounts of Rando. Brandt administrator of Edward Fitzgerrett (CH).
- accounts of Mathew Barns administrator of Johannah Hudson.
- accounts of Mathew Barns administrator of Philip Jones.
- inventory of Christopher Gregory (AA), by Mr. William Dent.
- accounts of Mr. Anthony Neale executor of Madam Ann Neale (CH).
- additional inventory of Col. George Robotham.

4 October. Mr. John Bayne (CH) vs. (N). Caveat exhibited.

Exhibited accounts of Mary Powell administratrix of William Powell (AA).

Exhibited accounts of William Osborn administrator of Thomas Dines.

18A:8 Mr. John Willmott (CV) exhibited:
- bond of Thomas Kingcart. Securities: Edward Wood, Jr., John Wood. Also inventory, by appraisers George Spicer & Nicholas Fountaine.
- bond of Joshuah Sedwick administrator of Thomas Sedwick. Securities: John Chittham, Thomas Tucker.
- bond of Elisabeth Purnall. Securities: James Dixon, William Woodard.

Exhibited accounts of widow Plumer (AA).

Further exhibited from CV:
- inventory of Thomas Sedwick.

Court Session: 1699

- accounts of George Wade.
- accounts of Francis Leaf.

Maj. Thomas Smithson (TA) exhibited:
- inventory of Robert Broadway.
- inventory of Susannah Vaughan.
- inventory of Andrew Orum.
- inventory of Sarah Yowler.
- inventory of James Meen.
- renunciation of Mary Mason on estate of Thomas Mason.
- inventory of Robert Macklein.
- inventory of William Hornby.
- inventory of Thomas Clemens.
- inventory of Henry Snowden.
- bond of Mary Dobbs administratrix of John Dobbs. Securities: George Vinson, Edmon Goodman.
- bond of Sarah Broadway administratrix of Samuell Broadway. Securities: George Bowes, Edward Clark.
- bond of William Stone administrator of Jacob Little. Security: William Edmundson.
- bond of Margarett Meen administratrix of James Meen. Securities: William Scott, Nath. Scott.

18A:9 ...
- accounts of John Salter administrator of Samuell Newton.
- accounts of Thomas Hopkins & his wife Elisabeth administratrix of Mortough Horney.
- accounts of Nathaniell Scott administrator of John Pickett.
- accounts of Vincent Hemsley administrator of Robert Broadway.
- will of James Meens.
- will of Charles Robinson.
- will of Thomas Skilington.
- will of Samuell Broadway.

Mr. John Hall (BA) exhibited:
- accounts of Joyce Marshall administratrix of Isaack Marshall.
- accounts of John Rouse executor of Richard Thompson.
- accounts of Joseph Peak administrator of Francis Robinson.
- inventory of Francis Chattam.

Court Session: 1699

- bond of Elisabeth Ebden administratrix of William Ebden. Also inventory.
- bond of William Macarty administrator of Richard Robinson.
- bond of Sarah Copas administratrix of John Copas.
- inventory of John Armstrong.
- bond of Abraham Taylor administrator of John Taylor.
- inventory of Ambros Prevett.
- bond of Jere. Royston administrator of John Royston.
- inventory of John Ferry. Administrator: Ch. Merryman.

Exhibited accounts of William Thomas administrator of Edward Edwards (TA).

Exhibited accounts of Dorothy George administratrix of James George (TA).

Exhibited accounts of Richard Jones & his wife Ann administrators of William Burgess (AA).

18A:10 23 October. Charles Fowler for Sarah Fouler exhibited accounts on estate of Edward Wood (CV). "Quietus est" was granted.

Exhibited accounts of Ralph Hawkins administrator of Flora Kyle (AA).

2 November. William Taylard (g, SM) exhibited:
- inventory of John Holland, by appraisers Benjamin Collman & Henry Freiks.
- inventory of John Roberts, by appraisers Jo. Gillum & James Wood.
- inventory of Robert Cooper, by appraisers John Evans & Samuell Wheeler.
- inventory of Anthony Evans, by appraisers William Aisquith & Benjamin Inman.
- inventory of Robert Blades, by appraisers John Henderson & William Hickman.
- inventory of Justinian Tenison, by appraisers John Brine & Benjamin

Page 160

Court Session: 1699

Reder.
- accounts of Owen Maclamy administrator of John Hammon.
- accounts of Dunnock Dennis administrator of Hope Taylor.
- accounts of Jane Price administratrix of James Price.
- accounts of Benjamin Cottman administrator of William Robinson.
- accounts of Mary Swayne administratrix of John Swayne.
- bond of Elisabeth Greenhalgh administratrix of John Watson. Securities: Richard Attwood, Thomas Haddock.
- bond of Patience Cooper administratrix of John Holland. Security: James Spence.
- bond of Robert Blades administrator of Robert Blades. Security: John Henderson.

Exhibited:
- inventory of Lewis Pether (TA), by appraisers John Dawson & William Aldern.
- inventory of Thomas Hall (SM), by appraisers Raphael Haywood & George Keeth.
- inventory of Richard Mason (CH), by appraisers Joseph Willson & Thomas Dixon.
- inventory of John Robinson (AA), by appraisers Richard Duckett & John Sellman.

18A:11 ...
- inventory of David Blaney (TA), by appraisers William Clayton & John King.

7 November. Exhibited inventory of Symon Finoe, by appraisers John Jacob & William Disney.

27 November. Thomas Stockett exhibited inventory of Mary Yates (AA), by appraisers James Sanders & Thomas Odell.

Bonds exhibited:
- Anthony Ruly administrator of James Dutchson. Securities: William Bladen, Richard Beard.

Page 161

Court Session: 1699

- William Taylard administrator of Richard Keen. Securities: Menas Devoran, (N).
- Sarah Griffith administratrix of William Griffith. Securities: William Maccubbins, Edward Rumney.
- Mary Rockhold administratrix of John Rockhold. Securities: Lancelott Todd, Thomas Blackwell.
- William Stone administrator of Samuell Broadway. Securities: George Bows, Edward Clark.
- Mary Dobbs administratrix of John Dobbs. Securities: George Clinson, Edward Goodman.
- Thomas Stockett administrator of Mary Yates. Securities: Thomas Sprigg, John Nutthall.
- Stephen Cole administrator of Thomas Tennsey. Security: Thomas Tench, Esq.
- Elisabeth Hunt administratrix of Dr. Hunt. Securities: Orlando Greenslade, John Freeman.
- Thomas & Cornelius Wade administrators of Jane Price. Security: John Taylor.
- Charles Merryman administrator of John Ferry. Securities: Samuell Sicklemore, Charles Adams.
- William Pennington administrator of Edward Duncalfe. Securities: Thomas Homewood, Ralph Moss.
- Thomas Homewood administrator of John Bennitt. Securities: William Pennington, William Lewis.
- William Osborn administrator of Thomas Dines. Securities: Edward Combs, William Scott.

18A:12 ...

- Ann Pettybon administratrix of Joseph Pettybone. Securities: Thomas Homewood, Ralph Hawkins.
- Sarah Fuller administratrix of Edward Fuller. Securities: John Hurst, Thomas Dossen.
- James Homewood administrator of George Robinson. Securities: Thomas Homewood, William Pennington.
- Ralph Hawkins administrator of Flora Kile. Securities: Margarett Downs, William Lewis.

Page 162

Court Session: 1699

- John Bayne administrator of Humphrey Warren. Security: Thomas Whichaley.

29 November. John Taylor (g, DO) for Mr. John Rawlings (DO) exhibited:
- will of Alexander Fisher.
- will of Manus Handly, constituting his widow executrix.
- will of John Cullison, constituting James Foxon executor.
- will of William Dean, constituting Richard Tubman & John Meredith executors.
- inventory of Ellis Thomas, by appraisers Thomas Taylor & Thomas Gray.
- inventory of William Woodgate, by appraisers Henry Griffith & Anthony Chilcott.
- inventory of Alexander Fisher, by appraisers William Messew & John Lecompt.
- inventory of Manus Hanley, by appraisers John Nichols & Nicholas Macleland.
- inventory of John Cullison, by appraisers Michael Todd & Edward Turner.
- inventory of William Dean, by appraisers Timothy McNemara & Edward Turner.
- accounts of Jane Read executrix of William Read.
- bond of Elisabeth Thomas administratrix of Ellis Thomas. Security: John Richard.
- bond of James Cannon administrator of William Woodgate. Security: John Taylor.
- bond of Elisabeth Fisher administratrix of Alexander Fisher. Securities: John Snelson, John Rawlings.

18A:13 ...
- bond of Mary Hanley administratrix of Manus Hanley. Securities: William Edmundson, Patrick Cavan.
- bond of James Foxon administrator of John Cullison. Security: John Meredith.
- bond of Elisabeth Dean administratrix of William Dean.

Page 163

Court Session: 1699

Securities: William Bird, John
Meredith.

Exhibited accounts of Mary Gary
administratrix of her husband Lawrence
Garry (AA).

Sarah widow & executrix of William
Griffith (AA) was granted administration
on his estate.

Exhibited will of Alexander Simms,
proved before John Carvill. Sarah Simms
executrix was granted administration on
his estate.

2 December. Exhibited will of Francis
Johnson, constituting his widow
Elisabeth Johnson executrix.

6 December. Richard Boughton (CH)
exhibited:
- inventory of Edward Sanders.
- inventory of Ignatius Wheeler, by
  appraisers Thomas Wheeler & Mathew
  Barns.
- inventory of John Fry, by appraisers
  Michael Marten & James Adam.
- inventory of Isabella Thompson, by
  appraisers Mathew Sanders & Griffin
  Davies.
- will of Henry Hawkins.
- accounts of Susan Delahay
  administratrix of George Delahay.
- bond of Elisabeth Hawkins
  administratrix of Henry Hawkins.
  Security: William Barton.

18A:14   ...
- bond of Mary Oneal administratrix of
  Arthur Oneale. Securities: William
  Glover, Morris Fitzgerratt.
- bond of Philip Lynes administrator
  of Isabell Thompson.
- bond of Dorothy Hunt administratrix
  of John Hunt. Securities: William
  Smith, Richard Estop.
- additional accounts of Robert
  Harrison & Richard Wade
  administrators of Jo. Write.
- inventory of Thomas Hillary.

Court Session: 1699

Exhibited will of Water Taley (KE), by
Mr. Elias King.

Exhibited accounts of Thomas Tench
administrator of Robert Hewett (AA).
Also inventory.

Exhibited inventory & accounts of Mr.
Lawrence Vanderbath (KE) late minister
of St. Paul's Parish (KE).

12 December. John Willymott (CV)
exhibited:
• bond of Darby Hornley. Securities:
  John Fisher, Bryant Maydaniell.
• accounts of Thomas Kingcart.
• inventory of Thomas Purnall.
• bond of Elisabeth Keen. Securities:
  George Young, John Manning.
• bond of John Leech. Securities:
  Ambrose Leech, Jeremy Leech.
• bond of John Clark. Securities:
  William Williams, Edward Evans.

Mr. Henry Ridgley (AA) exhibited oath
of Richard Wharfield & John Gater,
appraisers of Woolfran Hunt
(chirurgeon).

18A:15   Exhibited renunciation of Mrs. Sarah
Lumley relict of Alexander Lumley, Esq.
(BA), recommending Charles Carroll, Esq.
as administrator, as principle creditor.
Date: 16 November 1699.

15 December. Exhibited inventory of
Samuell Skidmore (AA), by appraisers
Humphrey Boon & Robert Eagle.

16 December. Exhibited bond of Charles
Carroll administrator of Alexander
Lumley. (AA). Security: W. Bladen.

Docket:
• Henry Low vs. Henry Darnall. Libel
  dismissed.
• Alexander Forbas vs. William
  Taylard. Continuance was granted.
• (N) Hoskins & (N) Dent
  administrators of (N) Smith vs.
  Cleborne Lomax. Said Lomax is
  "dead".

Court Session: 1699

William Watts vs. Gerrard Slye.
Attachment to issue unless Capt. Sly
renders full accounts.

Henry Darnall, Jr. vs. Henry Low & his
wife administrators of John Darnall.
Libel exhibited. Attachment issued for
want of an answer.

18A:16 (N) Rousby administrator of (N) Seth vs.
Robert Robinson. Said Robinson had no
right to the administration. His LoA
revoked.

(N) Johnson & wife vs. Thomas Hedge
executor of (N) Hedge. Libel exhibited.
Attachment issued for want of an answer.

John Sweatnam (KE) vs. (N) King
executor of (N). Sweatnam. Text of
libel. Plaintiff is nephew & heir to
Edward Sweatnam (high sheriff, KE,
dec'd). Said Edward left no issue
alive.
18A:17 Mentions: wife of Charles Tilden, other
relations in ENG,
18A:18 Elias King, said Elias King & Charles
Tilden since dec'd.
18A:19 Signed: J. Regnier.
18A:20 Text of answer.
18A:21 Signed: Char. Carroll (procurator).
Date: 6 October 1699.
• Andrew Cornelisson deposed.
18A:22 ...
• Catherine Heathcot deposed.
• Mr. John Salter deposed that he was
there at the same time as Jeffrey
Power, Nathaniel Hynson, William
Edwin, Henry Hosier, William Smith,
& the doctor. Mentions: Mr. Miller.
18A:23 ...
• Joshuah Sweatnam deposed that the
Monday before the will was made, he
desired to go over the Chester River
& desired Thomas Yewell & the
deponent to call on John Sweatnam.
Mentions: that said John was said
Edward's brother's son & he had no
relations in the Country.
18A:24 ...
• Thomas Yewell deposed.
• William Rice deposed.

Court Session: 1699

- Elisabeth North, age 40, deposed that "you will make a bastard of John Sweatnam as his father had done".

18A:25 ...

- Col. William Pearce, age 56, deposed.
- William Coker, age 45, deposed on 25 May 1699 that he was the physician to said Edward. Before: Robert Smith.
- Robert Smith, age 47, deposed on 29 November 1699

18A:26 ...

that said Edward was discoursing with said John about his father's will.
- James Williams, age 43, deposed on 29 November 1699.
- Henry Hosier, having taken the test, said.
- Edward Fry, having taken the test, said.
- Christopher Davison (KE), age 32, deposed before Col. John Hynson & Lt. Col. Thomas Smith.

18A:27 ...

Mentions: Peter Allaby, Mary Popper (servant).
- John Whittington, age 40, deposed on 30 November 1699.
- Peter Allaby deposed before Col. Thomas Smith & Col. John Hynson.

18A:28 ...

Mentions: 2 sisters of said Edward.
- William Harris, age 50, deposed. Mentioned: Mrs. Mary Tilden, "2 young women sisters' children of Mr. Sweatnam".

18A:29 ...

- Philip Holleger, age 62, deposed.
- Mary Popper, age 22, deposed before Col. John Hynson & Lt. Col. Thomas Smith. Mentions: 2 sisters (of said Edward) in ENG.

18A:30 ...

- William Smith (one of witnesses to will) deposed that he went with William Edwyn (neighbor). Mentions: Nath. Hynson, Jeffrey Power, John Salter, Henry Hosier.

18A:31 ...

18A:32

- Joshuah Sweatnam deposed.

...

Mentions: John Sweatnam & William
Sweatnam sons to Richard Sweatnam.

18A:33

...

- Ann Tilden (said Edward's
goddaughter) deposed before Thomas
Brooke. Date: 11 July 1699.
Ruling: will is good in law.

18A:34   Philip Hoskins, Esq. (CH) & his wife Ann
relict & executrix of Thomas Mudd (g,
CH) vs. Thomas Mudd (son & executor of
said Thomas) & William Boreman, Jr.
Text of libel. Said Thomas Mudd
constituted his wife Ann & his son
Thomas executors & MM Thomas Clark &
William Boreman, Jr. overseers or
assistants to his children. Said Clark
renounced as overseer.

18A:35   Said Phillip & Ann married on 14
November 1698.

18A:36   Said Phillip & Ann are guardians to 3
small children of said Thomas. Signed:
William Dent.

18A:37   Sentence:

18A:38   Plaintiffs removed to Portobacco CH.

18A:39   Said Boreman to render accounts.

18A:40   Signed: John Addison, Thomas Brooke.

Henry Darnall, Jr. vs. Henry Low & his
wife administratrix of John Darnall.
Continuance was granted.

William Pennington exhibited accounts on
estate of William Martin (AA).

Mr. Thomas Orell was granted
administration on estate of Dr. John
Hynde. Appraisers: Philip Briscoe,
Joseph Venor.

Thomas Warren & Abra. Warren vs. Notley
Warren. Thomas Warren exhibited summons
to Capt. Bayne. Attachment ordered.

Mr. Charles Carroll for Capt. Nicholas
Smith petitioned regarding Anthony Ruley
administrator of Dr. James Dutchson.
Said Ruley to proceed with
administration.

18A:41   Said Smith to give an accounting of said

Court Session: 1699

Dutchson's goods on his ship & to
deliver them to relations in ENG.

Mr. Thomas Warren exhibited summons to
Capt. Bayne. Attachment ordered.

John Kemble renounced administration on
estate of Edward Boothby (BA).

Allexander Magruder exhibited accounts
on estate of Thomas Hutchens (CH).
"Quietus est" was granted.

Capt. Lockwood for Francis Price
petitioned for will of Robert Philips
(BA) to be proved.

John Thompson for Mary Trundell
exhibited will of John Trundell (AA),
proved. Also exhibited inventory.

18A:42 John Thompson for Martha Carr relict &
administratrix of Walter (AA) was
granted administration on his estate.
Also, said Martha was granted
administration on estate of Walter Carr,
Sr. (AA).

William Edmundson for his mother-in-law
Elisabeth Sharp executrix of William
Sharp (TA) petitioned for Thomas
Robinson, Jr. to prove said Sharp's
will.

Maj. William Dent exhibited will of
Christopher Gregory (AA), proved by
Thomas Lawrence, Esq. & John Dowdall.

Robert Hopper petitioned for examination
of accounts of Rose Bruce administratrix
of George Bruce (AA).

John Thompson for Martha Carr exhibited
inventory of Walter Carr, Jr. (AA).
Also exhibited inventory of Walter Carr,
Sr. (AA).

18A:43 Exhibited bond of Mary Trundell.

Said John Thompson for Susannah Heiford
administratrix of Thomas Heiford (AA)
was granted administration on his

estate.

John Long administrator of William Dale was granted "quietus est".

Michael Miller was granted administration on his father's estate (KE).

Charles Fowler for Sarah Fowler exhibited accounts of Edward Wood (CV). "Quietus est" was granted.

Sarah executrix of William Griffin (AA) petitioned for his will to be proved.

Stephen Cole was granted administration on estate of John Towsey, a passenger on his vessel.

Elisabeth Hunt was granted administration on estate of Dr. Hunt (AA).

18A:44 John Stanley for Catherine Kullen petitioned for the appraisers of estate of James Cullen (AA) be sworn.

Thomas Taley executor of Walter Taley (KE) petitioned for appraisers.

Anthony Ruly was granted administration on estate of James Dutchson (AA).

John Thompson petitioned for examination of accounts of Sarah Horne executrix of William Horne (AA).

William Taylor was granted administration on estate of Richard Keen (CV), as principle creditor.

John Higgins petitioned for Thomas Hughes to prove will of Griffith Morley (AA).

Mr. Robert Finley to examine accounts of George Haddaway administrator of Stephen Benson (TA).

18A:45 Charles Carroll was granted administration on estate of Mr.

Court Session: 1699

Alexander Lumley (BA).

Capt. Richard Hill was granted administration on estate of Robert Handcock (AA).

John Thomson exhibited oath of Susan Heiford administratrix of Thomas Heiford (AA).

Randall Revell for Elisabeth Porter administratrix of William Porter (SO) exhibited accounts. "Quietus est" was granted.

Mr. Cromwell for Elisabeth Ashman executrix of George Ashman (BA) petitioned for will to be proved by Richard Cromwell (g).

Stephen Cole administrator of John Towsey (AA) exhibited accounts & inventory.

Stephen Gill administrator of Daniel Macomus (AA) was granted administration on his estate.

18A:46 George Plater, Esq. was granted administration on estate of Mrs. Burford (CV).

Mr. Robert Finley (TA) exhibited accounts of:
- John Salter administrator of (N). Sydes.
- John Salter administrator of (N). Newton.
- (N) Blane executor of (N) Blane.
- (N) Bickesteth administrator of Capt. Marshall.
- (N) Cleland administrator of (N) Cleland.
- (N) administrator of Samuell Withers.

Mary Chapell was granted administration on estate of Henry Chapell (AA).

Sicily Sadler was granted administration on estate of Joseph Sadler (TA). Mr. Copedge to administer oath.

Court Session: 1699

John Garterell was granted
administration on estate of Francis
Johnson (AA).

18A:47   Maj. William Dent for Barbarah Hynson
executrix of Randolph Hynson (CH)
petitioned for Richard Boughton to
examine accounts.

Thomas Atterbury & his wife Joan
exhibited accounts of John Smith (CV).
"Quietus est" was granted.

Thomas Hughes to prove will of Robert
Gover (AA).

Hercules Hume exhibited accounts on
estate of John Hume (CV). "Quietus est"
was granted.

Samuell Chew & Nehemiah Birkhead were
granted administration on estate of
Abraham Nayler (AA). Capt. Holland to
administer oath. Also, said Holland is
to prove will of Benjamin Chew (AA).

Katherine Ridgley executrix of Henry
Ridgley (AA) was granted administration
on his estate.

18A:48   Walter Smith administrator of Jeremy
Eldridge administrator of Roger Cooper
(CV) was dismissed, as said Cooper left
no books. Date: 1 December 1699.

William Boreman, Jr. executor of
Elisabeth Young (CH) exhibited accounts.

George Ayrs & his wife Elenor executors
of John Long executor of Clement Haly
were referred to County Court.

William Herbert executor of John
Cherribub was acquitted of incomplete
accounts.

Richard Harrison & Richard Wade
administrators of John Wright exhibited
accounts.

Samuell Mason & his wife Mary
administrators of Christopher More

Page 172

summoned to render accounts.

18A:49   Richard Harrison administrator of
Richard Carver (CH) was acquitted.

Thomas Coleman & his wife Mary
administratrix of Jonathon Samway
summoned to render accounts before
Thomas Brooke, Esq.

Heneage Robinson administrator of Capt.
Thomas Harman (PG) was acquitted.

John Harebottle administrator of Edward
Jones (AA) summoned to answer objections
of his wife [!]. No one was present to
prosecute.

Ann Fisher administratrix of Thomas
Fisher (TA) exhibited accounts.

18A:50   Edmond Goodman executor of Alexander
Toulson (TA) renewed his bond.

Amy Dolland executrix of William Dolland
renewed her bond.

Exhibited:
- inventory of John Holland.
- inventory of Elis Thomas.
- inventory of William Woodgate.
- accounts of Richard Rawlins.
- inventory of John Troughton (CH).
- inventory of William Selby.
- inventory of William Brown.
- inventory of Dr. Woolfran Hunt.
- inventory of Robert Hancock.
- accounts of Ann Taylor
administratrix of Thomas Taylor.

18A:51   ...
- accounts of Elisabeth Marshall
executrix of William Marshall (CH).
- accounts of Clement Haley.
- accounts of William Porter.
- additional accounts of Richard
Harrison & Richard Wade
administrators of John Wright.
- accounts of Alexander Magrugder &
his wife Ann executrix of Thomas
Hutchison.
- accounts of Ann Swayn administratrix
of John Swayn (SO).

- accounts of Benjamin Collman, Jr. administrator of William Robinson.
- accounts of Dunnock Dennis administrator of Hope Taylor.
- accounts of Thomas Jameson who married relict of Ignatius Mathews (CH).
- accounts of Jane Price administratrix of James Price (SO).
- accounts of Joseph Peak administrator of Francis Robinson (BA).
- accounts of John Nichols executor of John Sharp (DO).
- accounts of Randolph Brandt administrator of Edward FitzGerrard (CH).
- accounts of Francis Coffer administrator of Thomas Coffer.
- accounts of Mathew Barns administrator of Philip Jones.
- accounts of Jane Read executrix of William Read.
- <unspecified> of Eloner Wells administratrix of John Wells.

18A:52 ...

- accounts of Robert Noble.
- accounts of Margarett Mercer administratrix of John Mercer (AA).
- accounts of John Harebottle administrator of Henry Francis.
- additional inventory of John Rockhold. Mary Rockhold executrix exhibited accounts.
- inventory of Thomas Heiford.
- inventory of William Sharp (TA).
- inventory of John Bennett (AA).
- accounts of Ann Skidmore administratrix of Samuel Skidmore.
- accounts of Col. Henry Ridgley administrator of William Brown (BA).
- inventory of William Haslewood.
- accounts of Thomas Hedge administrator of Thomas Hedge.
- inventory of Alexander Lumley.
- inventory of John Royston.
- inventory of John Coopis.
- inventory of Richard Askew.
- inventory of Jane Price (SO).
- accounts of James French administrator of William Mickin (SM).

- inventory of Andrew Magrave (SM).

18A:53 ...
- accounts of Mary Cozens executrix of John Cosens (AA).
- accounts of Elisabeth North executrix of John North.
- inventory of Bartholomew Mackmurry.
- accounts of Henry Nowell & his wife Ann executrix of Solomon Rutte (SM).
- inventory of Daniel Richman.
- accounts of Charles Watts.
- additional inventory of Willmott Hill (SO).
- list of debts of William Knight (SM).
- accounts of Willmott Hill.
- accounts of James Round administrator of Howell Francis.
- inventory of William Garey (TA).
- inventory of James Clayland.
- inventory of Peter Hutchison. Henry Burt administrator exhibited accounts.
- accounts of John Jones administrator of John Magager.
- inventory of John Marshall.
- accounts of Mathew Smith & his wife Mary administratrix of John Dine (TA).
- inventory of Thomas Skillington.
- inventory of Ann Cosden.
- additional accounts of Thomas Hopkins & his wife Elisabeth administratrix of Mourtough Horney.

18A:54 ...
- accounts of Thomas Hillary.
- accounts of Ann Wheelock executrix of Edward Wheelock.

Court Session: May 1700

1 May. Henry Darnall, Jr. vs. Henry Lowe & his wife administratrix of John Darnall. Demurrer overruled. Defendants to file answer. Madam Lowe to swear to answer.

Alexander Forbas vs. William Taylard. Continuance was granted.

William Watts vs. Gerrard Slye. Capt. Slye to discharge himself of balance to estate.

(N) Johnson & his wife vs. (N) Hedge
executor of (N) Hedge. Attachment of
contempt to defendant.

William Smith has attended court for
several days to prove will of John
Bennett (AA).

18A:55 After taking oath before Col. John
Addison, executors of Mr. Homewood to
compensate him.

Exhibited inventory of Elisabeth Smith,
found among effects of William Smith
(dec'd) by appraisers John Booker &
Lewis Jones. Mr. William Dent & Capt.
Philip Hoskins to take possession
thereof in satisfaction for costs of
recent suit of said Hoskins & said Dent
administrators of (N) Smith & Cleborne
Lomax.

Thomas Smith & Elias King vs. Michael
Miller (KE) administrator of Michael
Miller. Said Smith & King are guardians
to Arthur Miller (son of dec'd). Said
Michael summoned.

Exhibited accounts of Thomas Tench, Esq.
administrator of Lyonel Copley, Esq.
Col. John Addison exhibited objections.
Mentions: payment to Henry Fernley.
Objections of Mr. Richard Mason read.

18A:56 Mathew Scarborough for Hannah Maynard
executrix of James Maynard (SO)
petitioned for Mr. Peter Dent to
examine accounts.

Mr. Robert Mason was granted
administration on estate of Thomas
Ashwick (CH), by Maj. William Dent
(CH).

Col. John Thompson (CE) to examine
accounts of Philip Rasin & Thomas
Thackstone administrators of Thomas
Thackstone.

Capt. Philip Hoskins (CH) to examine
accounts of Jane Sanders executrix of

Court Session: May 1700

Edward Sanders.

John Thompson (AA) to administer oath to
administrators of Mary Trundell.

Mary Barnet was granted administration
on estate of Mary Smith (AA).

Exhibited accounts of Mrs. Rachael
Killburne widow & administratrix of
Richard Killburne (AA).

18A:57   Petition. Date: 22 April 1700.
Anthony Neale was summoned to exhibit
accounts on estate of Capt. Joseph
Pile. Continuance was granted for 6
months to provide final accounts & for 2
more orphans to be paid.

John Nuttall vs. Maj. Walter Smith
executor of Thomas Hillary (CV). Case
dismissed.

Col. John Bigger administrator of
Robert Carvy summoned to proved
inventory & accounts. Case dismissed.

Thomas Blake & his wife Ann
administratrix of Edward Isaack
exhibited that estate is overpaid.

Daniell Robertson & his wife Mary vs.
Edward Ball & his wife Priscilla
administratrix of William Lyle. Case
dismissed.

18A:58   Thomas Smallwood executor of John
Smallwood (CH) exhibited accounts filed
with Mr. Cleborne Lomax, who gave
"quietus est".

Samuell Burman executor of William
Burman summoned to exhibit accounts.
Case dismissed.

Henry Powller administrator of Joseph
Huniford (SM) to provide accounts to Mr.
Keech.

John Riley administrator of Bartholomew
Murris exhibited accounts.

Page 177

Court Session: May 1700

Gabriel Parrot administrator of John
Briscoe (AA) exhibited that he cannot
exhibit accounts until he has recovered
from (N) Elzey.

Gabriel Parrott administrator of Daniell
Longman exhibited that estate is
overpaid.

Christopher Waters & his wife Elisabeth
executrix of John Powell were granted
continuance.

Thomas Lee & his wife Alice executrix of
William Burman exhibited that estate is
overpaid.

18A:59 Joshuah Meriken administrator of Richard
Baily (AA) exhibited that he had
provided accounts to Mr. Cheseldyn.

Elisabeth Boothby & James Philips
executors of Edward Boothby exhibited
accounts on estate of (N) Johnson.
Continuance was granted.

John Dawson administrator of Bryan Omely
(TA) was granted dismissal.

Lazarus Madox administrator of Elener
Cane summoned to exhibit inventory &
accounts on estate of Lazarus Madox, Sr.
(SO). There is no estate.

Hannah Maynard executrix of James
Maynard was granted continuance.

Exhibited:
* inventory of Charles Bevan (PG), by
  appraisers Thomas Greenfield &
  Robert Orum.
* inventory of Capt. Richard
  Brightwell, by appraisers David
  Small & Edward Willet.
18A:60 ...
* inventory of John Joyce, by
  appraisers John Pottenger &
  Christopher Thompson.
* accounts of Bartholomew Goff & his
  wife Hannah executrix of Thomas Hide
  (PG).
* accounts of Thomas Johnson & his

Page 178

wife Mary administratrix of Charles
Hay.
- additional inventory of William
Hutchison.
- inventory of George Plater, Esq., by
appraisers Joseph West & John
Hutten.
- accounts of John Lennam
administrator of Michael Kersey.
- inventory of Joseph Lockworth (PG),
by appraisers William Mosten &
George Nayler.
- accounts of Elisabeth Hunton
executrix of Thomas Dixon (CV).
- inventory of Robert Brothers, by
appraisers Robert Wood & Daniell
Brown.
- inventory of Peter Hill, by
appraisers George Spicer & John
Lloyd.
- inventory of Henry Tucks, by
appraisers Thomas Atterbury &
Charles Richardson.
- inventory of Elisabeth How, by
appraisers William Braban & Henry
Hough.
- accounts of Darby Hernley
administrator of Henry Tucks.
- accounts of Elisabeth Hunton
executrix of Timothy Hunton.

18A:61 ...
- accounts of Sarah Stinet
administratrix of Joseph Stinett
(CV).
- inventory of Samuell Scott, by
appraisers Thomas Johnson & John
Bradhurst.
- accounts of Thomas Atterbury
administrator of John Cornelius.
- accounts of Darby Hernley
administrator of Edward Armstrong.
- accounts of Hercules Hume executor
of John Hume.
- additional accounts of Philip
Hoskins & his wife Ann executrix of
Thomas Mudd.
- inventory of Philip Clark (SM), by
appraisers William Watts & Peter
Watts.
- accounts of Martha Bowen
administratrix of Jonas Bowen (BA).
- inventory of William Reycrof, by

Court Session: May 1700

appraisers Thomas Greenfield &
Richard Marsham.
● accounts of John Salter & his wife
Bridgett executrix of John Sides
(TA).
● accounts of Mary Jarvis
administratrix of Henry Jarvis (AA).
● additional accounts of John Salter
administrator of Samuell Newton
(TA).
● accounts of Henry Eldesly & his wife
Parnell & Elisabeth Ladmore
executors of Robert Crook.
● inventory of James Cranford (CV), by
appraisers George Cole & Henry
Botler.
● inventory of Arthur Oneale, by
appraisers Morris FitzGerrard &
William Glover.
● inventory of Cleborne Lomax, by
appraisers John Theobalds & Michael
Marten.

18A:62   ...
● inventory of John Hunt (CH), by
appraisers William Smith & Richard
Justept.
● accounts of Constance Frye
administratrix of John Frye.
● inventory of Jacob Jennifer (DO), by
appraisers Robert Don & William
Harris.
● inventory of Patrick Donelly, by
appraisers David Jenkins & John
Willis.
● inventory of Alexander Fraiser, by
appraisers John Nichols & Mathias
Allford.
● inventory of John Vincent, by
appraisers William Mishew & Peter
Stawks.
● accounts of Elisabeth Dean
administratrix of William Dean (DO).
● inventory of Giles Porter, by
appraisers Richard Ken & Humphrey
Tilton.
● inventory of John James, by
appraisers Richard Kenword & Darby
Haley.
● inventory of John Eldridge, by
appraisers Thomas Pierce & John
Brownton.
● accounts of Owen Hughes executor of

Page 180

Court Session: May 1700

Edward Johnson. Also inventory, by appraisers Samson George & Edward Nevell.
- accounts of John Atkins & his wife Mary relict & executrix of Peter Sefferson.

18A:63 ...

- accounts of Thomas Tench, Esq. administrator of Lyonel Copley, Esq. (AA).
- additional accounts of John Pemberton executor of George Robotham.
- inventory of Henry Chapell, by appraisers Robert Eagle & Humphrey Boon.
- accounts of John Fisher administrator dbn of Dr. Symon Wooten (CV), unadministered by Col. John Bigger.
- accounts of Edward Boothby & his wife Elisabeth administratrix of Capt. Henry Johnson (BA).
- accounts of Samuell & Mary Mason administrators of Christopher Mire (CH).
- additional accounts of John Hall & his wife Martha administratrix of Edward Beadle (BA).
- accounts of Mark Richardson & John Hall administrators of George Uty & his wife Mary.
- additional accounts of John Hall & his wife Martha relict of George Gouldsmith.
- accounts of John Farthing administrator of Samuell Dolson (AA).
- accounts of Stephen Cole administrator of John Towsey.
- inventory of Clement Parks, by appraisers Jos. Guibert & James Hay.
- additional accounts of John Wright administrator of Thomas Gault.

18A:64 Wills exhibited:
- Robert Philips (AA).
- Ignatius Wheeler (CH).
- Francis Johnson (AA).
- Robert Benger (BA).
- Roger Philips (SO).
- Michael Williams.

- William Nox.
- Francis Martin.
- Dominick Kirwan (TA).
- Thomas Russam.
- William Watts.
- James Clayland.
- James Berry.
- Thomas DelaHay.
- Griffith Morley (AA).
- Thomas Townsing.
- Thomas Wakefield (CH).
- John Wattson (SM).
- George Asman (BA).
- James Finley (CH).

Court Session: July 1700

18A:65 Henry Darnall, Jr. vs. Henry Lowe & his wife administratrix of John Darnall. Answer due from the defendant.

Alexander Forbas vs. William Taylard. Continuance was granted.

William Watts vs. Gerrard Slye. Defendant discharged.
- John Shanks deposed that his father John Shanks had a Negro woman & Col. Coode bought her & a child of Charles Watts, Negro Sam (boy), & Negro Mattox another.
- John Gootherick deposed. Mentions: Charles Watts.
- William Sandy deposed.

18A:66 (N) Johnson vs. Thomas Hedge executor of (N) Hedge. Attachment issued against said Hedge.

Mary Barnett vs. Henry Meryday. Said Meryday summoned.

John Ewin & his wife vs. Robert Cutchin administrator of Moses Groom. Said Cutchin summoned.

Thomas Winter & his wife vs. John Garterell. If said Winter posts security, then he will be given LoA.

Maj. Thomas Smith & Elias King guardians to Arthur Miller vs. Michael

Court Session: July 1700

Miller administrator of Michael Miller.
Said Miller summoned

Thomas Edmondson & his wife
administratrix of (N) Grason vs. Robert
Allen. No information.

Susannah Wooten administratrix of Symon
Wooten vs. John Fisher. Said Fisher
summoned.

18A:67 Exhibited:
- accounts of William Dent executor of
  Christopher Gregory (AA).
- inventory of John Leach, by
  appraisers James Heigh & Benjamin
  Ball.
- inventory of Edward Evans (CV), by
  appraisers John Jenkins & William
  Williams.
- inventory of John Fields, by
  appraisers William Stinnet & William
  Bradley.
- inventory of Robert Catlyn, by
  appraisers James Curtis & George
  Lane.
- accounts of Jonathon Showell &
  Armell Showell executors of Samuel
  Showell (SO).
- accounts of Francis Jenkins
  administrator of Richard Wharton.
- accounts of Robert Blades
  administrator of Robert Blades.
- accounts of Ann Holland
  administratrix of William Holland.
- accounts of Henry Rich who married
  widow & administratrix of John
  Williams.
- accounts of Thomas Adams
  administrator of Philip Adams.
- accounts of Elisabeth Townsend
  administratrix of John Townsend.
- accounts of George Hutchins
  administrator of Thomas Hillman.
- accounts of Sarah Smith executrix of
  Ra. Smith (CH).
- inventory of John Townsend (AA).
- inventory of William Smith (CH), by
  appraisers John Booker & Lewis
  Jones.

18A:68 ...
- inventory of Elisabeth Smith (widow,

Page 183

Court Session: July 1700

CH), by appraisers John Brook &
Lewis Jones.
- accounts of Philip Hoskins executor
of Mary Hall.
- inventory of Jeremiah Eldridge, by
appraisers William Wadsworth & John
Bowls.
- accounts of Sarah Horne widow &
administratrix of William Horne
(AA).
- inventory of James George (TA), by
appraisers Lewis Meredith & John
Oldson.
- inventory of Edward Fowler, by
appraisers Thomas Horsman & Samuell
Flewelyn.
- inventory of James Stanfield (SO),
by appraisers John Hendry & Edward
Green.
- inventory of Erasmus Harrison, by
appraisers John Franklyn & Edward
Green.
- inventory of James Stanfield & James
Macoom, by appraisers John Hendry &
Edward Green.
- inventory of Roger Philips, by
appraisers Philip Carr & Joseph
Venabs.
- inventory of Michael Harrison, by
appraisers Richard Chambarett &
Robert Carey.
- inventory of Samuell Baker (BA), by
appraisers George Smith & Samuel
Brown.

18A:69   ...
- accounts of William White & his wife
Ann administrators of Samuell Baker
(BA).
- accounts of Margarett Mark
administratrix of John Mark.
- accounts of Edward Lloyd, Richard
Tilghman, & Thomas Thomas
administrators of William Gary (TA),
during minority of John Gary &
George Gary.
- additional accounts of Benjamin
Hall, William Boreman, & Anthony
Neale executors of Richard Hubbart
(CH).
- accounts of John Givin who married
widow of Thomas Tallar (CH).
- accounts of Thomas Tench, Esq.

Page 184

administrator of Benjamin Scrivener (AA).

- inventory of Griffin Morley, by appraisers Seaborne Tucker & Daniel Brown.
- accounts of Charles Daft executor of Thomas Warren (SM).
- accounts of Joseph Edwards administrator of John Roberts (SM).
- inventory of John Fardery, by appraisers Edward Parson & Thomas Haddock.
- accounts of Edward Miller administrator of Daniell Moy.
- additional accounts of Ann Abell executrix of Samuell Abell.

18A:70 ...

- accounts of John Nevitt for Ann Jarboe relict & executrix of Peter Jarboe (SM).
- inventory of Benjamin Chew (AA), by appraisers Abraham Birkhead & Thomas Hughes.
- inventory of Abraham Nayler, by appraisers Josias Towgood & Thomas Hughes.
- accounts of Job Evans & his wife Sarah administratrix of John Perry.
- accounts of Christopher Bayne executor of Christopher Bayne (CV).
- inventory of Daniell Macomus, by appraisers Nicholas Sheppard & John Marriott.
- inventory of Joseph Sadler (TA), by appraisers Mathew Eareckson & Thomas Baxter.
- inventory of George Ashman (BA), by appraisers Edward Dorsey & Thomas Hedge.
- inventory of Timothy Wakefield, by appraisers John Barron & John Roby.
- inventory of Robert Benson (CH), by appraisers Thomas Chapman & Evan Jones.
- inventory of Thomas Mitchell, by appraisers Francis Green & Andrew Simpson.
- inventory of Allin Steward, by appraisers Mathew Sander & Peter Mackhlan.

18A:71 ...

- inventory of Richard Jones (CH), by

- appraisers John Higgins & John Ford.
- inventory of Charles Tracey (PG), by appraisers James Stoddart & Joshuah Hill. Mentions: leased land.
- inventory of Richard Keen (CV), by appraisers William Williams, Jr. & Jere. Sheredine.
- accounts of Richard Waplington administrator of William Raycroft.
- accounts of Philip Griffin who married relict & administratrix of Richard Rawlings (AA).
- inventory of Robert Gover, Sr., by appraisers Robert Wood & John Stephens.
- accounts of Elisabeth Nicholson executrix of John Nicholson.
- accounts of Cornelius Innis administrator of William Innis (SO).
- accounts of William Turvile who married executrix of William Tomkins.
- inventory of Leonard Camperson (TA), by appraisers George Vinson & Richard Kempstone.
- accounts of Richard Jones & his wife Ann administratrix of William Burgess (AA).
- additional accounts of Clement Hill & Luke Gardiner executors of Richard Gardner (SM).
- accounts of Henry Ridgley, Sr. administrator of William Brown (AA).

18A:72 ...
- accounts of Charles Low who married relict of Thomas Johnson (SO).

Wills exhibited:
- John Scott (CV).
- Samuel Copeland (PG).
- Elisabeth Cades (CV).
- Peter Hill.
- William Atchison (PG).
- Richard Chaffee.
- Robert Catlen (SO).
- John Leach (CV).
- John Sallers.
- John Pennington (CE).
- Garrett Murrey.
- Daniell Macknell.
- John Hodgson.
- Francis Child.

Court Session: July 1700

18A:73   . . .
- John Willis (CE).
- James Holloway.
- Robert Gover (AA).
- Robert Jones (CH).
- nuncupative will of Robert Benson, proved by John Elder & Mary Miller.
- nuncupative will of William Robinson.
- Henry Ridgley, Jr. (AA).

(no surname)
   Christian 14
   James 135
   John 38
   Samuell 133
   Thomas 125
   Walter 169

Abell
   Ann 76, 77, 185
   Samuell 76, 77, 185
Abington
   John 10, 23, 32,
     94, 151
Abott
   Samuell 72
Abotthe
   Samuell 39
Abrams
   Jacob 81
Adam
   James 164
Adams
   Charles 12, 162
   Francis 127, 133
   Grace 127
   Mary 12
   Philip 183
   Richard 12
   Thomas 183
Addams
   Francis 128
Addison
   John 48, 74, 155,
     168, 176
   Joseph 65
Aisquith
   William 36, 115,
     125, 160
Aketh
   George 75
Alcock
   Thomas 53, 54, 60
Alden
   William 152
Aldern
   William 161
Alderne
   William 137

Aldredge
   Mary 26, 34
Aldridge
   Henry 14
   Mary 14, 54, 82,
     130
Alford
   John 22, 73, 82
   Mathias 14, 22
Allaby
   Peter 167
Allen
   John 70, 97, 107,
     128, 133
   Mull 113
   Philip 70
   Phillip 128
   Robert 183
   William 107
   Zachariah 86
Alleson
   Charles 55
Allford
   Mathias 83, 180
Allin
   William 18
Allison
   Charles 55, 74
Althea
   John 49
Ambross
   Frances 84
Anderson
   Andrew 89
   John 98, 150
   Peter 136, 137
   William 28, 91, 143
Andrew
   Nathaniell 139, 141
Andrews
   Anthony 6
Annis
   Thomas 77
Armestrong
   Edward 112
Armstrong
   Edward 109, 179
   Francis 20
   John 160
Arnall

Susannah 90
Arnold
John 150
Susannah 139, 146
Arnoll
Thomas 59
Arterby
Thomas 109
Asbestone
William 30
Ashdale
(N) 56
Ashdell
John 49
Ashford
Michaell 108
Ashman
Ann 59, 63
Elisabeth 171
George 33, 35, 40,
47, 48, 140,
171, 185
Richard 59, 60, 63,
75
Ashwick
Thomas 176
Askew
John 144
Richard 174
Askin
John 134
Askins
John 30, 92
Askue
Philip 71
Richard 90
Asman
George 182
Asquith
William 49, 114
Atchison
William 98, 186
Atckison
Robert 11
Athe
John 142
Athea
John 142
Atheson
William 108
Athey
George 25
John 142
Atkin

John 71
Atkins
John 20, 69, 84,
130, 181
Mary 130, 181
Attaway
Thomas 12
Atterbury
Joan 172
Thomas 172, 179
Attkins
John 98
Attway
Thomas 57
Attwood
John 156
Richard 77, 125,
161
Thomas 123
Atwood
Richard 15
Auger
Nicholas 132
Auld
James 103
Austin
Samuell 85
Thomas 55
Ayrs
Elenor 172
George 172

Bacon
John 70
Bagg
Mary 17, 142
Thomas 17, 142
Bailley
John 37
Baily
Richard 178
Baker
Ann 139
Isaack 151
James 57
John 20
Joseph 106
Michaell 18
Samuell 139, 184
Thomas 50, 51, 156
Baldwin
John 66, 85, 102
Baldwyn

John 110, 139, 147
Baley
   Richard 52
Ball
   Benjamin 183
   Edmond 109
   Edward 69, 105,
     111, 143, 177
   Pricilla 143
   Priscilla 177
Ballamy
   Mathew 52
Ballard
   Mr. 100, 121
Baly
   Edward 92
Bane
   Christopher 19
Banister
   John 53, 65
Bannester
   John 55, 74
   William 76
Barber
   Newman 109, 111
   Stephen 112
Bardwell
   Ann 7
Barey
   Daniell 30
Barker
   John 55, 65
   Mary 33, 83, 140
   Richard 73
   Thomas 33, 75, 140
   William 83
Barkr
   John 60
Barner
   Mary 107
   Thomas 107
Barnes
   Henry 70, 97
   Math. 158
   Mathew 55, 97
Barnet
   Mary 177
Barnett
   Mary 156, 182
   Thomas 36, 136
Barns
   Mathew 70, 74, 158,
     164, 174
Barrett

John 48
Barron
   John 185
Barrott
   James 87
Bartlett
   John 80
   Sarah 80
Barton
   John 128
   William 22, 62,
     141, 148, 164
Bass
   Charles 130
Batchelour
   Catherine 13
   William 13, 23
Bates
   William 88, 95
Batie
   John 20
Batson
   Christopher 91
   E. 140
   Edward 48, 52, 68,
     72, 95, 100,
     102, 110, 116,
     117, 118, 120,
     124, 134, 142,
     143
Batten
   John 26
Battery
   John 128
Battes
   William 151
Battson
   Edward 87
Batty
   John 56
Baxter
   Thomas 185
Bayle
   John 76
Bayley
   John 15
   Richard 54
   Robert 58, 115
Bayly
   John 29
   Margret 31
   Robert 31
Bayne
   Capt. 168, 169

Christopher 185
John 4, 62, 70,
     158, 163
Beach
   Elias 115
Bead
   Nicholas 55
Beadle
   Edward 181
Beale
   Col. 143
   James 78, 111
   Ninian 34, 123,
      143, 149
   Thomas 42
Bean
   Francis 142
   John 48
Beane
   Christopher 122
   John 48
Beanes
   Christopher 122,
      149
Beard
   John 53
   Nich. 53
   Richard 4, 54, 100,
      104, 139, 161
   William 53
Bearne
   Elisabeth 71
Beason
   Thomas 24
Beaumond
   Richard 144
Beaumont
   Richard 20
Beck
   Charles 31
   Edward 93
   Elias 29
   John 93
   Mary 93
Beddle
   Edward 18
Beech
   Elias 58
   John 61
Beecher
   John 63
Beedle
   Edward 147
Bell

Daniell 76, 114
James 103
Major 120
Bellamy
   Mathew 103
Bellford
   William 18
Belt
   Elisabeth 96
   John 96
Bembridge
   Christopher 89, 125
Benger
   Robert 181
Bennet
   Richard 28
Bennett
   Elisabeth 116
   John 78, 102, 116,
      131, 132, 143,
      149, 151, 174,
      176
   Mr. 1
   R. 41
   Richard 1, 36, 37,
      41, 47, 118,
      120, 121, 122
Benning
   Henry 73
Bennitt
   John 162
Bensher
   Richard 90
Benson 171
   Ann 25
   Elisabeth 25
   James 17, 25, 26,
      38, 80, 90, 134,
      147
   Perry 25
   Robert 58, 70, 129,
      131, 185, 187
   Stephen 104, 126,
      170
Benton
   Marke 22
   Richard 15, 30, 49
   Sarah 49
Berckhead
   Richard 73
Berkhead
   Richard 29
Bermont
   Charles 72

Berry
  Benjamin 3
  James 149, 182
Bevan
  Charles 178
Beven
  Charles 148
  Mary 148
Bexley
  W. 21
Bickesteth
  (N) 171
Bigger
  (N) 23
  John 7, 9, 21, 46,
    78, 79, 101,
    124, 152, 177,
    181
Biggs
  Robert 69
  Seth 10, 113, 114
Bile
  James 58
Birckhead
  Margatt 106
Bird
  Abraham 109, 111,
    112
  William 164
Birkhead
  Abraham 185
  Margarett 105
  Nehemiah 172
Bishop
  Roger 20
Bishopp
  Roger 56
Biston
  George 72
Black
  Charles 71
Blackenden
  Thomas 81
Blacketter
  John 152
Blackiston
  Col. 22
  Madam 10
  Nehemiah 10, 119,
    152
Blackman
  Thomas 92
Blackmore
  John 67

Blackner
  Elisabeth 149
  John 149
Blackston
  Ebenezar 50
Blackstone
  Ebenezar 51
Blackwell
  Sarah 113
  Thomas 47, 74, 105,
    113, 123, 133,
    146, 156, 162
Bladen
  W. 49, 64, 165
  William 10, 21, 22,
    50, 54, 88, 95,
    110, 123, 155,
    161
Blades
  Robert 160, 161,
    183
Blake
  Ann 177
  Charles 37, 143
  Hen. Mar. 18
  Jane 19
  Thomas 19, 25, 27,
    110, 112, 129,
    177
Blakiston
  Ebenezar 156
  N. 122
  Nathaniel 155
  Nathaniell 122
  Nehemiah 124
Bland
  James 93
  Thomas 122
Blane
  (N) 171
Blaney
  Da. 127
  Daniell 136
  David 96, 103, 161
  Katherine 136
Blanford
  Tabitha 54
  Thomas 54, 66
Blany
  David 91
Blare
  John 138
Blatchford
  Stephen 48, 66

Blay
    Edward 2, 21, 29,
      130
Blinckhorne
    Robert 94
Blinkhorne
    Robert 94, 109, 147
Blunt
    Robert 72, 120, 138
Boarman
    William 75
Bodkin
    Peter 7
Bojo
    John 144
Bole
    David 109
Boly
    James 119
Bond
    Benjamin 87, 103,
      132, 134
    Giles 52, 64
    Peter 88, 95
Bonner
    Henry 24, 40
Booker
    John 53, 176, 183
    Thomas 38
Bookr
    John 60
Boon
    Humphrey 165, 181
    Richard 52
Boone
    Humfrey 94
    Humphrey 22, 48,
      118, 148
    Humphry 110, 140,
      151
    Humply 132
    Jane 81
    John 12, 81
Boorne
    William 15
Booth
    John 71, 83, 84, 98
Boothbey
    Edward 124
Boothby
    Edward 1, 9, 12,
      169, 178, 181
    Elisabeth 178, 181
Boram

John 39, 62
Boreman
    William 144, 151,
      168, 172, 184
Bosman
    William 137
Boston
    Henry 18, 81
Boswell
    William 115
Botler
    Henry 180
Botton
    Christopher 127
Bouge
    John 26
    Mr. 26
Boughton
    Katherine 55
    Mr. 21
    Ri. 49
    Richard 13, 16, 37,
      39, 42, 43, 61,
      73, 97, 113,
      133, 151, 164,
      172
    Samuell 43
Boulay
    James 146, 147
Boules
    Crout 142
    John 142
Bourne
    Elisabeth 30, 119,
      146, 147
    Samuell 30, 146
Bouye
    John 32, 62, 64, 67
Bowdell
    John 126
Bowdle
    Phebe 17
    Thomas 17
Bowen
    Jonas 12, 139, 140,
      179
    Martha 139, 179
Bowers
    Jonas 125
Bowes
    George 159
Bowlery
    Fran. 60
    Francis 58

Bowles
    Anthony 125
    Cicllia 143
    James 125
    John 143
Bowling
    James 35
    John 97
Bowls
    John 184
Bown
    Mary 124
    William 125
Bows
    George 162
Box
    Thomas 149
Boy
    Jennett 129
    John 129
Boyce
    Ailce 37
    John 48, 140
    Ruth 48
Boyd
    John 69
Boye
    John 58
Boyer
    William 72
Boyle
    James 74
Bozman
    John 3
Braban
    William 179
Braborne
    William 30
Brace
    John 16
Bradhurst
    John 179
Bradley
    Robert 98, 133
    William 112, 129,
      183
Bradly
    R. 62
    Robert 62, 100
Braff
    Thomas 126
Braine
    Benjamin 141
Brandt

Rando. 158
Randolph 174
Branham
    Cornelius 125
Brannock
    John 120
Brasheire
    John 63
Braunan
    Cornelius 96
Brawner
    Henry 113, 129,
      131, 133
    Mary 113
Bray
    James 149
    Peirce 97
Brent
    Capt. 21
    George 11, 19, 43,
      44
    Henry 9, 98, 151
    Jane 43
    Rando. 128, 131
Brett
    George 16, 59, 129
Brewarton
    William 84
Brewer
    William 89
Brewerton
    William 84
Brewnett
    Robert 23
Brickenden
    Thomas 78
Bridge
    Joseph 124
Bridges
    Thomas 69, 123
Bright
    John 31, 92, 115
    William 57
Brightwell
    Richard 20, 100,
      103, 133, 178
Brimmer
    Elisabeth 76
Brine
    John 160
Brisco
    Thomas 45
Briscoe
    John 178

Mr. 5
Philip 168
Thomas 54
Britt
  George 16, 120, 143
Brittaine
  John 130
Britten
  John 130
Brittingham
  William 8
BroadWay
  Elisabeth 127
  Robert 127, 159
  Samuell 159, 162
  Sarah 159
Brockson
  Bridget 129
  Elisabeth 82
  John 72, 129
  William 72, 82
Brook
  John 184
Brooke
  Abraham 77
  Baker 6, 20, 56
  Catherine 56
  Charles 1, 6, 9,
    77, 109
  James 149
  John 53, 85
  Judith 8, 21, 85
  Leonard 77
  Mary 85
  Roger 7, 77, 105
  Sarah 85
  Thomas 155, 168,
    173
Brookes
  Charles 20
  John 40, 53, 149
  Judith 40
Broom
  John 38
Broome
  John 38, 121
Brothers
  Robert 149, 152,
    179
Brown
  Ann 53
  Daniel 185
  Daniell 179
  David 71, 84

Edward 138
James 106
John 31
Samuel 184
Samuell 25, 90
William 173, 174,
  186
Browne
  Alexander 146
  Ann 53, 60
  Daniell 26, 149
  David 146
  Edward 116
  Elisabeth 96, 103
  Francis 106, 126
  James 15, 96, 113,
    125, 126
  Jane 117
  John 31, 57, 96,
    103
  Lewe de Roche 50
  Margarett 146
  Robert 11
  Samuell 12, 124
  Thomas 12, 123
  William 116, 117
Browner
  Henry 53, 55
  Mary 53
Brownton
  John 180
Bruce
  George 116, 157,
    169
  Rose 116, 169
Bruff
  Rhoda 96
  Thomas 127
Bruse
  Rose 157
Bryan
  Daniel 56
  Elinor 35
  William 35, 59
Bryant
  Lydia 136
Buckle
  (N) 7
Buckley
  Patrick 134
Buckmaster
  Daniell 149
Bull
  William 31

Bullett
  Elisabeth 20
Bullock
  Thomas 135
Burch
  George 124
Burdett
  Parthania 42
Burdit
  Parthenia 42
Burditt
  Parthania 43
  Parthenia 43, 55,
    65
Burford
  Anne 42, 43
  Madam 49
  Mr. 49
  Mrs. 171
  Thomas 53, 55
Burges
  Anne 66
  Charles 61
  Edward 63, 64
  George 95
  John 28
  Susan 61
  William 3, 47, 55,
    61, 63, 64, 66,
    85, 101, 106,
    112, 113, 139
Burgess
  Ann 101
  William 61, 101,
    110, 156, 160,
    186
Burgis
  Edward 96
Burgiss
  Capt. 87
  Edward 103
  George 89
Burket
  Patience 92
  Richard 30
Burkett
  Patience 115
Burman
  Samuell 177
  William 177, 178
Burnett
  Elisabeth 148
  Mary 148
  Thomas 137

Burrill
  Proomce 115
Burrows
  John 58
Burt
  Henry 175
Busey
  Paul 111
Bussey
  Hezekiah 149
Butler
  Charles 141
  Henry 78, 129
Butterie
  Francis 70
Butterworth
  Michaell 12, 32
Buttery
  Francis 133
Buttler
  Cecill 114
  Henry 149
Button
  Nathaniell 93
Buttons
  Nathaniell 74
Byles
  James 128

Cades
  Elisabeth 186
Cadle
  Zacariah 66
  Zacharia 50
Caldwell
  James 83
Cale
  Peter 130
Cambell
  Alexander 130
  John 30
  Thomas 30
  Walter 82, 120, 140
Camble
  Walter 34
Camperson
  Leonard 48, 134,
    186
  Margaret 134
Cample
  Walter 26
Cane
  Elener 178

John 86
Canelly
    Bryan 135
Cannon
    James 93, 157, 163
    Stephen 138
Cape
    John 127, 135
Capell
    Benjamin 119, 145
    Thomas 139
Carbery
    John Bap. 72
    John Baptista 2,
        37, 114
    John Bta. 96
Carbury
    John Bapt. 123
Carey
    Robert 184
Carles
    Charles 77
Carnall
    Daniell 38
Carnell
    Daniell 24
    Deborah 24
Carpenter
    Henry 51, 59, 60
    Humphrey 60
Carr
    James 107
    Martha 156, 157,
        169
    Philip 184
    Walter 156, 157,
        169
    William 6, 80
Carroll
    (N) 100, 101
    Char. 166
    Charles 1, 19, 21,
        25, 34, 44, 63,
        86, 100, 101,
        145, 165, 168,
        170
    Mr. 21, 32, 101
Carsey
    (N) 87
    Elisabeth 4
    James 4, 87
Carss
    Robert 12
Carter

Jane 140
John 122
Philip 4
Valentine 116, 121
William 60, 138,
    140
Carver
    Richard 173
Carvil
    Mr. 119
Carvile
    (N) 100, 101
    John 93
    Mr. 26, 32
    Ro. 43
    Robert 1, 10, 19,
        20, 45, 68, 86
Carvill
    John 86, 115, 130,
        164
    Robert 40
    Thomas 114
Carvy
    Robert 177
Catlen
    Robert 186
Catlyn
    Robert 183
Cattae
    Benjamin 138
Catterson
    Katherine 137
Catterton
    Michael 59
Cattrell
    William 130
Causeen
    Ignatius 55
Cavan
    Patrick 163
Cawser
    Philip 8
Ceason
    Ann 125
    James 125
Ceciell
    Joshua 50
Cecill
    Jo. 111
    John 57
    Joshua 3, 25, 50,
        64, 98, 100,
        108, 111, 133,
        143, 148

Jossuah 77
Josuah 78
Ceecill
  Joshua 65, 66
Certain
  Robert 16, 52
Certaine
  Mary 16
Cesing
  John 73
Chafe
  John 41
  Richard 41, 127
Chaffee
  Ann 149
  Richard 120, 123,
    135, 149, 186
Chaires
  John 17, 84
Chambarett
  Richard 184
Chamberline
  Samuell 76
Chambers
  Richard 84
Chandler
  (N) 21
  Col. 11
  Jane 11, 42, 43
  Mary 11
  Richard 19, 42, 43,
    44, 48, 58, 61
  William 11, 19, 42,
    43, 44, 55, 74,
    129
Chapell
  Alexander 50
  Henry 171, 181
  John 4, 24, 145
  Mary 171
Chaplin
  Francis 39
Chapman
  John 69, 78, 98
  Thomas 70, 185
Chappell
  Alexander 86, 104,
    110, 158
  Allexander 66, 67,
    106, 108
  Elisabeth 104, 110
  Henry 89, 94, 99
  John 68, 88, 94,
    103, 119

Charlett
  Richard 2, 9, 21,
    64, 123
Chatham
  Francis 139
  Joane 139
Chattam
  Francis 159
Cheason
  Ann 125
  James 125
Cheires
  John 52
Cherribub
  John 172
Cheseldyn
  Esq. 7, 29
  Kenelm 15, 26, 48,
    106
  Mr. 178
Cheshire
  Richard 52
Chessum
  William 29, 58
Cheverell
  John 15
Chevirell
  John 92
Chew
  Ann 104, 105, 110
  Benjamin 25, 172,
    185
  Calleb 85
  Joseph 25, 88, 95
  Samuell 18, 85,
    104, 105, 172
Chilcock
  James 41
  Mary 41
Chilcott
  Anthony 163
Child
  Abraham 64, 85
  Francis 186
Chishire
  Richard 10
Chittham
  John 112, 158
Chrichley
  James 104
Chrismas
  Charles 30
Churbey
  Peter 138

Church
   Thomas 144
Clapcott
   William 7
Clare
   Marke 20, 25
Clark
   (N) 101
   Andrew 97
   Conier 70
   Coniers 99
   Edward 71, 159, 162
   John 70, 99, 165
   Peter 73, 84
   Philip 45, 179
   Phillip 37, 45
   Richard 103
   Thomas 168
   William 35
Clarke
   Abraham 99
   Benoni 16
   Daniel 54
   Daniell 13, 25, 60
   John 14, 96
   Peter 68, 91, 116
   Petter 37
   Phil. 40
   Philip 5, 6, 11,
      15, 19, 21, 23,
      34, 46
   Phillip 37, 40, 85
   Ro. 76
   Robert 32, 60, 98
   Thomas 3, 54
   William 25, 68, 98,
      118
Claxon
   Thomas 151
Clayland
   James 175, 182
Clayton
   Henry 136
   William 82, 136,
      161
Clegett
   Thomas 102
Cleland
   (N) 171
Clemens
   Thomas 159
Clement
   John 61, 74
Clements

Elisabeth 80
   Thomas 80, 127
Clerk
   John 128
Clerke
   Daniel 54
Clift
   Ellinor 33
   John 33
Clifts
   Eleanor 53
   John 54
Clinson
   George 162
Clouds
   Nicholas 84
   Richard 31, 92
Coale
   Edward 77
   John 83
   William 47
Coard
   Thomas 139
Coates
   Leonard 40
   Nicholas 77
Coats
   Honorable 141
Cobbage
   John 116
Cockey
   Sarah 47, 67
   Thomas 47, 67
   William 4
Coffer
   Francis 70, 174
   Thomas 70, 97, 158,
      174
Coker
   Dr. 141
   William 167
Cole
   Edward 30, 70, 77,
      109
   George 67, 105,
      109, 180
   Peter 29
   Stephen 162, 170,
      171, 181
Coleman
   Mary 173
   Thomas 173
Coles
   Henry 104

Coley
    John 115
Collens
    Barbara 84
    Thomas 84
Colliar
    William 95
Collier
    Alice 85
    Francis 99
    Robert 137
    Thomas 89, 90, 132
    William 89
Collins
    Samuell 14
Collman
    Ben. 84
    Benjamin 84, 160,
      174
Collyer
    Francis 122
    Sarah 122
    William 123
Colory
    Francis 75
Comberford
    Garrett 6
Combs
    Edward 162
Comegis
    Cornelius 15
Comegys
    William 4
Conely
    Bryan 147
Conley
    William 111
Connell
    Daniell 98
    James 75
Conner
    John 27, 28, 137
Conneway
    Joseph 89, 100, 109
Connorrll
    Dennis 35
    Mary 35
Connoway
    Joseph 110, 132
Connter
    Jarvis 60
Connworth
    Michaell 89
Consene

Elisabeth 82
    John 82
Constable
    Henry 22
    Kathern 48
Conwith
    Michaell 125
Coode
    Col. 182
Cook
    Morgan 89
Cooke
    (N) 56
    Jane 99
    Morgan 94, 95, 99
    Thomas 5, 49, 81
Cookery
    Samuell 73
Cookesey
    Sarah 75
Cooksey
    Philip 13, 61
    Samuell 92, 96
    Sarah 55, 61
Cooley
    William 123
Cooper
    John 92
    Nicholas 42
    Patience 161
    Robert 66, 72, 120,
      160
    Roger 172
    William 3, 7, 27
Coopis
    John 174
Copage
    John 47, 48
Copas
    John 160
    Sarah 160
Copedge
    Mr. 171
Copeland
    Samuel 186
    Samuell 69
Copley
    Lyonel 176, 181
Copnell
    Edward 30
    Margrett 30
Coppage
    John 107, 116, 134,
      138, 140

Coppedge
  John 47, 66, 80
Corben
  Nicholas 12
Corbin
  Alice 12
  Nicholas 12
Cordea
  Marke 10
Cork
  Philip 36
Cornelisson
  Andrew 166
Cornelius
  John 119, 179
  Peter 51, 59
Cornish
  John 16, 124, 129
  Martha 16, 129
  Peter 131
Cornoly
  Petter 150
Cosden
  (N) 5, 32
  Alfonso 122
  Alphonso 122
  Ann 149, 175
  Thomas 122
Cosens
  John 175
Costen
  Stephen 27
Costin
  Henry 72
  Stephen 27
Coston
  Comfort 56
  Henry 82
Cottman
  Benjamin 161
Cottrill
  Elisabeth 49
  Ja. 49
Coulbourne
  William 84
Coursey
  Elisabeth 99
  Henry 22
  William 18, 23, 80,
    81, 91, 99, 126
Court
  John 155
Courtis
  William 28

Courtney
  Thomas 36
Courts
  John 7
Coventry
  Ralph 128
  William 117, 128,
    156
Cowly
  John 76
Cox
  Henry 67, 71
  Thomas 73, 82
Coxnell
  Edward 58
Cozens
  John 64, 85
  Mary 64, 175
Crane
  John 108
Cranford
  J. 106
  James 10, 23, 32,
    33, 144, 145,
    147, 152, 180
  Mr. 32
  Nathaniell 71, 105,
    129
Craxon
  Thomas 129
Craxton
  John 61
  Thomas 58, 59, 60
Craycroft
  Ignatius 50, 54
  John 50, 54
Cromwell
  Mr. 171
  Richard 13, 171
  William 47, 48
Crook
  John 76, 77
  Robert 180
  Sarah 76
Crooke
  John 59, 143
  Robert 15, 28
  Sarah 58
Crudgentone
  Roger 85
Crumwell
  Richard 35
Cuccens
  John 3

Cullen
    James 107, 122,
        132, 170
    Katherine 122, 132
Cullens
    James 10
Cullison
    John 163
Culver
    Henry 65
Cumberford
    Garrat 20
Cumberland
    John 115
Cunnerell
    Dennis 59
Curry
    John 30, 115
Curtis
    James 183
    William 68
Curtiss
    Michaell 125
Cutchin
    Robert 182

Daft
    Charles 57, 185
Dakins
    William 109
Dale
    William 18, 170
Dallahide
    Francis 69, 90
Dalton
    Nathaniell 112
Danee
    William 146
Danelly
    Ann 130
    Patrick 130
Daniell
    Humphrey 124
    Richard 127, 132,
        134
Daniellson
    Daniell 65
Danielly
    Ann 63
    Patrick 34, 63
Dannelly
    Ann 85
    Patrick 85

Dant
    Thomas 57
Danverin
    Manus 87
Danvies
    Thomas 86
Danvis
    Thomas 50, 86, 108
Darbin
    Thomas 13
Dare
    Nathaniel 56
    Nathaniell 102, 105
Darnall
    Henry 34, 62, 68,
        86, 98, 100,
        101, 165, 166,
        168, 175, 182
    John 101, 166, 168,
        175, 182
    Mary 98
Darnell
    Col. 20
Dasheill
    George 137
    James 137
    Robert 137
    Thomas 137
Dashell
    James 27
Dashiell
    James 27, 28, 71,
        84
Daught
    Charles 30, 31
Dauson
    Thomas 114
Dauvas
    Thomas 66, 67
Davenish
    Ann 132
    Robert 132, 134
Davidson
    Isbell 124
Davies
    Griffin 164
    John 71
    Thomas 78
Davis
    Ann 35
    Griffin 128
    John 18, 31, 32,
        55, 56, 114, 135
    Joseph 142

Mary 31, 32
Phillip 95
Richard 3, 97
Thomas 60, 67
Davison
   Christopher 167
   Patrick 124
Dawkins
   James 78, 112
   Joseph 109, 112
   William 105, 112
Dawson
   Edward 65
   John 38, 90, 102,
     161, 178
   Ralph 38, 123
   Thomas 108, 148
Day
   Edward 138
   Humphry 90
   Mary 138
   Robert 59, 79, 102
Dayne
   Dennis 124
Deakins
   Thomas 57
Dean
   Elisabeth 163, 180
   William 163, 180
Deaver
   John 10, 140
   Richard 86
Deavor
   Richard 67
Deavour
   Richard 25, 26
Debbs
   John 152
Dehiniossia
   Allexander 73
DelaGeorge
   Arnoldus 130
Delahay
   George 128, 131,
     164
   Susan 164
   Susannah 128, 131
   Thomas 182
Delehay
   Thomas 38
Deliniosa
   Alexander 123
   Mary 123
Demondidier

Anthony 24
Denew
   Thomas 107, 123
Dennis
   Dannock 27
   Dunnock 27, 161,
     174
Denny
   Christopher 81, 82
Denro
   Thomas 138
Dent
   (N) 101, 165
   Elisabeth 42
   John 6
   Maj. 113
   Michaell 6
   Mr. 23, 59
   Peter 8, 124, 137,
     176
   William 11, 19, 21,
     26, 39, 42, 43,
     44, 48, 53, 55,
     58, 62, 101,
     117, 122, 145,
     156, 158, 168,
     169, 172, 176,
     183
Denton
   Henry 24, 34, 42
   Mary 42
   Mr. 24
   William 13, 80
Denwood
   Leven 28
   Levin 27, 144
Derrumple
   William 79
Deserton
   John 56
Devall
   John 117
Devoran
   Menas 162
Devoren
   Manus 145
Devorin
   Manus 117
Devorriland
   Manus 95
Dickenson
   Edward 79
Dickinson
   Edward 71

Sarah 71
Dickson
    Thomas 105, 106,
        108
Digges
    Col. 29
    Edward 10, 16
    Elisabeth 10
    William 10
Dike
    Mary 53
    Mathew 53, 60
Dine
    John 175
Dines
    Thomas 158, 162
Dinnes
    Thomas 60
Disharoone
    Joane 4
    Michaell 3
Disney
    William 104, 161
Diston
    Ralph 138
Divall
    Marreen 113
Dixon
    James 19, 152, 158
    John 152
    Thomas 97, 108,
        111, 161, 179
    William 38, 80, 91
Dobbs
    John 159, 162
    Mary 159, 162
Dodd
    Jane 49
    Richard 49
Dodson
    Samuell 53
Doland
    Amy 116, 138
    William 116, 138
Dolland
    Amy 173
    William 173
Dolons
    Nathaniell 123
Dolson
    Samuell 181
Don
    Robert 180
Done

Robert 99
Donelly
    Patrick 180
Donelson
    Thomas 136
Dooman
    John 131
Dorington
    William 63
Dorman
    Thomas 53, 74
Dorrington
    Ann 5
    William 5, 23, 33,
        83, 85, 130
Dorsett
    John 65
Dorsey
    Edward 185
Dorson
    John 68, 81
Dossen
    Thomas 162
Dotton
    Nat 111
Douch
    Hugh 93
Douglas
    Mary 20
Dove
    Robert 105
Dowdall
    John 47, 113, 169
Dowdell
    John 88
Down
    Mary 8
    Robert 8
Downes
    John 117
    Margarett 118
Downs
    Margarett 162
Dowse
    William 26
Doxey
    John 92, 126
Doyn
    Dennis 75
    Joshua 92
Doyne
    Dennis 55
    Jane 55, 92, 96
    Jesse 43, 74, 111

John 70, 116
Joshua 91, 96
Mary 116
Robert 11, 34, 74
Draper
    Lawrence 50, 51,
        117, 133
Drew
    Anthony 12
Drue
    Anthony 89
Dryden
    Henry 20, 50, 69
Duccat
    Richard 139
Duckett
    Richard 117, 161
Duckworth
    Ann 125
    John 125
Duggins
    John 29
Duglass
    Mary 144
    Robert 144
Duncalfe
    Edmond 108, 109
    Edward 162
Duncon
    (N) 61
    Elisabeth 61
Dunevan
    Cornelius 76
Dunkean
    Elisabeth 3
    James 3
Dunkin
    John 65, 78
    Sarah 65, 78
Durdon
    Stephen 17
Dutchson
    James 161, 168, 170
Duvall
    Elisabeth 13
    Lewis 104
    Mareen 120, 146
    Samuell 13, 54
Dworen
    Manus 100
Dwyer
    Edmond 74
    Edward 70

Eagle
    Robert 107, 110,
        118, 132, 148,
        151, 165, 181
Eareckson
    Mathew 103, 185
Earle
    Michaell 81, 82
Earp
    Thomas 107
Easterling
    John 105, 109
Eastop
    Richard 16
Ebden
    Elisabeth 160
    William 160
Eccleston
    Hu. 99
    Hugh 24, 40, 150
    Mr. 23
Edelen
    Richard 97
Edgar
    Richard 151
Edlen
    Richard 75
Edloe
    Joseph 11
Edmans
    Thomas 79
Edmondson
    James 28, 39
    John 2, 11, 17, 26,
        28, 33, 39, 53,
        68, 80, 81, 119
    Sarah 28
    Thomas 28, 148, 183
    William 17, 28, 68,
        80, 119
Edmundson
    James 72
    John 72
    Sarah 72
    Thomas 69, 72, 99
    William 72, 156,
        157, 159, 163,
        169
Edwards
    Ann 56
    Edward 160
    John 32
    Joseph 79, 185

Page 205

Edwin
    William 166
Edwyn
    William 167
Egcleston
    Mr. 23
Egerton
    Ann 125
    Charles 125, 126,
       133
    John 125, 126
Eggleston
    Hugh 54
Elburn
    Hugh 2
Elder
    John 187
Elders
    William 124
Elderseley
    Henry 28
Eldersley
    Henry 15, 72, 130
    Parnell 15
Eldesly
    Henry 180
    Parnell 180
Eldridge
    Jeremiah 108, 129,
       149, 184
    Jeremy 172
    John 93, 180
Eley
    Mathias 145
Elget
    William 4
Elles
    Hugh 59
    Ruth 59
    William 36
Ellett
    Daniell 98
Elliott
    Daniell 108
    William 53, 65
Ellis
    Hugh 5, 7, 21, 24,
       26, 32, 45, 78,
       79, 123
    John 93
    Ruth 32, 78
Ellit
    William 128
Ellsey

John 45, 112
Elmes
    William 82
Elsey
    Arnold 40, 100,
       101, 119, 121
    John 5, 21, 67, 71,
       86
Elzey
    (N) 178
    Arnold 4, 19, 25
    John 22
Emerson
    John 68, 91, 103,
       136
    Thomas 103
Emery
    Arthur 135
    Katherine 135
Emett
    John 69
Emmett
    Hannah 69, 78
    John 78, 98
Endley
    Richard 5
Ennalls
    Thomas 2
Ennis
    Thomas 29, 115
Ereckson
    Margarett 146
    Mary 146
    Mathew 121
Erickson
    Hugh 130
    Mathew 47, 116, 123
Erreckson
    Math. 2
Errickson
    Mathew 107, 152
Estall
    John 80
Estell
    John 5
Esterling
    Henry 79
Estop
    Richard 164
Eubanc
    Thomas 89
Eubanks
    Richard 71
    Thomas 81

Evans
    Anthony 114, 160
    Benjamin 49
    Edward 165, 183
    Elisabeth 79
    Job 185
    John 74, 114, 122,
        125, 133, 160
    Nicholas 84, 138
    Peter 127
    Richard 67
    Sarah 185
    Thomas 18, 90, 135
    Walter 56
Evens
    Obadia 26
Ewbanks
    Richard 91
Eweings
    John 90
Ewin
    John 182
Exerkson
    Mathew 121

Fairbanck
    David 135
Falkener
    Martin 65
Falkner
    Martin 65
    Mary 65
Fardery
    John 185
Farfar
    William 90, 124
Farmer
    Elisabeth 72
    Samuell 72, 81
Farrell
    Patrick 57
Farthing
    John 181
Fary
    Joseph 67
Feanly
    John 109
Fenix
    John 32
Fenoe
    Symon 146, 147
Fenox
    Symon 106

Fenwick
    John 60, 76, 77
Fernely
    Henry 25
Fernley
    Henry 38, 121, 176
    Margaret 38
    Winnifred 121
Fernly
    Henry 20, 24
Ferret
    Mary 56
Ferry
    John 124, 160, 162
Fida
    Richard 20
Fido
    Richard 147
Fields
    John 183
Finch
    Hugh 16
Finley
    James 182
    Robert 170, 171
Finoe
    Symon 161
Fisher
    (N) 23
    Alexander 163
    Ann 35, 91, 147,
        173
    Elisabeth 163
    John 7, 9, 21, 25,
        46, 96, 113,
        165, 181, 183
    Richard 60
    Robert 59, 79
    Thomas 35, 65, 91,
        173
    William 7, 131
Fitchsimons
    Nicholas 42, 48
Fitzgarrett
    Edward 131
Fitzgerald
    Edmund 79
    William 79
FitzGerrard
    Edward 174
    Morris 180
Fitzgerratt
    Morris 164
Fitzgerrett

Edward 158
Fitzsimons
    Martha 32
    Nicholas 32
Fitzsymons
    Mr. 13
    Nicholas 83
Fleasham
    Michaell 140
Fleathear
    Nicholas 117
Fletcher
    Elisabeth 142
Fletham
    Nicholas 64
Flewelyn
    Samuell 184
Floorewood
    Daniel 58
Florewood
    Daniel 56
Floyd
    Daniel 54
    David 25
    James 107, 108, 110
    John 108, 114
    Mary 54
Floyde
    John 109
Fooke
    Anne 42
Forbas
    Alexander 165, 175,
        182
Forbes
    Allexander 101
Ford
    Christopher 53, 60,
        74
    James 41, 47, 109,
        112
    John 79, 186
    Robert 56
Foreman
    Thomas 138
    William 108, 112
Former
    Doroty 75
Forrest
    Elisabeth 50
    John 39, 50, 54
    Richard 15
Foster
    Ralph 73, 92, 106,

110
Robert 31, 114
Fouck
    Hugh 29
Fouke
    Gerrard 19
Fouler
    Sarah 160
Foulkes
    Gerrard 58
Fountaine
    Nicholas 105, 109,
        111, 158
Fout
    Hugh 73
Fowke
    (N) 21
    Anne 42, 43
    Gerard 42
    Gerrard 42, 43, 44,
        48
    Mary 42
Fowkes
    Gerrard 43
Fowler
    Charles 160, 170
    Edward 184
    Sarah 170
Foxon
    James 157, 163
Fraiser
    Alexander 180
Frampton
    Francis 129, 158
Francis
    Frances 96
    Henry 38, 94, 174
    Howell 8, 175
    Mary 88
    Stephen 145, 146,
        147
    Thomas 35, 88, 96
Francklin
    John 8
Francklyn
    Robert 88
Franklin
    John 59, 60
    Richard 82
    Robert 95
Franklyn
    John 184
    Robert 88
Fraughton

Francis 151
Freeborne
   Thomas 148
Freeman
   Ann 31, 56
   Francis 25, 31, 56
   John 88, 145, 147,
     162
   William 24
Freiks
   Henry 160
French
   James 15, 30, 57,
     75, 77, 174
Frisbey
   Benjamin 132
   William 133
Frisby
   William 133
Frisdell
   William 126
Frith
   Henry 127, 137
   Hugh 135
Frizell
   Mary 102
Fry
   Constance 127
   Constant 151
   Edward 167
   John 127, 151, 164
Frye
   Constance 180
   John 180
Fuller
   Edward 4, 38, 94,
     122, 123, 162
   Sarah 122, 162
   William 14, 37,
     102, 103
Furbush
   Alexander 120

Gadsbuy
   Johanna 40
   John 40
Gadsby
   Johannah 54
   John 34, 51, 54, 86
Gaile
   John 68, 94
Gale
   John 20, 156

Margarett 20
Gallampton
   Francis 97
Gallion
   Joseph 12
Galloway
   Richard 68, 148
   Samuell 148
Gambing
   James 25
Gamblin
   James 50, 98
Gambling
   Elisabeth 69, 78
   James 69, 78
Gannt
   Thomas 77
Gardiner
   John 48
   Luke 56, 77, 92,
     97, 115, 186
Gardner
   Alexander 114, 116
   James 129
   John 35
   Luke 125
   Mary 123
   Mathew 129
   Richard 186
Garey
   Lawrence 117, 121
   Mary 117
   William 127, 134,
     175
Garland
   Randall 151
   Randolph 127
Garrett
   Amos 140
   Richard 133, 143
Garruttson
   Garrett 90
Garry
   Lawrence 164
Garterell
   John 172, 182
Gartrill
   John 49
Gary
   George 184
   John 184
   Mary 164
   William 184
Gaskin

William 99
Gasling
  Thomas 60
Gassaway
  Ann 113
  Elisabeth 68
  John 68, 94
  Nicholas 13, 52,
    87, 88, 89, 104,
    113, 147
Gater
  John 165
Gates
  Dorithy 75
  Dorothy 70
  Robert 70, 75
Gather
  John 116, 146, 147
Gatrell
  Jane 49
Gattrell
  John 33
Gault
  Thomas 181
Gaunt
  Thomas 119
Gawdard
  John 76
Gee
  Joshua 144
Gellett
  Walter 79
Gendron
  Mark 33
George
  Dorothy 140, 160
  James 16, 140, 157,
    160, 184
  Sampson 15
  Samson 181
Gerard
  J. 61
  John 96
German
  Lewis 67, 90
Gerrard
  John 61
  Justinian 125
Geskin
  William 99
Gibbs
  Edward 52, 108,
    122, 123, 133
  Richard 9

Gibson
  Elisabeth 90
  Mr. 67
  Robert 82, 130
  William 81
Gilders
  John 82
Gill
  John 88, 95
  Mary 113
  Stephen 171
Gillam
  John 34
Gillens
  John 58
Gilley
  William 94
Gillum
  Jo. 160
Gilly
  Elisabeth 39
  William 39
Ginrood
  Richard 130
Givan
  Robert 138
Givin
  John 184
Glandering
  John 87
Glanfeild
  William 133
Glanvell
  William 36, 84
Glover
  Daniell 135
  Henry 78
  John 18, 81, 150
  William 164, 180
Godard
  Petter 39
Goddard
  Christian 22
  Elias 22
  Sarah 21, 22, 62
Godfrey
  George 74, 75, 127,
    128
Godsgrace
  John 79
Godshall
  John 13, 70, 131
Godson
  John 55

Godward
  Elias 14
Goff
  Bartholomew 65, 178
  Charles 29, 73
  Hannah 178
Goffe
  Charles 30
Goldsborough
  Robert 46
Goodfellow
  (N). 9
Goodman
  Edmon 159
  Edmond 116, 138,
    173
  Edward 162
Goodrick
  Francis 127
Goodwick
  Francis 151
Goosey
  Jonathon 105
Gootherick
  John 182
Gorsuch
  Charles 15
Gosey
  Richard 58
Gosling
  William 27
Gott
  Richard 88, 95
  Robert 40, 102
Gouerly
  Barbara 129
Gough
  Stephen 2, 6, 15,
    31, 76, 77
Gouldbury
  Robert 37
Gouldesborough
  Mr. 29
  R. 40, 46
  Robert 3, 9, 15,
    33, 38, 40, 64,
    68, 85, 102
Gouldesborrough
  Robert 28
Gouldesbury
  Robert 86
Goulds.
  (N) 101
Gouldsmith

George 19, 181
Gourley
  John 129
Gouty
  John 157
Gover
  Robert 172, 186,
    187
Grafton
  Mary 71
  Robert 71
Grason
  (N) 183
Gray
  Andrew 151
  Clary 130
  George 78, 144
  James 29, 87, 130
  John 44, 55, 74,
    83, 124, 139
  Miles 3
  Philladelphia 151
  Thomas 139, 163
  William 139
Green
  Christopher 102
  Edward 8, 184
  Francis 185
  Joshua 43
  Mr. 43
Greenberry
  Ann 28
  Charles 36, 102
  Nicholas 14, 28, 94
Greenbery
  Charles 28
  Nicholas 36
Greenbury
  Charles 117
  Nicholas 140
Greene
  Jane 43
Greenfeild
  Thomas 2, 3, 9, 21,
    62, 64, 100,
    103, 123, 134,
    139
Greenfield
  Thomas 178, 180
Greenhalch
  Edward 152
Greenhalgh
  Elisabeth 161
Greenhall

Elisabeth 126
Greenhaulgh
    Edward 126
Greenslad
    Orlando 145
Greenslade
    Orlando 100, 162
    Orlandoe 66, 133
Greenwell
    James 31, 77
Greenwood
    Samuell 13, 37, 140
Gregory
    Christopher 65,
        117, 156, 158,
        169, 183
Gresham
    John 88, 102
Gressam
    John 96, 118
    Richard 119
Gressum
    Mary 102
    Robert 102
Grey
    John 55
Griffin
    Jane 107
    Philip 186
    Phillip 107, 121,
        122
    Sarah 170
    William 122, 170
Griffith
    Henry 163
    Sarah 162, 164
    William 162, 164
Grigory
    Christopher 88
Groce
    Nicholas 104
Groom
    Moses 12, 182
Groome
    Moses 125, 139
    Samuell 38
Groomelight
    George 95
Groomlight
    George 89
Grover
    John 105
Groves
    Joan 78

John 78
Robert 78
William 51, 61, 63,
    85, 123
Grubb
    Ann 96
    John 92, 96
Grundy
    Robert 38, 134
    Thomas 134
Grunwen
    Thomas 42
Grunwin
    Thomas 31, 96, 104,
        106
Grunwyn
    Thomas 114, 122,
        123, 126, 132
Guibert
    Jos. 15, 181
    Joshua 75, 91
Guilder
    Henry 73
    John 73
Guither
    William 123
Gunnell
    Jane 90
Gunton
    Elisabeth 67, 105,
        111
    Timothy 67, 105
Gutridge
    Henry 26
    Mary 26
Guyatt
    John 20, 93
Guybert
    Josh. 120
    Joshua 124
Guyston
    Joseph 124
Guyther
    Owen 6
    Thomas 125
    William 96, 122,
        125
Gwin
    Christopher 29
Gwinn
    Christopher 76
    John 81
    Sarah 91
    William 91

Gwither
  Owen 73
  Thomas 73, 77
  William 73
Gwyn
  William 143

Hacker
  John 18, 80, 136
Hackett
  Theophilus 107
  Thomas 107
  William 17
Hadaway
  George 104
  Mary 103
  Peter 103
Haddaway
  George 170
  Peter 127
Haddock
  Elisabeth 38
  Richard 38, 56
  Thomas 69, 77, 126,
    132, 133, 161,
    185
Hadly
  John 135
Hagan
  James 113
  Thomas 70, 128
Hagen
  James 75
Haile
  Nicholas 147
Hainer
  John 17
Haleid
  Edward 76
Haley
  Clement 173
  Darby 150, 180
Hall
  Aaron 79
  Alice 8
  Ann 79
  Benjamin 35, 146,
    147, 184
  Charles 8
  Edward 112
  Eli 145
  Elisabeth 114
  Elisha 10, 71, 143,

    145, 147, 148
  John 1, 12, 18, 19,
    34, 83, 89, 90,
    102, 120, 146,
    156, 159, 181
  Joseph 93
  Joshua 133
  Josuah 78
  Martha 1, 12, 18,
    181
  Mary 61, 120, 143,
    184
  Mr. 12
  Sarah 148
  Thomas 59, 77, 92,
    114, 161
  William 13, 61, 71
Haly
  Clement 172
Hambleton
  John 30
  Samuell 91
Hamilton
  Gavin 108
  Gawham 111
  John 42
Hammon
  John 137, 161
Hammond
  John 69
Hamond
  Elisabeth 59
  John 59, 60
  Mr. 116
Hance
  John 49
Hancock
  Robert 173
  Stephen 88
Handcock
  Robert 171
  Stephen 95
Handly
  Manus 163
Hanley
  Manus 163
  Mary 163
Hanslap
  Capt. 61
  Elisabeth 96
  Henry 24, 88, 96,
    102
  Joseph 95, 102
Hanslop

Elisabeth 95
Henry 95
Hanslopp
Elisabeth 88
Joseph 88
Hanson
Hance 133
Hans 17, 96
Haunce 88
John 74
Mary 88
Harbent
William 94
Harbert
William 15, 69, 87,
129, 134, 152
Harbett
Elisabeth 58
Harbotle
John 95
Harbottle
Ann 38
John 38, 89, 99
Hardesty
George 142
Harding
Thomas 102
Hardistey
George 143
Hardman
Jeffy 80
Hardy
Henry 59
William 63
Harebottle
Ann 102
John 102, 173, 174
Harman
Casp. 87
Casparus 93
Katherine 89
Kathern 112
Thomas 147, 173
Harney
Elisabeth 91
Mortaugh 91
Harniss
Jacob 133, 143
Harpam
William 57, 64
Harpham
William 70, 128
Harrington
Charles 93

James 114
John 148
Harris
Edward 135, 136
Elisabeth 105
Francis 53
George 105
John 87, 112
Moses 136
Peter 56
Peter William 56
Richard 103, 105,
126
William 78, 105,
115, 145, 167,
180
Harrison
Charles 104
Edward 52
Elisabeth 52
Erasmus 184
James 17, 148
Joseph 131, 149
Michael 184
Michaell 137
Richard 13, 44, 61,
75, 131, 172,
173
Robert 73, 127,
137, 164
William 17
Hartley
Ann 58
Joseph 58, 92
Hartly
Ann 92
Joseph 92
Hartshorne
George 108
Harvey
Robert 47
Thomas 149
Wenfred 47
Harvy
Robert 103
Harwood
John 120
Haryson
John 6
Haselwood
Henry 139
John 130
Haslewood
John 59

William 174
Hatfeild
William 18
Hatfield
William 127
Hatton
John 103, 129
William 128
Hawkins
Elisabeth 132, 146, 164
Henry 141, 146, 164
John 87, 90, 127
Joseph 132
Ralph 117, 118, 156, 160, 162
William 89, 100
Hawthorne
Jeremiah 7
Hawton
William 131
Hay
Charles 54, 65, 179
James 181
Hayes
John 48
Hays
Mary 54
Haywood
Ralph 20
Raphael 161
Raphaell 6
Hazelwood
John 130
Hazlon
Lewis 76
Head
Adam 57, 75
William 7, 79, 152
Heade
Adam 57
Healey
Clement 92
Heard
John 6, 58
Susannah 58
Heath
James 107
Sarah 69, 83
Thomas 12, 69, 83, 90
Heathcot
Catherine 166
Hebb

Thomas 76
Hedge
(N) 166, 176, 182
Thomas 24, 69, 83, 145, 166, 174, 182, 185
Hedger
Bridgett 112
John 112, 149
Heifer
Thomas 62
Heiford
Susan 157, 171
Susannah 169
Thomas 157, 169, 171, 174
Heigh
James 10, 39, 78, 183
Height
James 118
Hellen
David 109, 119
Hely
Darby 72
Hemesley
Jane 152
William 41, 152
Hemsley
Charles 126
Phil. 127
Phillimon 80
Phillip 136
Phillomen 126
Vincent 80, 126, 127, 159
William 20, 34, 55, 82, 89, 101, 136
Henderson
John 160, 161
Hendrixon
Mathias 82
Hendrixson
Mathias 82
Hendry
John 7, 8, 184
Henington
Ann 58
Henly
Daniell 126
Darbey 26
Hennington
Henry 58
Henry

John 60
Hensley
   Edmond 83
Henson
   Barbara 131
   Rando. 131
Herbert
   Elinor 31
   William 31, 172
Herkin
   Cornelius 82
Herman
   Casparus 2
   Casparus Augustin
      2, 5
   Casparus Augustine
      21
   Casper 29
   Cateryne 2
   Catherine 2
   Katerine 5
   Katherine 29
Herne
   Sarah 88
   William 88
Hernley
   Darby 109, 112, 179
Hewes
   John 60
   Owen 15, 73, 93
   Robert 15
Hewett
   Robert 165
Hewitt
   John 84
Hewley
   Samuell 138
Hews
   Owen 82
   Thomas 140
Heyden
   Francis 72
   Thomasin 95
   Thomeson 72
Heydon
   Francis 95
Heyfer
   Thomas 51, 63
Hickman
   Mary 20
   Timothy 129
   William 10, 20, 160
Hicks
   Thomas 2

William 125
Hide
   Ruth 19
   Thomas 54, 178
Higer
   John 59
Higgens
   Michaell 93
Higgins
   John 170, 186
   Michaell 20
Higham
   Francis 39, 94
Hill
   (N) 5
   Benjamin 60, 105,
      109
   Clement 32, 92,
      120, 124, 186
   Francis 5, 41, 141,
      142
   Johnson 8, 27
   Joseph 50
   Joshuah 186
   Peter 179, 186
   Richard 50, 133,
      139, 171
   Robert 16, 129
   Samuell 72
   Thomas 141
   William 23, 78
   Willmott 56, 175
Hillary
   Thomas 35, 164,
      175, 177
Hillman
   Thomas 56, 183
Hillory
   Thomas 87
Hinington
   William 75
Hinson
   Charles 36, 52
   John 17
   Nathaniell 141
   Richard 127
   William 38
Hinton
   Thomas 59, 94, 152
   William 4
Hinwood
   Robert 121
Hirst
   Daniell 78

Hitchcock
  Thomas 93
Hobart
  Ric. 7
Hobes
  Robert 94
Hodges
  (N) vs. 23
  John 11, 19, 36,
    45, 46, 51
  William 11, 19, 36,
    45, 51, 84
Hodgeson
  Mary 73
  William 73
Hodgson
  John 186
  Mary 77
  William 77
Hoges
  Thomas 96
Hogg
  Ambross 147
Holdsworth
  Thomas 125
Holladay
  Thomas 54
Holland
  Ann 183
  Capt. 51, 145, 172
  Frances 8
  John 160, 161, 173
  Richard 8
  William 25, 50, 63,
    87, 100, 104,
    105, 106, 113,
    116, 128, 139,
    143, 145, 183
Holleger
  Philip 167
Hollensworth
  John 16
Hollett
  John 118
Hollins
  John 30
Hollinsworth
  John 84
Hollon
  William 76
Holloway
  James 187
  John 78, 79
  Mathew 79

Hollyday
  Thomas 100, 133
  William 61
Holton
  Jesse 17
Homewood
  James 27, 108, 109,
    110, 111, 118,
    132, 162
  Mr. 176
  Thomas 117, 132,
    162
Hood
  Elisabeth 96
Hooke
  Annable 65
  Thomas 65
Hooks
  Thomas 149
Hooper
  Maurice 2
  Morris 50
Hopewell
  (N) 5
  Elisabeth 5, 141,
    142
  Joseph 125
  Richard 125
Hopkins
  Clement 81
  Elisabeth 81, 159,
    175
  Ger. 68
  Gerratt 95
  John 52
  Mr. 27
  Phillip 52
  Samuell 2, 3, 7,
    14, 27, 66, 71,
    83, 97, 137, 138
  Thomas 81, 127,
    159, 175
  William 60, 61, 93
Hopper
  Robert 13, 25, 96,
    116, 117, 140,
    146, 147, 157,
    169
Horn
  William 83
Hornby
  William 159
Horne
  John 114

Sarah 95, 170, 184
William 90, 95,
    156, 170, 184
Hornely
    William 135
Horner
    Richard 34
Horney
    Mortaugh 91
    Mortough 159
    Mourtough 175
Hornley
    Darby 165
Horrell
    Christopher 134
Horsey
    Isaac 98
    Isaack 71
    Nathaniell 8
    Stephen 8, 23
Horsman
    Thomas 83, 84, 184
Hosier
    Henry 95, 166, 167
Hoskins
    (N) 101, 165
    Ann 115, 120, 168,
        179
    Philip 58, 168,
        176, 179, 184
    Phillip 39, 55,
        115, 117, 120,
        124, 143, 144,
        145
Hotten
    William 115
Houblon
    John 9
Hough
    Henry 179
Houghton
    William 131
Houldsworth
    Joshua 76
Houlton
    John 140
How
    Elisabeth 151, 179
    Thomas 30, 151
Howard
    Cornelius 47, 64,
        113
    Edmund 14
    John 47, 113, 133

Martha 111
Mathew 47, 67, 88,
    151
Phillip 47, 64,
    113, 122
Ralph 114
William 106, 111
Howe
    Elisabeth 19
    John 19
    Thomas 94, 109
Howell
    (N) 24
    John 37, 54
    Thomas 21, 45
Howes
    John 94
Hubbard
    Humphrey 130
    Richard 128
Hubbart
    Richard 184
Hubert
    Richard 97
Hudson
    Johann 55
    Johanna 75
    Johannah 158
    William 109
Hues
    James 139
    Owen 26
Hughes
    John 54
    Owen 26, 180
    Thomas 170, 172,
        185
Hughs
    Thomas 50, 51, 66,
        85, 100
Huitt
    John 71
    Rachell 71
Hull
    Edward 79
    Nathaniell 134
Hulse
    Sarah 73
Hume
    Hercules 172, 179
    John 111, 118, 172,
        179
    William 142
Humes

Hercules 112
John 112
Humfris
    Thomas 4
Hunam
    John 71
Hungerford
    Edmond 109
    Edmund 105
Huniford
    Joseph 177
Hunt
    Ann 130
    Benjamin 83, 123,
        130
    Dorothy 164
    Dr. 162, 170
    Elisabeth 162, 170
    John 67, 75, 135,
        149, 164, 180
    Mary 13
    Richard 13
    Thomas 13, 16
    Wolfran 2
    Woolfran 165, 173
Hunter
    William 97, 108
Hunton
    (N) 32
    Ann 5, 24, 26, 45
    Elisabeth 5, 24,
        45, 79, 94, 179
    Mordeca 45
    Mordecai. 79
    Mordecay 122
    Mordica 5
    Sarah 45
    Thomas 94
    Timothy 179
Hurley
    Roger 150
Hurst
    John 89, 100, 114,
        122, 123, 131,
        147, 148, 162
Hurt
    (N) 23
    John 11, 19, 45, 51
Husbands
    William 30, 31, 57,
        126
Hussey
    Thomas 58
Hutchens

Thomas 169
Hutchings
    Franc. 7
    Francis 7
Hutchins
    Charles 107
    Elisabeth 67, 112
    Francis 67, 112,
        122
    George 56, 97, 183
    Thomas 132, 145,
        147, 156
    William 19, 74, 79,
        102
Hutchinson
    Anne 70
    John 72
    Thomas 70, 129
Hutchison
    Peter 175
    Thomas 173
    William 98, 179
Hutten
    John 179
Hyde
    John. 7
    Thomas 65
Hyden
    Francis 37
Hynde
    John 168
Hynson
    Barbarah 172
    Charles 24, 84
    John 167
    Nath. 167
    Nathaniel 166
    Nathaniell 53, 141
    Randolph 172
    Richard 135
    William 84, 135

Ingerson
    Daniell 136
Ingram
    Daniell 118
    John 47, 118
    Seth 118
Inman
    Benjamin 64, 160
Innes
    Cornelius 27
Innis

Cornelius 27, 186
Nathaniell 8
William 27, 186
Insly
Andrew 157
Isaack
Edward 19, 177
Richard 139
Ives
John 139

Jackson
Ezakell 82
George 104, 116
Henry 90, 139
James 47, 48
Mary 105, 112
Richard 105, 109,
112
Samuell 139
Jacob
John 146, 161
James
Ann 150
Charles 72, 82
Edward 13, 23
George 11
Henry 58
John 129, 150, 180
Jone 11
Joseph 17, 126
Jameson
Thomas 174
Jarboe
Ann 57, 185
Elisabeth 126
John 76
Peter 57, 77, 185
Jarman
Lewis 67, 86, 124
Jarvice
Humphry 87
Mary 87
Jarvis
Henry 180
Humphry 95, 103
Mary 95, 180
Jay
John 81
Jeffres
Richard 8
Jelf
William 117

Jenkins
Ann 105
David 180
Francis 97, 183
Jeremiah 7
John 19, 106, 183
Richard 70, 74
Thomas 41, 53
Jennifer
Jacob 180
Jerman
Lewis 90
Jesup
Joseph 96
Joanes
Sollomon 76
Joans
John 76
Philip 74
Johns
Richard 146
Johnson
(N) 166, 176, 178,
182
Alice 114
Ann 26, 28
Cornelius 147, 148
Edward 26, 28, 73,
82, 181
Elisabeth 164
Francis 28, 33, 49,
164, 172, 181
George 102
Henry 181
John 23, 106, 114,
135
Mary 179
Peter 96
Robert 96
Stephen 139, 145
Thomas 125, 138,
151, 178, 179,
186
William 26, 28, 33,
49, 50
Jolly
Peter 80
Jones
Alice 16
Ann 106, 110, 112,
160, 186
Ann administrators
of 156
Anne 106

John 169
Kemp
  (N) 39
Kempston
  Richard 66
Kempstone
  Richard 186
Kempton
  Richard 134
Kemston
  Thomas 111
Ken
  Richard 180
Kendall
  John 108, 109
Kendle
  Jane 21
  Richard 21
Kenerly
  Alice 50, 118
  William 50, 118
Kennard
  Richard 82
Kent
  Absolom 105
  Absolon 9
  John 56
Kenword
  Richard 180
Keristed
  Jochem 79
Kersey
  Elisabeth 52
  Martha 137
  Michael 179
  William 103, 108
Kerstead
  Joachim 59
  Margrett 59
Kersteed
  Joakim 101
  Margrett 101
Kertley
  Thomas 76
Kerwyn
  Daniell 137
Key
  Henry 70
  Sarah 70
Kible
  William 83
Kilbourn
  Charles 106
Kilburn

Rachell 100
Kilburne
  Charles 64, 66, 67
  Richard 66, 100
Kile
  Flora 162
  Florah 118
Kiles
  Flora 156
Killam
  Thomas 97
Killburne
  Rachael 177
  Richard 37, 177
Killton
  Thomas 29, 93
Kimball
  John 125
Kincraft
  Thomas 111
Kinemount
  Andrew 127
King
  (N) 5, 166
  Elazar 88
  Elias 4, 16, 22,
    37, 52, 73, 84,
    95, 110, 112,
    116, 118, 121,
    144, 165, 166,
    176, 182
  Elisabeth 150
  Henry 29, 33, 37,
    38, 40, 46
  John 3, 8, 13, 23,
    59, 83, 84, 136,
    161
  Mary 23
  Obadia 51
  Obadiah 14, 59
  Obediah 150
  Robert 3, 23, 137
  Tabitha 37, 40, 46
Kingcart
  Thomas 105, 106,
    108, 158, 165
Kingcroft
  Thomas 67
Kings
  Richard 9
Kinimont
  Ambros 71
Kinnard
  Richard 150

Kinnerly
   Richard 150
Kirke
   John 83
Kirkley
   Thomas 15
Kirwan
   Dominick 182
Kitten
   Theophilus 122
Knigh
   John 60
Knight
   George 144
   John 58, 129, 144
   William 57, 77,
      133, 175
Knighton
   Thomas 113
Knightsmith
   Thomas 112
Knightson
   Thomas 107
Knott
   Francis 109
Knowles
   Lawrence 80, 91,
      96, 99, 123
Korry
   Will. 135
Kullen
   Catherine 170
Kyle
   Flora 160

Laddimore
   Edward 87
Lademore
   Edward 93
Ladimore
   Edward 130
Ladmor
   George 82
Ladmore
   Elisabeth 73, 82,
      180
   George 73
Lambe
   Nicholas 24
Lambert
   John 89
Lamberty
   John 90

Lancaster
   Richard 69, 148
Land
   Mathew 127
Landerkin
   John 112
Landiferr
   Samuell 125
Lane
   George 3, 183
   Walter 138
Langsley
   Ann 63
   Charles 63
Large
   Elisabeth 6
   Robert 6, 15, 77
   Thomas 6
Larkin
   Thomas 61, 66
Latham
   Edward 38
Launam
   John 65
Lauterkin
   John 19
Lawes
   John 14, 98
   Katherine 14, 98
Lawrence
   John 67, 94
   Margerett 67
   Phillip 50
   Thomas 52, 169
Lawson
   Thomas 55, 70, 74,
      75, 128
Lawyer
   William 59
Layton
   Henry 98
   Margrett 98
Leach
   John 78, 183, 186
Leaf
   Ann 105
   Francis 105, 159
Leaff
   Francis 149
Leake
   John 107
   Richard 6
Lean
   George 3

Phillip 64, 107,
   120
Lyon
   Daniell 104

Mabbet
   Kempton 35
Mabbot
   Mrs. 107
Mabbott
   Kympton 99
   Mr. 107
Macarty
   William 160
Maccubbins
   William 162
Mackachy
   John 16
   Mary 15
MackDowell
   John 109
Mackeel
   William 120
Mackeele
   David 138
Mackeetas
   Patrick 53
Mackell
   John 2
   Thomas 2
   William 2
Mackhlan
   Peter 185
Macklein
   Robert 159
Macklyn
   Richard 135
   Robert 135, 136
Mackmilion
   Peter 16, 20
Mackmillion
   Peter 74
MackMurry
   (N) 57
   Bartholomew 175
Macknell
   Daniell 186
Macknitt
   John 66, 71, 97
Maclamy
   Owen 161
Macleland
   Nicholas 163

Macomus
   Daniel 171
   Daniell 185
Macoom
   James 184
Maddox
   Alexander 14
   Notly 31
   William 106
Madox
   Cornelius 58
   Lazarus 178
Magager
   John 175
Maghall
   Timothy 69
Magra
   Andrew 126
Magrave
   Andrew 175
Magrooder
   Samuell 66, 111
Magrow
   Andrew 134
Magruder
   Allexander 169
   Samuell 87
Magrugder
   Alexander 173
   Ann 173
Main
   George 117
Mainardoe
   Peter 82
Makacky
   John 28
   Mary 28
Makett
   John 138
Makey
   Fer. 150
Malden
   Francis 112
Maldin
   Frances 9
Man
   Edward 38
   Lucy 38
Mang
   Edward 131
Maning
   John 70, 92
Mankin
   Maurice 70

Stephen 70, 128,
    131
Manly
    Cornelius 57, 73
Manning
    John 123, 126, 165
    Jos. 43
    Joseph 70
    Rachel 123
Manthorpe
    Samuell 110
Manthrop
    Mr. 2
    Samuell 5, 112
Manyng
    John 79
    Ruth 79
Mark
    John 184
    Margarett 184
Marke
    Ann 88, 94
    John 25, 32
    Margarett 25
    William 88, 94, 103
Markes
    William 130
Marriott
    John 185
Marrow
    Anguish 138
Marsh
    Isaack 116
    Thomas 66, 96, 116,
        123
Marshall
    Capt. 171
    Elisabeth 70, 173
    Isaack 159
    John 175
    Joseph 74
    Joyce 159
    William 70, 74, 75,
        173
Marsham
    Ann 98
    Richard 1, 9, 54,
        56, 62, 98, 148,
        180
Marston
    Robert 151
Marten
    Michael 164, 180
Martin

Francis 182
James 57, 59, 60,
    94
John 53, 70, 131,
    133
Mary 70
Michaell 70
Robert 87
Will. 89
William 100, 109,
    168
Mary 56
Masheell
    Isaack 124
Mason
    (N) 23
    Edward 24
    Mary 159, 172, 181
    Richard 11, 19, 45,
        51, 161, 176
    Robert 6, 176
    Samuell 172, 181
    Thomas 159
Massee
    Philip 18
Massey
    Nicholas 87
    William 88
Massum
    Richard 49
Masters
    John 30, 34, 65
    William 151
Mathew
    Roger 12
Mathews
    Ignatius 74, 111,
        174
    Isaac 70
    Mary 70, 74
    Morrice 14
    Roger 90
Mathiason
    Mathias 150
Mattax
    William 114
Mattox
    Jonas 29
Maud
    Francis 151
Maude
    Francis 114
Maunaur
    Henry 127

Maydaniell
  Bryant 165
Maynard
  Hannah 176, 178
  James 176, 178
  widow 26
Mayward
  Francis 130
McNemara
  Timothy 163
Mead
  Francis 88
  John 149
Meadcalfe
  Alderman 26
  John 64
Meade
  Francis 147, 148
Meads
  John 111
  William 152
Meaney
  James 151
Meares
  Elisabeth 152
  William 102, 152
Meckley
  Christopher 119
Medcalfe
  John 47
Medford
  Thomas 57
Medley
  John 30
  William 76
Medly
  Anne 31
  William 31
Meech
  Thomas 29, 34
Meek
  Francis 61
Meeke
  Mary 61
Meekes
  Walter 19
Meeks
  Francis 13
  Mary 13
Meen
  James 159
  Margarett 159
Meende
  James 81

Meens
  James 72, 159
Megee
  George 71
Melton
  Thomas 96
Mercer
  John 174
  Margarett 174
Meredith
  Henry 38
  John 157, 163, 164
  Lewis 184
Merekin
  Hugh 52
Meren
  William 75
Mereton
  Jacob 70
Merica
  Anne 64
  Hugh 64
  Joshua 64
Meriken
  Hugh 47
  Joshua 47
  Joshuah 178
Merikin
  Joshua 52
Meriton
  John 103
Merrekin
  Ann 52
Merrican
  Heugh 55
Merriday
  Henry 102
  Hugh 115
  Lewes 140
  Lewis 140
  William 88
Merrikin
  Ann 52
  Joshua 52
Merriman
  Charles 124
Merriton
  John 68
Merritt
  John 96
Merryman
  Ch. 160
  Charles 162
Meryday

Henry 103, 182
Meshew
    William 130, 131,
        150
Messer
    John 102
    Margrett 102
Messew
    William 163
Messick
    Julian 138
Methven
    James 64
Mickin
    William 174
Middleton
    Richard 2
Milborne
    Nich. 26
Milburne
    Nicholas 5, 18
Miles
    Edward 101
    Henry 8
    John 31, 32, 56,
        58, 60, 76
    Margery 56
    Samuell 8
    Susanna 36
    Thomas 29, 36, 115
Millbourne
    Nicholas 134
Miller
    (N) 119
    Arthur 176, 182
    Edward 57, 114, 185
    John 31, 76, 137
    Mary 187
    Michael 170, 176,
        183
    Michaell 17, 21,
        23, 29, 84, 112,
        121, 122, 141,
        144, 146, 147
    Mr. 166
    Willhm 137
Mills
    Elisabeth 103
    William 103
Millstead
    Edward 44
    Elisabeth 44
Milson
    Edward 55

Minching
    Richard 57
Ming
    Edward 13
Mire
    Christopher 181
Mishew
    William 180
Miskall
    John 14
    Teague 14
Mitchell
    Henry 30
    Thomas 185
Mitchen
    Margarett 134
Mitley
    Christopher 145
Moate
    William 109
Mogbee
    Martha 98
Mogiah
    Andrew 57
Mole
    William 118
Moll
    John 89
Moone
    Ralph 137
Mooney
    Thomas 115
    widow 22
Moor
    Henry 70, 74
    Thomas 70, 72
Moore
    Ann 135
    Hannah 91
    Henry 62
    James 65, 69
    John 58
    M. 61
    Mordica 61, 101
    Mordicay 113, 141
    Richard 126, 135
    Thomas 62, 93, 129
    Ursula 113
    William 17, 54, 91
Moot
    William 108
More
    Ann 135
    Christopher 172

Moreland
Jacob 33, 115, 129,
140, 141
Morgan
Abraham 72
Edward 92
Elisabeth 77
Harbert 116, 134
Jarvis 119, 143
Thomas 32, 42, 48,
83
William 15, 76, 77
Morgann
William 6
Morgin
Jarvis 104
Morley
Griffin 185
Griffith 170, 182
Morris
John 82
Richard 127, 131
Thomas 8, 137
Morrison
William 11
Morrough
John 95
Morrow
Anguish 131
Morry
Bartholomew 76
Timo. 5
Morse
William 68
Morss
Richard 67
Morton
Mary 80
Moseley
Joseph 66
Thomas 15
Mosely
Joseph 48
Moss
Elisabeth 15
Joseph 89, 100
Ralph 108, 162
Richard 109
William 15, 128,
133
Mosten
William 179
Mould
Frances 51, 59

Humphrey 51
Humphry 59, 60
Mounfeild
John 12
Mounts
Laurence 15
Laurens 15
Sarah 15
Moy
Daniell 114, 185
Muckgiver
John 127
Mudd
Ann 168
Thomas 13, 115,
120, 144, 168,
179
Mulattoes
Betty 42
Billey 42
Charles 42
Jane 42
Lewis 42
Mullen
John 138
Mulraine
Cornelius 17
Munday
Robert 134
Murphey
James 18, 23, 25,
37, 41, 136
John 76
Murphy
Charles 13
James 37
Murray
John 88
Murrey
Garrett 186
James 35
Murris
Bartholomew 177
Murry
Bartholomew 92
James 48
Muschamp
George 6
Muschett
Henry 125
Mutchin
Richard 134

Page 230

Nailer
    George 99
Nayler
    Abraham 172, 185
    George 179
Naylor
    George 103
Neale
    Ann 1, 41, 55, 158
    Anthony 1, 7, 10,
        41, 131, 158,
        177, 184
    Fra. 72
    James 1, 41
    Jonathon 27, 37,
        102, 107, 117,
        118, 132
    Madam 1
    Mathew 110
    Nicholas 140
    Susannah 80
Neall
    Charles 135
    Jonathon 115
Needles
    John 5, 41
Negro
    Black Jack 86
Negroes
    Anne 42
    Billy 43
    Ellinor 42
    Harrie 43
    Lewis 42
    Mattox 182
    Sam 182
Nellson
    Thomas 65
Nelson
    John 128, 133
    Mary 128
    Richard 120, 143
Nevell
    Edward 181
Nevett
    John 57
Nevit
    John 31
Nevitt
    John 31, 185
Newham
    John 89
Newland
    Henry 17

Newman
    Jane 18
    John 18, 89
    Richard 75, 76, 77,
        133
    Roger 13, 48, 94,
        100, 118, 140
Newnam
    Daniell 91
    Joseph 91
Newton
    (N). 171
    Elisabeth 105, 113,
        156
    Henry 96
    John 88, 95, 105,
        113
    Owen 30
    Samuell 90, 91,
        103, 159, 180
Nicholls
    John 82, 83, 140
    Simon 99
    William 47, 111,
        112
Nichols
    John 157, 163, 174,
        180
    Thomas 67
Nicholson
    Elisabeth 16, 106,
        186
    Francis 107
    John 106, 186
    Rebbecca 146
    Rebecca 106, 147
    Thomas 16, 82
Nickolls
    Thomas 106, 114
Nixon
    Ralph 103
Noble
    John 57, 115
    Robert 55, 174
Nollett
    Thomas 118
Norman
    Daniell 134
    Elisabeth 35, 40,
        48
    George 35, 40, 48,
        51, 54, 86
Norrest
    Robert 52, 84

Norris
    Christopher 77
    Edward 39
    William 75, 105
North
    Elisabeth 107, 109,
        167, 175
    John 107, 109, 112,
        175
Nowell
    Ann 175
    Henry 175
    William 118
Nox
    William 182
Nunan
    John 81
Nuttall
    John 177
Nutthall
    John 75, 146, 162

Odaham
    George 106
Odeell
    Mr. 139
Odell
    Phillip 146
    Thomas 66, 85, 146,
        161
Offitt
    William 149
Offley
    Edward 84
OKeith
    George 58, 59
Oldson
    John 184
Olesse
    Robert 90
Oliver
    Dorothy 105
Olwis
    Robert 124
Omely
    Bryan 178
Oneal
    Mary 164
Oneale
    Arthur 164, 180
Onorton
    John 8
    William 8

Oram
    Andrew 136
    Thomas 89, 95
Orell
    Thomas 168
Orme
    Robert 134
Orrell
    Thomas 74
Orum
    Andrew 159
    Robert 178
Osborn
    William 158, 162
Osborne
    William 107
Osbourne
    William 138
Osburn
    Hannah 84
    William 84
Osen
    Francis 79
Oubeer
    Elisabeth 65
    Stephen 65
Outen
    John 97
Owen
    Edward 85
    Joseph 79
    Mr. 107
    Richard 40, 54, 99,
        107, 121, 150
Owens
    Ann 138
    Will 138
    William 138
Owns
    Stephen 123

Paca
    Aquilla 90
Pagan
    Peter 144
Paggett
    Thomas 98
Paine
    John 127, 128
Palmer
    Daniell 1, 89, 139
    William 10
Panter

John 8, 14, 138
Pargrave
  James 152
Parker
  Andrew 59
  George 122
  John 8, 60
  Thomas 82, 145
  William 7, 122
Parks
  Clement 181
Parrett
  Elisabeth 49, 61,
    66
  Gabriell 46, 49,
    61, 66
Parrish
  Edward 119
Parrot
  Gabriel 178
Parrott
  Gabriel 54, 178
  Gabriell 10, 13,
    21, 22, 25, 45
  Mr. 5
Parson
  Edward 185
  William 112
Parsons
  Amos 66, 97
  David 57, 76, 96
  John 4, 87
Pattison
  Ann 116
  Gilbert 54, 116,
    140
  Jacob 6
  James 10, 22, 31,
    58, 69
Pawlett
  Martha 48
  Richard 48
  William 48
Paws
  James 123
Payne
  Isaack 30
Peak
  Jane 46
  Joseph 46, 159, 174
  Mary 11
Peake
  Jane 13, 29, 38,
    40, 41, 46

Joseph 13, 29, 34,
  37, 38, 40, 83,
  90, 124
  Peter 76
Pearce
  John 129
  Mary 129
  Thomas 73
  William 29, 72, 167
Peare
  Thomas 76
Peasly
  John 111
Peck
  Benjamin 103, 134
Peddoe
  Lazarus 140
Peddow
  Sarah 140
Peeckley
  John 110
Peirce
  Thomas 16, 82
Pemberton
  John 41, 80, 181
Pen
  William 3
Penington
  William 4, 38, 108
Penn
  Elisabeth 62
  William 53, 62
Pennington
  John 186
  Thomas 132, 134
  William 35, 89, 94,
    100, 109, 162,
    168
Perce
  William 93
Percifull
  John 84
Perrey
  Robert 137
  Thomas 16
Perry
  Joell 132
  John 88, 95, 104,
    185
  Sarah 88, 95
Person
  Simon 90
Persons
  John 35

Pery
  James 156
Peterson
  Henry 16
Pether
  Lewis 161
Pettibone
  Ann 117
  Joseph 117, 148
Pettybon
  Ann 162
Pettybone
  Joseph 162
Peunis
  Elisabeth 151
  James 151
Pew
  (N) 59
  David 60
  Dinah 59
Phelpes
  Walter 103
Philips
  James 9, 178
  Robert 156, 169,
    181
  Roger 181, 184
Phillips
  Anthony 90, 124,
    139, 146
  Capt. 107
  James 4, 12, 89,
    90, 139
  Robert 64, 67, 108,
    110, 113, 119
Phillpott
  Edward 75
Philpot
  Edward 70
Philpott
  Edward 75
Phips
  Elisabeth 15
Pickard
  John 81
Pickett
  John 159
  William 12
Pierce
  Thomas 180
Pile
  Joseph 177
Pindar
  Edward 2, 9

Sarah 2, 9
Pinder
  Edward 23, 53
  Sarah 23
Pinnard
  John 72
Pinton
  Hugh 109
Pitcher
  Emanuell 6
Pitt
  Ann 130, 150
  John 49, 80, 81
  Phillip 130
  William 150
Pitts
  John 56
  Philip 59
  Phillip 130
Planner
  William 23
Plater
  Ann 49
  George 11, 33, 34,
    49, 140, 171,
    179
Plumer
  Elisabeth 117
  widow 158
Plummer
  Thomas 117
Plunkett
  Richard 137
  Thomas 53
Pollard
  Edward 24
Polley
  Richard 109
Polman
  Elias 30
Poor
  Walter 131
Pope
  Henry 78
  John 126
  Mary 54
  Robert 157
Popper
  Mary 167
Porter
  Elisabeth 8, 171
  Giles 150, 180
  John 66, 97
  Joseph 150

Rabbitts
    William 107
Rabett
    William 121
Rabitts
    Mary 107
Racheford
    Lawrence 44
Racklife
    Charles 4
    Elisabeth 4
Rackliffe
    Charles 2
Racliffe
    Elisabeth 2
Radford
    Sarah 63
Ragles
    James 72
Raines
    Ri. 62
Ralfe
    Thomas 4
Randall
    Robert 93
Rasin
    Philip 176
Ratcliff
    Milenex 70
Ratclyff
    Mathew 128
Ratford
    John 63
Raulings
    Richard 158
Rawlings
    Anthony 14, 150
    Jane 122
    John 5, 14, 23, 26,
        33, 51, 82, 125,
        130, 150, 163
    Ralph 115
    Richard 107, 121,
        122, 186
Rawlins
    Paule 65
    Richard 63, 173
Raycroft
    William 186
Rayos
    John 93
Read
    Jane 14, 163, 174
    John 115

William 14, 33,
    163, 174
Reason
    Philip 72
Reaves
    Thomas 142
Record
    Thomas 52
Redar
    Thomas 99
Reder
    Benjamin 161
Redgrave
    Abraham 82
Reed
    Jane 33
    Mathew 135
Reeves
    Ann 31
    John 143
    Thomas 31, 77, 142,
        143
    Upgatt 55
Regester
    Robert 38
Register
    Robert 80
Regneir
    Jacob 142
Regnier
    J. 166
Regon
    James 74
Reigneir
    Jacob 119
Rencha
    John 14
Renolds
    Thomas 52, 104
Respeer
    William 143
Revell
    Randall 171
Reycrof
    William 179
Reynolds
    Edward 129
    Henry 146
    John 34
    Thomas 35
Rice
    Evan 79
    William 166
Rich

Henry 14, 66, 183
William 17, 54
Richant
  Stephen 17
Richard
  Ashman 75
  John 163
Richards
  John 126
  William 17
Richardson
  Anne 83
  Charles 179
  Daniell 148
  David 97
  Elisabeth 86, 95,
    148
  John 130
  Joseph 86, 95, 148
  Mark 181
  Marke 1, 12, 89
  Martha 24
  Nicholas 48
  Simon 23
  Sisley 23
  Susanah 12
  Susanna 1
  Susannah 83
  Thomas 24, 29, 124
  William 63, 68, 86,
    95, 97, 103,
    148, 152
Richman
  Daniel 175
  Daniell 92
Ricketts
  John 8, 93, 150
  Penellope 150
  Penelope 93
Rickins
  Thomas 54
Rider
  Thomas 94
Ridgley
  Charles 117
  Col. 116
  Henry 28, 37, 104,
    117, 120, 165,
    172, 174, 186,
    187
  Katherine 172
  Mary 120
Ridgly
  Henry 117

Rigbey
  James 119, 146
Rigby
  Arthur 136
  Ellioner 136
  James 110, 139
Riggby
  James 47
  John 47
Riley
  John 177
Ringold
  James 152
  Martha 136
  William 136
Roach
  John 84
Roades
  Abraham 134
  Charles 134
Roads
  Nicholas 100
Robert
  Gates 75
Roberts
  Ann 56
  Charles 10
  John 56, 160, 185
  Robert 71, 151
  Sarah 71
Robertson
  Daniell 177
  Katherine 33
  Margret 91
  Mary 177
  Richard 33
  Robert 91
Robinett
  Allen 1
Robins
  George 80
  John 68
  Thomas 28, 33, 40,
    53, 68, 80, 136,
    156, 157
Robinson
  Charles 159
  Elisabeth 27
  Francis 90, 124,
    159, 174
  George 108, 109,
    132, 162
  Heneage 173
  James 56

John 112, 136, 139, 161
Richard 160
Robert 166
Thomas 169
William 7, 8, 27, 60, 138, 139, 161, 174, 187
Robotham
George 17, 18, 37, 41, 68, 158, 181
Robothem
George 80
Roby
John 185
Rochford
Laurence 42, 44
Rockhold
Edward 128
John 113, 133, 162, 174
Mary 111, 113, 128, 162, 174
Rockwood
Edward 127
Rogers
David 91, 96
Isabell 90
Joseph 11
Rogerson
Philip 9
Rookwood
Edward 133
Roper
William 104, 119
Rose
John 114
Mable 51
Mayble 59
Thomas 6, 57, 125
Rosewell
William 29
Roswell
Joseph 142
William 2
Rotchford
Lawrence 44
Rottee
Sollomon 77
Round
James 8, 175
Rousbey
Elisabeth 96
Rousby

(N) 166
Elisabeth 101
Rouse
John 69, 159
Rout
William 39
Rowl
William 49
Rowles
Christopher 132
Rowlin
Richard 112
Royston
Jere. 160
John 36, 160, 174
Rozier
Benjamin 32, 147
Notley 115, 120
Ruarke
William 96
Rule
Stanhope 29
Ruley
Anthony 168
Ruly
Anthony 161, 170
Rumball
Anthony 18, 103, 126, 127
Rumney
Edward 102, 162
Russam
Thomas 182
Russell
John 131, 150
Mary 130, 150
Michaell 126
Ruston
Thomas 124
Rutte
Solomon 175
Ruxton
Nathaniell 139
Ryder
Thomas 89
Ryland
John 16
Ryley
Hugh 65
John 92
Rymer
Ralph 32

Sadler
    Joseph 171, 185
    Sicily 171
Salamstone
    Mathew 53
Sales
    Robert 135
Sallers
    John 186
Salter
    Bridgett 180
    John 90, 91, 112,
      159, 166, 167,
      171, 180
Samesberry
    Richard 111
Samuell
    Ignatius 106
Samway
    Jonathon 173
Sander
    Mathew 185
Sanders
    Edward 164, 177
    James 102, 110, 161
    Jane 176
    John 111
    Jonathon 109
    Mathew 151, 164
    Richard 28
Sands
    Richard 79
Sandy
    William 182
Sandys
    Richard 47, 112
Sangster
    John 61
Sanner
    John 92
    Mary 92
Santee
    Christopher 18, 39
Sape
    Margrett 74
Sargent
    Dameres 44
    John 80, 81, 126
    Mary 80
    William 44
Sargoon
    John 126
Sauage
    John 114

Saunder
    James 88
Saunders
    Edward 113, 127,
      131
    James 66, 113, 114,
      117, 123, 146
    Jane 113, 127
    John 128
    Joseph 155
    Mathew 128, 133
    Matt. 53
Savidge
    John 6
Sawell
    Ignatius 112
    James 112
Sayer
    Frances 36, 37
    Francis 71
    Peter 143
    Petter 37
Sayers
    Frances 96
    Peter 91
Saywell
    Ja. 137
Scaley
    Thomas 124
Scanbrough
    Tobias 140
Scarborough
    Mathew 176
Scarbrough
    Mathew 8
    Matthew 26
Scarff
    Nicholas 149
Scidmore
    Samuell 37
Scott
    Charles 67, 86
    Cuthbert 2
    James 71, 103, 126
    John 10, 20, 39,
      56, 186
    Nath. 72, 159
    Nathaniell 81, 159
    Samuell 71, 79,
      105, 109, 112,
      179
    William 71, 72,
      102, 103, 138,
      159, 162

Scrivener
   Benjamin 94, 100,
     155, 185
Scromingk
   Robert 130
Seagar
   Margrett 94
   Thomas 94
Seale
   John 69
Seargent
   Damaris 44
Sedgewick
   Thomas 149
Sedgwick
   Elish 152
   Joshua 111
   Thomas 111
Sedwick
   Joshua 105
   Joshuah 158
   Thomas 105, 158
Sefferson
   Peter 181
Selbey
   Edward 118
   Elisabeth 119
   Mathew 119
Selby
   Daniell 27, 28
   Mary 28, 111
   Parker 28
   William 111, 157,
     173
Sellman
   John 139, 161
Sequence
   John 15
Sergant
   William 44
Sergent
   William 53
Seth
   (N) 101, 166
   Jacob 36, 71
   Jacobus 79, 80, 91
Seuerwright
   Robert 93
Sewall
   Ignatius 59, 60
   Nicholas 16
Sewell
   Ann 56
   James 80

   John 56, 134
   Maj. 61
   Nicholas 101
   Peter 79
Shank
   Thomas 76
Shankam
   Thomas 130
Shankes
   John 126
Shanks
   John 57, 182
   Thomas 115
Sharp
   Elisabeth 156, 157,
     169
   John 139, 157, 174
   William 2, 5, 33,
     62, 63, 68, 71,
     72, 80, 102,
     156, 157, 169,
     174
Sharpe
   John 138, 140
   William 39
Shaw
   Christopher 89, 125
   John 4
   Ralph 13, 70, 128
Sheircliffe
   William 76
Shepard
   Charles 44
   Robert 152
Shephard
   Barthollomew 92
   Charles 44
   Robert 74, 102
Sheppard
   John 126
   Mary 126
   Nicholas 185
   Thomas 111, 149
Sherclift
   William 58
Sherdne
   Daniell 106
Shereden
   Daniell 25
Sheredine
   Daniel 59
   Jere. 186
Sheridin
   Daniell 15

Sherrwood
  Hugh 135
Sherwight
  Robert 112
Sherwood
  Daniell 38, 103,
    148
  Hugh 8, 21, 40, 64,
    85
  John 38
Shield
  John 125
Shimey
  Joseph 149
Shinsllin
  Samuel 138
Short
  John 71, 79, 109
Shorte
  Anne 71
Showell
  Armell 183
  Jonathon 183
  Samuel 183
  Samuell 137
Shrine
  William 129
Shrive
  Jane 105
  William 105
Sickamore
  Samuell 25
Sicklemore
  Daniell 83
  Samuell 12, 69, 162
Sides
  John 91, 180
Simes
  Allexander 115
Simmons
  Daniell 78
  Thomas 79
Simms
  Alexander 164
  Sarah 115, 164
Simons
  Daniell 74
  James 32, 57
Simpson
  Andrew 185
  Thomas 104
Simson
  Thomas 151
Sinnett

  Garrett 97
Sinnott
  John 106
Sissill
  John 77
Sisson
  Edward 93
  Olive 93
Sissons
  Edward 92
Skellington
  Thomas 21
Skidmore
  Amy 110
  Ann 174
  Samuel 174
  Samuell 110, 165
Skilington
  Thomas 159
Skilleton
  Thomas 136
Skillington
  Ken. 62
  Kenelm 62
  Penelope 63
  Thomas 22, 62, 63,
    175
Skillton
  Thomas 15
Skinner
  Robert 7, 79
  Rogert 7
  Thomas 150
Skiper
  John 19
Skynner
  Clarke 149
Slacon
  George 145
Slade
  William 48
Slaid
  William 47
Sly
  Capt. 166
  Gerrard 63
  Priscilla 92, 114
  Prisilla 152
  Robert 92, 114,
    142, 143, 152
Slye
  Capt. 175
  Gerrard 101, 166,
    175, 182

Richard 34
Sotheron
  John 129
  Richard 70
Sothorne
  Richard 31
Southee
  John 33
Southerne
  Richard 58, 75
Sowright
  Robert 89
Sparrow
  Anne 47
  Solomon 68
  Thomas 47, 148
Spence
  James 71, 83, 161
Spice
  George 67
Spicer
  George 106, 108,
    111, 158, 179
Spickman
  William 151
Spink
  Henry 75, 77
Spinke
  Henry 57, 58, 76
  William 76
Sporne
  Nicholas 13
Sprigg
  Thomas 65, 149, 162
Spring
  Robert 80
Stafford
  Joyce 137
Staley
  Mr. 32
  Thomas 25, 32, 125
Staly
  Thomas 90
Standbauck
  Thomas 111
Standly
  John 16
Stanes
  Samuell 126
Stanfield
  James 184
Stanley
  John 66, 88, 95,
    170

Stawks
  Peter 180
Steevens
  Francis 123
  John 5
Stephens
  John 186
  William 157
Stepkin
  Garrett 86
Stevens
  Charles 123
  Edward 130
  Francis 52, 107
Stevenson
  Edward 96
Steward
  Allin 185
  David 85
  Margrett 85
  Mery 80
Stewart
  John 55
Stinchcome
  Nathaniell 51
Stinet
  Sarah 179
Stinett
  Joseph 179
Stinnet
  William 183
Stoakes
  Peter 131
Stockett
  Thomas 161, 162
Stoddard
  James 65, 147
Stoddart
  James 78, 186
Stoddert
  James 98
Stone
  Dorothy 55
  Elenor 70
  Ellinor 74
  John 55, 70, 73,
    74, 75, 113, 128
  Mathew 44
  Matthusalem 97
  Thomas 70, 129
  William 44, 61, 70,
    92, 159, 162
Stoop
  John 130

Storey
  Walter 118, 128
Story
  Walter 53, 70, 75
Stowe
  Jane 59
Strawbridge
  Joseph 69, 83, 147
  Sarah 83, 140
Stringer
  Edmond 18
Sulevant
  Darby 111
Sumerland
  John 2
Sumner
  Robert 94, 149
Sunderland
  John 64, 94
Sury
  Henry 10
Sutton
  Alce 83
Swaile
  Francis 76, 92
Swaine
  John 33, 81
Swakes
  Peter 150
Swalles
  Flrances 57
  Mary 57
Swallow
  John 81
Swan
  James 114
Swann
  Richard 105
Swawell
  John 141
Swayn
  Ann 173
  John 173
Swayne
  John 161
  Mary 161
Sweatnam
  (N). 166
  Edward 17, 34, 37,
    68, 72, 73, 91,
    99, 101, 110,
    116, 121, 122,
    144, 166
  Jane 17

  John 122, 144, 166,
    167, 168
  Joshuah 166, 168
  Richard 17, 34, 81,
    91, 99, 121, 168
  William 168
Sweatname
  Edward 118
Sweettnam
  John 141
Swettnam
  Edward 36, 37, 112,
    141
  Richard 36
Swift
  John 71
  William 71
Swindell
  Daniell 124
Swinster
  John 25
Swyer
  Anne 79
Sydes
  (N). 171
  Bridget 127
  John 127
Sykes
  Thomas 92
Symmons
  James 29
Symons
  Elisabeth 104, 106
  George 104, 106
  James 12
  John 135
Synnodd
  John 126
Synnott
  John 96
Synodd
  John 126

Talbott
  Edward 148
  Elisabeth 148
  John 148
  Sophia 148
Taley
  Thomas 170
  Walter 170
  Water 165
Tallar

Thomas 184
Tally
    Thomas 133
    Walter 133
Taney
    John 79
    Margrett 101
    Michaell 15, 68,
        101
    Thomas 58, 70
Tannehill
    William 78, 98, 108
Tanner
    Henry 60
Tant
    John 6, 31, 76, 92
    Thomas 57
Tany
    Margrett 101
    Thomas 22, 101
Tanyhill
    William 98
Tarr
    John 8, 27
Tarry
    Thomas 82
Tate
    Thomas 135
Tatersall
    Phillip 110
Tattershall
    Lawrence 57
Tawney
    Michaell 22
Taylard
    William 34, 64, 65,
        73, 101, 114,
        115, 123, 126,
        142, 145, 160,
        162, 165, 175,
        182
Taylor
    Abraham 25, 124,
        160
    Ann 127, 173
    Edward 33
    Henry 144
    Hope 27, 161, 174
    James 72, 82, 129
    John 14, 106, 107,
        112, 129, 130,
        137, 160, 162,
        163
    Laurence 18

Lawrence 140
Magdelen 75
Margret 31
Mary 112, 129
Michaell 119
Robert 133
Thomas 23, 28, 97,
    127, 163, 173
Walter 31, 76
William 12, 29, 32,
    75, 120, 132,
    151, 170
Tears
    Hugh 74
Teege
    Edward 16, 28
Tench
    Edward 138
    Esq. 111
    Mr. 110
    Thomas 47, 52, 61,
        66, 87, 88, 94,
        100, 108, 112,
        129, 155, 162,
        165, 176, 181,
        184
Tendall
    Thomas 41
Tenison
    Justinian 160
Tennis
    Justinian 151
    Katherine 151
Tennison
    Elisabeth 125
    Justinian 126
Tennsey
    Thomas 162
Terrett
    Nicholas 10, 103
Teton
    Thomas 125
Tettersall
    Lawrence 115
Thacker
    Thomas 59
Thackstone
    Thomas 130, 176
Thatcher
    (N) 5
Theobalds
    John 131, 180
Theobely
    John 53

Thetcher
  Mordant 33
Thomas
  Benjamin 55
  Elis 173
  Elisabeth 163
  Ellis 163
  Evan 88, 110, 155
  Henry 19
  John 39, 42, 48,
    139
  Samuell 148
  Stephen 72
  Thomas 91, 127,
    136, 184
  William 160
Thompson
  Anthony 26
  Christopher 178
  Henry 83
  Isabell 164
  Isabella 127, 164
  James 97, 134
  John 15, 19, 24,
    28, 29, 82, 87,
    93, 150, 156,
    157, 169, 170,
    176, 177
  Mary 15
  Richard 69, 83, 159
  Robert 15, 30
  Will. 6
  William 13, 70, 75
Thomson
  Henry 127
  John 171
Thornborough
  Rouland 36
Thorne
  William 58
ThorneBurne
  Richard 63
Thornson
  Richard 130
Thornton
  Richard 29
Thoroughgood
  Francis 97
Thranstone
  Thomas 72
Thrift
  John 96
Throwgood
  Fran. 14

Thurston
  Thomas 25
Tidings
  John 96, 152
Tilden
  Ann 168
  Charles 16, 121,
    166
  Mary 167
Tiley
  John 6
Tilgham
  Richard 17
Tilghman
  Mr. 33
  Richard 13, 41,
    127, 184
Till
  Edward 53, 59, 60,
    133
  Sarah 59, 129
Tilletson
  John 17
Tillgman
  Mr. 135
  Richard 136
Tillman
  Richard 136
Tillotson
  John 54
Tillsley
  Thomas 112
Tilly
  Joseph 49
Tilton
  Humphrey 72, 150,
    180
  Humphry 150
Timothy
  William 97
Tindall
  Thomas 51
Toas
  Daniell 24, 38, 80
Todd
  Lancellott 113
  Lancelott 162
  Michael 163
  Michaell 157
Toes
  Daniell 120
Tole
  Thomas 76, 115
Toley

John 18
Tyre
    Jacob 19

Ubgat
    John 77
Underwood
    John 149
Ungle
    Robert 5, 135, 156
Unky
    Thomas 126
Utie
    George 1, 12
    Mary 1, 12, 18
    Susanna 1
Uty
    George 181
    Mary 181

Vahan
    Susannah 136
Vanderbath
    Lawrence 165
Vanderford
    Charles 84
    George 84, 135
    John 84
Vanderhay
    Dan. 93
Vanderhayden
    Math. 29
VanderHeyden
    Mathew 21
    Mathias 2, 130
Vangaesill
    Jacob 2
Vanreswick
    John 15
Vanswearingen
    Garrett 88
Vansweringen
    Garrett 10, 114
    Gerrard 114
    Joseph 114
    Mary 114
    Zachar. 125
Vaugezell
    Jacob 29
Vaugezlow
    Jacob 29
Vaughan

Susannah 159
Vaughop
    Thomas 128
Veezey
    John 15
Venables
    William 84
Venabs
    Joseph 184
Venor
    Joseph 168
Vernon
    Christopher 4
Vesey
    John 93
Viccory
    John 51
    Margarett 51
    Margrett 59
Viccous
    John 59, 60
Vickers
    Thomas 131
Vincent
    George 134
    John 180
Vine
    Mary 140
Vines
    John 121
Vinson
    George 66, 103,
      159, 186
Vivers
    Nathaniell 75, 92
Voss
    Robert 91
Vowles
    Richard 76

Wabbe
    John 59
Wade
    Cornelius 162
    George 59, 159
    John 83, 133
    Richard 131, 164,
      172, 173
    Thomas 162
Wadsworth
    Elisabeth 105
    William 105, 184
Waggen

James 70
Waggitt
  John 16
Wahop
  (N) 145
Wakefield
  Thomas 182
  Timothy 185
Wales
  Mary 25
  Richard 25
Walken
  John 39
Walker
  Ann 27, 57, 151
  Daniell 38, 134
  John 50, 54
  Richard 57, 76, 151
  Thomas 27
Walkinson
  Cornelius 34
Wallace
  William 66
Wallass
  William 83
Walle
  Elisabeth 4
Waller
  William 14
Wallice
  James 71
  William 71
Wallis
  Ann 132
  Mary 50
  Richard 30, 50,
    132, 134
Wallter
  Ann 8
  Thomas 8
Walson
  Charles 131
Walter
  Anne 27
Walters
  Alexander 140
Walton
  Stephen 30, 69, 87,
    126
Walwin
  Edward 95
  Susanah 95
Waple
  James 20

Waplington
  Richard 186
Ward
  Edward 22
  Elisabeth 44
  James 44
  John 44, 55, 74,
    131
  Joseph 70, 113
  Katherine 44
  Murphy 113
  Thomas 44
Warden
  William 59
Warfoot
  Mary 90
Wargent
  William 51, 150
Warman
  Stephen 89, 96
Warner
  Samuell 65, 94
Warren
  Abra. 168
  Abraham 11, 20, 21,
    24, 45
  Bazell 22
  Christopher 54
  Elisabeth 54
  Humph. 21
  Humphrey 24, 45,
    163
  Humphry 45
  Ignatius 29, 30, 92
  Notley 11, 20, 24,
    70, 168
  Notly 21, 45
  Nottley 114
  Samuel 54
  Samuell 143
  Sarah 143
  Thomas 11, 20, 21,
    24, 45, 57, 76,
    168, 169, 185
Warthinton
  John 48
Washfield
  Robert 73, 83
  Susannah 73
Waterman
  Ann 108
  Nicholas 108
Waters
  Christopher 178

Elisabeth 178
John 119
Joseph 92, 115
Thomas 78
Watkins
Ann 3
Francis 83
James 22
John 3, 21, 24, 98
Katherine 98
Richard 19
Samuell 8, 11, 22,
41, 137, 142
Watkinson
Cornelius 60, 109
Watson
Charles 55
John 90, 129, 161
William 100, 103
Watters
John 111
Wattkins
Richard 112
Samuell 45
Watts
(N) 57
Charles 32, 58, 74,
175, 182
Elisabeth 57
James 78, 111, 149
Margret 21
Peter 179
William 21, 63,
101, 166, 175,
179, 182
Wattson
John 182
Waughob
Thomas 57
Waughop
Archibald 122
Thomas 73
Wauhop
Archibald 145, 146
Wayman
Lenard 103
Leonard 104, 116,
117, 140
Weales
John 139
Webb
John 7, 8, 56, 152
William 104, 126,
127

Webbe
John 60
Webster
John 124
Weeks
Joseph 17
Welham
Thomas 62
Wellham
Thomas 52
Wells
Benjamin 4, 9
Blanch 4
Elenor 140
Eloner 174
George 4, 9
Isaack 116
John 17, 138, 140,
174
Katherine 90
Margarett 40
Mary 25, 40
Richard 24, 25, 40
Zorababell 90
Wenman
Edward 79
Wessells
Gerrardus 150
West
Francis 67, 86
John 3, 8, 24, 71,
83, 84
Joseph 179
Westby
Samuell 65
Weyman
Leonard 52, 117,
119
Wharfield
Richard 165
Wharton
Henry 16
Richard 14, 97, 183
Thomas 7, 46, 141
Wheateley
Arthur 64
Wheatley
Arthur 85, 131
Wheatly
Arthur 40
William 138
Wheeler
Charles 85
Elisabeth 72, 150

Frances 158
Henry 14, 51, 59, 60
Ignatius 70, 75, 97, 158, 164, 181
John 72, 150
Samuell 74, 160
Susana 51
Susannah 59
Thomas 164
Wheelock
  Ann 175
  Edward 175
Whellock
  Ann 108, 110
  Edward 108, 110, 111
Wherrett
  William 92
Whichaley
  Thomas 70, 163
Whigler
  Alice 33
  Henry 33
Whitall
  Elisabeth 16
  John 16
Whitchell
  Mary 111
White
  Ann 184
  John 56, 77
  Nicholas 62, 63
  William 184
Whiteaker
  Henry 73
Whitehead
  Charles 35, 133, 139, 143
  Sarah 133
Whitehed
  Sarah 139
Whiteley
  John 59
Whitom
  William 74
Whittaker
  Mary 135, 136
Whittam
  William 74
Whittington
  John 167
  William 66

Wiatt
  Robert 95
Wickham
  Nathaniell 36
  Sebina 36
Wickman
  Timothy 147
Wigganer
  Giles 142
Wigginer
  Giles 64
Wiggins
  John 137
Wiggott
  Joseph 6, 80
Wight
  Ann 119
  John 62, 119
Wightt
  John 50
Wilder
  John 70
Wilkinson
  Cornelius 56
  John 53, 70, 128
  William 139, 140
Wilkison
  William 78, 147
Wille
  John 157
Willet
  Edward 178
Willett
  Edward 133, 149
Williamforeman
  William 108
Williams
  (N) 136
  Charles 119
  Edward 14, 150
  Enion 104
  Enionn 103
  Ester 57
  Francis 116
  Hester 58
  Hugh 69
  Isaack 19, 25
  Isacc 50
  James 37, 68, 69, 78, 87, 98, 167
  John 9, 14, 31, 66, 183
  Michael 181
  Thomas 93

William 56, 70,
106, 165, 183,
186
Williamson
Christopher 74, 92
Samuell 32
Willimot
John 78
Willimott
John 71
Willis
John 180, 187
Richard 78
Williston
James 116
Willmer
Lambert 17
Simon 17
Willmott
Henry 14
John 129, 149, 158
Susanah 14
Willought
John 119
Willowby
John 110
Wills
Jane 57
Orias 57
Osias 58
Willson
Eph. 138
Ephraim 23, 137
John 62, 105
Jonathon 64, 78, 98
Joseph 127, 161
Katherin 64
Katherine 69, 78
Sarah 98
William 98, 110,
149
Willymott
Joan 40
John 52, 67, 86,
94, 111, 112,
152, 165
Richard 40
Wilmer
Simon 17
Wilson
Ephraim 3
Jonathon 143
Moses 104
Thomas 71

Winchen
John 126
Margarett 126
Winchester
Isaac 96
Isaack 36, 72
Isaatt 65
John 123
Thomas 103
Wincoll
John 58
Windall
Thomas 29
Windell
Thomas 130
Winder
John 137, 138
Thomas 8
Winfeild
Jonathon 148
Winfield
Jonah 147
Winslow
John 131
Winsmore
Elisabeth 131
John 131
Winsor
John 14
Winter
Thomas 182
Winterford
Gilbert 66
Wiseman
John 36, 125
Wither
Samuell 26
Withers
John 78
Samuell 17, 25, 26,
38, 123, 171
Witton
Thomas 15
Wood
Edward 46, 60, 149,
158, 160, 170
James 51, 56, 62,
123, 160
John 53, 70, 74,
75, 97, 128, 158
Robert 26, 149,
179, 186
Thomas 2
Woodard

William 158
Woodgate
    William 163, 173
Woodward
    John 92
Wooland
    Edward 138
Wooler
    Edward 147
Wooley
    Ezekiell 144
Woolsey
    Ezekiell 144
Wooten
    Susannah 183
    Symon 124, 181, 183
Wooton
    Simon 46
Wootten
    Symon 25
Wootton
    Anne 7, 46
    Simon 7, 9
    Susanna 7
    Symon 23
Worgane
    William 85
Workman
    Anthony 66
Worthington
    John 22, 34, 35,
        38, 88, 89, 100,
        106, 107, 108,
        110, 114, 115,
        116, 118, 122,
        132
    Mr. 144
    Samuell 71, 84, 146
Wotton
    Ann 7
    Symon 46
Wouldhave
    William 56
Wridgley
    Henry 116
Wright
    Anthony 62
    Edward 14
    Francis 138
    Henry 64, 85
    John 81, 89, 90,
        151, 172, 173,
        181
    Nath. 17

Nathaniell 84
    William 138
Wriogley
    Henry 113
Wriothesley
    Henry 4
Write
    Jo. 164
Wroth
    James 11, 118, 121
Wyatt
    Isabella 89
Wyeat
    Thomas 4
Wyott
    Robert 89

Yate
    Mary 141, 146
Yates
    Mary 161, 162
    Robert 10
Yewell
    Sarah 82
    Thomas 82, 166
Yorke
    William 102
Yorkenson
    Mary 29
    York 29
Young
    Elisabeth 152, 172
    George 149, 165
    Jacob 15
    John 51, 52
    Juliana 81
    Mary 35
    Samuell 35, 96, 102
Yowle
    Sarah 72
    Thomas 72
Yowler
    Sarah 159

INDEX OF EQUITY CASES

Lingan vs. Cranford 23
Lloyd vs. est. of Lloyd 121
Lloyd vs. executors of Lloyd 101
Lowe vs. Darnall 34, 68, 86, 100, 165
Lynes vs. Toes 120

Mabbott vs. Owen 99
Millstead vs. Sargent 44

Nicholls vs. est. of Sandys 47
Nicholson vs. est. of Fenox 106
Nuttall vs. Smith 177

Parrott vs. Elzey 22, 45
Pattison & Vansweringen vs. Cullens 10
Pawlett vs. Pawlett 48

Ridgley vs. est. of Browne 116
Robertson vs. Ball 177
Robinett vs. est. of Snellen 1
Robotham vs. Bennett 37
Rockhold vs. est. of Dotton 111
Rousby vs. administrators of Seth 101
Rousby vs. Robinson 166

Smith & King vs. Miller 176, 183
Smith vs. Gadsby 86
Smith vs. Smith 48
Smith vs. Wells 40
Stinchcome vs. Gadsby & Smith 51
Sweatnam vs. King 144, 166

Thurston vs. Brown 25

Warren vs. Warren 11, 20, 21, 24, 45, 168
Watkins vs. Morrison 11
Watts vs. Slye 63, 101, 166, 175, 182
Wheatley vs. Sherwood 40, 64, 85
Whitchell vs. est. of Standbauck 111
Williams vs. est. of Sweatnam 37
Winter vs. Garterell 182
Wooten vs. Fisher 183